THE GREAT AGE OF DISCOVERY

FERDINAND, "KING OF SPAIN," SENDING FORTH HIS SHIPS FOR THE DISCOVERY OF NEW ISLANDS.

Wood-cut from the first account of Columbus's voyage in Italian. Published by Giuliano Dati in 1493. The ending of the tract indicates the character attached to the discoveries.

Finita lastoria della ĩuẽtione delle nuoue isole dicãnaria ĩdiane tracte duna pistola dixp̃ofano colõbo & p messer Giuliano dati tradocta dilatino ĩ uersi uulgari . . . di xxvi doctobre 14.93.

(See p. 97.)

THE GREAT AGE OF DISCOVERY

Edited by
ARTHUR PERCIVAL NEWTON

*With eight
collotype and twenty-three
other plates*

Essay Index Reprint Series

BOOKS FOR LIBRARIES PRESS
FREEPORT, NEW YORK

First Published 1932
Reprinted 1969

STANDARD BOOK NUMBER:
8369-1366-3

LIBRARY OF CONGRESS CATALOG CARD NUMBER:
79-99713

PRINTED IN THE UNITED STATES OF AMERICA

PREFACE

T H E substance of the contributions that are here published was included in a course of public lectures delivered in the Departments of History and Geography in KING'S COLLEGE, LONDON, in the Lent Term of 1931. They have been collected and provided with some references as guides to further study in the hope that they will be of interest and use not only to the general reader, but also to the increasing number of students who are now taking up the scientific study of historical geography. The maps and illustrations have been reproduced in almost every case from contemporary sources, and explanatory notes have been added.

Our especial thanks are due to the Royal Geographical Society for permission to reproduce certain illustrations and maps from their publications. My own thanks are due to my collaborators for their courteous acceptance of my editorial suggestions. For the planning and arrangement of the book I alone am responsible. The index has been prepared by Dr. H. J. Wood.

A. P. N.

KING'S COLLEGE,
    LONDON,
    February 1932.

CONTENTS

CONTENTS

CHAPTER VI

By H. P. BIGGAR, D.Litt., *Chief Archivist for Canada in Europe.*

CHAPTER VII

By H. J. WOOD, B.Sc. (Econ.), Ph.D., *Assistant Lecturer in Geography in King's College, London.*

CHAPTER VIII

By JAMES A. WILLIAMSON, M.A., D.Lit.

CHAPTER IX

By E. G. R. TAYLOR, D.Sc., *Professor of Geography in the University of London.*

LIST OF ILLUSTRATIONS
AND MAPS

b   ix

LIST OF ILLUSTRATIONS

x

LIST OF ILLUSTRATIONS

CHAPTER I

INTRODUCTION—THE TRANSITION FROM THE MEDIEVAL TO THE MODERN AGE

T H E traditional fashion of historical writers of dividing up the story of the past into great chapters or " ages," marked off by abrupt and arbitrary limits, may be of convenience for textbooks or examinations, but it has little relation to reality. Since the modern revival of the historian's art in the nineteenth century the true emphasis has been laid upon continuity and the gradual evolution of human society. We have come to realise that the extreme complexity of world conditions has been reached not by a succession of jerky catastrophes, but by a gradual and continuous process of " becoming." The more we study historical processes in detail, the more we are convinced that there are few or no abrupt and dramatic transitions after the manner of the theatre. One set of conditions gradually changes into another, but the more thoroughly the period is studied, the more it is found impossible to date exactly a point of transformation. There was no sudden and cataclysmic collapse of ancient Rome into barbarian darkness, nor any moment of abrupt emergence from the prison of medievalism into the brightness of the Renaissance such as some writers have fondly imagined.

Certain modern scholars, over-impressed by the essential continuity of history, have been led to question even the validity of such a universal conception as that of the " middle ages," for they have been baffled by the impossibility of choosing any criteria which will assign a particular year or years at the critical period of change either to the medieval or the modern age. But such an over-mathematical emphasis on continuity brings its own dangers, for it introduces the rigid theoretical canons of physical

B

science into the utterly different and subtler scheme of human relations and obscures undoubted facts and movements of the highest importance.

There is no more general consensus of opinion among students of the past than in their recognition that about the end of the fifteenth century there was in Western Europe a profound change in men's outlook upon the world. This change was so fundamental and so rapid that it is one of the outstanding facts in history, and marks a real change from one era to another. To quote the words of one of the greatest historians of the time : " Anyone who works through the records of the fifteenth and the sixteenth century becomes conscious of an extraordinary change of mental outlook showing itself on all sides in unexpected ways. He finds at the same time that all attempts to analyse and account for this change are to a great extent unsatisfactory. After marshalling all the forces and ideas which were at work to produce it, he still feels that there was behind all these an animating spirit which he cannot but most imperfectly catch, whose power blended all else together and gave a sudden cohesion to the whole." [1]

At one point the reader is deep in an old medieval world that seems to differ little from what it had been for centuries. He is surrounded by remote conceptions, shackled and bound by rigid principles and technical ideas that are expounded by men whose extraordinary cleverness and logical subtlety seem inextricably mingled with a childish naïveté and credulity. A very little farther and he is in the full light of modern times. Mankind seems to have come in that short interval to a stage of civilisation that in its broad outlines is entirely familiar. The problems that still occupy us have come into conscious recognition, and they are dealt with in ways that are easily intelligible and congenial to us because they so closely resemble our own. On the farther side of a line drawn across the centuries men speak strangely, and

[1] Mandell Creighton, Bishop of London.

their minds seem to work in unexpected ways. On the hither side they are animated by ideas and aspirations like those of to-day. The forms in which they express their thoughts and the records of their activity are more readily understandable than the earlier ones, because they resemble those that still prevail among us.

We have, in fact, passed from the middle ages into modern times, and as we look back we note that the change has come with amazing rapidity. It is comprised within the lifetime of a single generation, and however widely we stretch its limits, they will not extend beyond the half-century between 1477 and 1527. In the earlier of those years a certain Genoese, one Cristoforo Colombo, left his native city to seek his fortune— the beginning of a series of extraordinary and unprecedented adventures. In the later Charles V and his German soldiery sacked medieval Rome, and struck the last blow in the ancient quarrel between the Empire and the Papacy. Somewhere between those dates lies our critical line, whatever be the sphere of human activity that we are considering. The process of change that then took place is generally known as the " Renaissance," and the causes that brought it about must be sought in many directions. In the intellectual sphere men were profoundly influenced by the revival of ancient learning, and that also brought about great changes in the world of art, but such things were confined to the few, and they only slowly filtered down to the masses. The revival of learning might well have taken place without any great or rapid change in general social conditions. In the sphere of politics, it is true, great changes were taking place in the direction of centralisation of government, but these might not have led on to those stirrings of nationality that finally broke down the unity of Christendom if they had not been accompanied by other vital changes.

The one central and unprecedented fact of the time which never can be repeated or even paralleled in any future age

was the sudden expansion of the habitable world by geographical discovery. To quote the words of the historian
of the Renaissance in Italy : "The discoveries displaced the
centre of gravity in politics and commerce, substituting the
ocean for the Mediterranean, dethroning Italy from her seat of
central importance in traffic, depressing the eastern and elevating
the western powers of Europe, opening up a path for Anglo-
Saxon expansiveness, and forcing philosophers and statesmen to
regard the Occidental nations as a single group in counterpoise to
other groups of nations, the European community as one unit
correlated to other units of humanity upon this planet."[1] A large
part of the political and economic history of modern times has
been concerned with the rivalry of Europeans for opportunities of
exploiting and developing the new lands revealed in the fateful
half-century, and we may unhesitatingly call it the " Great Age of
Discovery," for there is no other to dispute its pre-eminence.

It is not our purpose here to attempt to recount the course of
the discoveries in detail or enter into the mazes of controversy in
which expert Americanists delight to exhibit their dialectic skill.
Our aim is the simpler one of tracing out some undisputed facts
concerning a few of the greatest of the explorers, and by setting
them against the background of their times to recover something
of the spirit in which all unconsciously they broke the prison
bonds of the medieval world in which they had been reared and
led the mass of mankind into a new era. Few of them, with one
striking exception, were theorists or pursuers of ideas of cosmogony. They were hard, practical men, who took the generally
accepted ideas for granted, and hunted for wealth for themselves
or their employers with a single-minded zeal. They left to
others the interpretation and explanation of what else they found.
Hardly any of the explorers gave any description of their own
adventures, and we are left to recover the story from scattered
and fragmentary sources. ,Their contemporaries were little

[1] John Addington Symonds.

better off, and it can hardly be wondered at that the assembly and correlation of world knowledge led to much misunderstanding and lagged far behind the discoveries themselves. It was many years before fairly accurate details of the new lands became a part of general knowledge, and even the broader facts only gradually became known. But the essential knowledge that there were strange, new lands beyond the sea crammed with wonders that surpassed all the old travellers' tales spread fast when once it had started, and it was undoubtedly one of the most potent factors in bringing about the change in men's outlook upon the universe that is the most striking feature of the first quarter of the sixteenth century.

Though the three men who have won the widest fame as discoverers, Cristoforo Colombo, a Genoese, Giovanni Caboto, a Genoese naturalised in Venice, and Amerigo Vespucci, a Florentine, were all Italians, in reality the work of revealing the new sea routes and exploring the lands to which they led was almost entirely the achievement of men of the Iberian nations— the Castilians and Portuguese, who were closely related. Their ancestry and historical development were so much the same that they belonged to a special national group, and only political accidents had made them subjects of rival crowns. With the exception of the voyages of John Cabot and the obscure work of the Englishmen associated with Hugh Eliot and Robert Nicolas Thorne, which lie apart from the main current of discovery, it may be claimed that until after the first quarter of the sixteenth century, when the main outlines had been set, everything was done by Spaniards or Portuguese or by a few Italians in their employ. In later years, when Frenchmen, English and Netherlanders came to follow up their work, this fact was neglected, and for reasons of national propaganda the magnificent achievements of the Iberians were minimised or the credit for their inspiration unjustly attributed to Italians. But, in truth, the task of revealing the new world beyond the Ocean and the conquest of the sea road to the East was accomplished almost wholly by men of a single national group, governed by peculiar historical circumstances, and far removed from the general stream of European development.

How did it come about that in the course of two or three generations there was such a vast outburst of virile energy from this group ? Was it merely due to political circumstances, or was there some deeper psychological cause at work which alone made it possible for men to put forth such heroic exertions ?

To answer these questions we must go farther than a narrative of the discoveries themselves, and Professor Antonio Pastor opens our enquiry. He provides for us a background against which the narratives may be set, and he shows that the vigour and dæmonic energy of the Iberians in the great age was due to survival among them of medieval inspiration and methods of thought. The Spaniards and the Portuguese became the leaders of the movement that brought in the new age, not because they were the first people to be imbued with the modern spirit of enquiry, but paradoxically they were the last to retain the medieval inspiration of the crusaders, the paladins and the knights-errant long after the ages of faith had waned among the other nations of Western Europe into the scepticism of the Renaissance.

The great age of discovery was, in fact, ushered in by the action of a spiritual movement of compelling force on minds ready to respond to it. Four centuries earlier a similar wave of spiritual energy had brought about the Crusades, and there is no contradiction of the essentially idealistic inspiration of both movements to be found in the fact that the lasting results of each were only material, and that both were stained by greed and cruelty. Unless the idealism of the explorers and conquerors is borne clearly in mind, we must fail to interpret rightly the way in which their heroic achievements were accomplished with an almost incredible poverty of means.

Before the first successful voyages across the Atlantic, the

6

Portuguese had been actively engaged in oceanic navigation and trade with savage lands for thirty years. Their explorations had begun thirty years earlier still, so that for more than half a century they had been winning experience of the organisation and conduct of distant expeditions. Sailors of other nations, Flemings, Frenchmen and English, had attempted to follow in their tracks and steal their profits, but little of that maritime activity was known to the general public, and it produced no reactions in the intellectual sphere. The official expeditions and their results were kept confidential, and the poachers of other nations were not anxious to incur the penalties of piracy. Professor Prestage in this volume carries further the story of Portuguese discovery that he began elsewhere,[1] and describes the voyages that were a direct prelude to the opening of the ocean routes. He continues his narrative down to the very end of our period, when China and Japan had been reached, and only the vast expanse of the Pacific remained to shroud its wonders from knowledge for two centuries more.

We next return to take up the story of Columbus which, as we shall see, springs naturally and directly from the earlier work of the Portuguese. It was his startling and widely published first discovery that opened the new age, and we must say something as to how the news was made generally known. If we deny to the Italians some of the credit that has been bestowed on them in undue measure, we cannot refuse to the men of that nation a foremost place in the movement. Save in a few cases, however, that was not upon the ocean, but must be awarded to them for what they did in making the discoveries and their significance known to the world. In that they stood alone. The Spaniards were self-centred and unvocal ; the Portuguese in the interest of their monopoly endeavoured to conceal their discoveries rather than make them known. Only Italians, the most cosmopolitan of people, had both access to the new geographical knowledge and

[1] See *Travel and Travellers of the Middle Ages,* ed. A. P. Newton, chap. x.

the power of interpreting and correlating it. If it be true, as was suggested above, that a new conception of the world was one of the vital influences that brought in a new era, then it must properly form part of our task to show how the knowledge upon which it was based was spread abroad. But to trace more than the beginning of that diffusion is impossible, for it would carry us in innumerable directions into the literature of thought. We must confine ourselves to the first quarter of the sixteenth century, wherein the destructive work of the new concepts was most marked.

When we turn to the actual discoverers and their discoveries, we consider certain of the most notable navigators and their geographical ideas as illustrative of the gradual increase of sound knowledge and the building upon it of a more accurate cosmogony. But such narratives of particular voyages can be nothing more than illustrations of the prevailing notions at work, for they were all successful, and the average venture was not. They were but a few among many, but they were recorded, though even for them the narratives are frequently scattered and imperfect. Most of the others have left little trace. All alike were inspired by the same spirit of credulous hope in the possibilities of a world of wonders. None knew or could even imagine what their efforts might bring forth, and what was true for the seamen was even truer for the land explorers and for the scholars who in their studies were striving to weave the newly discovered facts into an orderly cosmogony. For the tropical and temperate zones the accumulated experiences of the explorers enabled them to do this, but to the north they were baffled and their speculations were vain. In our last chapter Professor Taylor shows that the great age was characterised in this direction rather by a conflict of geographical ideas than by actual attempts at discovery, and that those were left for a later generation.

The period was above all an age of wonder. Miracle was piled on miracle as the story of adventure was unfolded, and gradually men passed from a time when the impossible fables of Mandeville were swallowed like a modern "best-seller" to a new-shaped real world infinitely more varied and marvellous. It seemed crammed with opportunities such as their ancestors had never credited, and it was with a sense of joyous exhilaration that adventurers burst forth from their medieval confines in search of fame and fortune. But not for that alone. The romantic quests of their predecessors still lured them. Where lay the "Earthly Paradise" and where the "Fountain of Eternal Youth"? None could tell, but any fortunate voyager might find them as they had done the islands of Antilia, the Golden Chersonese, or the Land of Prester John. Only a century or more of experience could prove what was real and what merely legend. Till then Utopia might lie just beyond any horizon, and all the treasures of Manoa await the first bold venturer who would scale the far-flung peaks that closed his distant view.

The theme has inspired great poets from Camoens to Keats and romantic writers from Washington Irving to Cunninghame Graham, with a host of lesser imitators. But here our task is a humbler one. It is to assemble the background of the historical facts of the principal voyages and trace something of the change in geographical ideas to which they gave rise. The task lies somewhere in the sphere of Historical Geography, and professed geographers and historians in association have attempted it.

CHAPTER II

SPANISH CIVILISATION IN THE GREAT AGE OF DISCOVERY

T H E task of the historian is a quest à *la recherche du temps perdu*. The data afforded by documents alone are insufficient for the task of re-creation, and only when they are interpreted, put through a process of juxtaposition and opposition, does there emerge from the lifeless material—perhaps when we least expect it—the significant concept that brings life to the labours of the research-worker. To envisage the more intimate aspects of the period that we usually call the " Renaissance," we must view it from a truly historical standpoint and avoid such a literal interpretation of the word as is too often the starting-point. It is certain that nothing is ever " re-born " in history.

At once the danger of indiscreet rationalisation threatens, that of projecting an academic Utopia, some fanciful evolution into the past. Political events are very secondary manifestations of human life. What during a generation has been an accepted principle of a minority takes shape in political moulds decades later. History is thus the history of ideas in relation, on the one hand, to the personalities that held them and, on the other, to the events which they affect or to which they give rise or which counteract their influence. It is of the greatest importance to emphasise the second point—the distance and tension between ideal and practice—if we are ever to oppose a real experience of time in history—the ultimate goal of all historical endeavour—to the chaotic disorder of modern historical science, oscillating between the nihilism—in so far as ideas are concerned—of the research-worker pure and simple and the fuliginous lucubrations of fashionable prophets who, in their anxiety to predict the future according to certain principles, impose these on the past, anchoring the frail and topheavy structure on a barely sufficient number of arbitrarily chosen circumstances of the past to give to an inverted Utopia an appearance of inevitability, of empirical as well as logical determinism. The fundamental datum of the experience of history is the experience of men in the past, and this experience cannot be only, nor even mainly, deduced from their social and political activities. It must be sought in individual activities and in the peculiar atmosphere surrounding ideas at a given moment, rather than in the ideas themselves.

As we review the past, three fundamental attitudes towards life seem to define themselves [1]. The first is an attitude of negation, and the autumn of the middle ages is of such melancholy renunciation all compact—not in the sense that the late fourteenth century and nearly the whole of the fifteenth were unhappier or less satisfactory to the generations that lived in that phase of European culture than any other age has been to those who lived in it. As we look back to this period, everything seems steeped in cruelty, disease, death, chaos and hatred, but all periods perhaps leave more traces of their sufferings than of their joys, and the historian of the future will find cruelty, disease, death, chaos and hatred in our own age to the same degree of horror. But whereas *we* try to act with powerful means on our environment and a note of not always conscious optimism is predominant, or was predominant in the nineteenth century, the opposite was the case during the later phases of Gothic culture. To express happiness was thought not only insincere but vulgar. Eustache Deschamps, the Court poet of Charles V of France, as a man a jovial lover of wine and hater of women—especially his own—laments as a fact that all good things have departed from this world. In despair he praises the simple bourgeois who eats " du potage et du chou," and weeps for the down-trodden people of France and their hero Du Guesclin—

"Temps de douleur et de temptacion,
  Aages de plour, d'envie et de tourment"—

and it is to be remembered that the age of Deschamps was that of an attempted Renaissance that bore no fruit. La Marche, the poet and chronicler of the magnificent Charles the Bold, fine flower of late chivalry, chose as his motto, *Tant a souffert La Marche.* In Spain they found a parchment on the dead body of the great Jorge Manrique, the most typical poet of the age of the Catholic Queen of Castile, slaughtered miserably, according to Hernando del Pulgar, before the castle of Garci Muñoz in 1478 by the men of the Marqués de Villena, one of the grandees who were resisting the anti-feudal policy of the Crown. Just before his death he had been writing some couplets—*Contra el mundo*— against the world :

> " Oh, world—thou who killest us !
> Yet might the life thou givest us
>   Be all living !
> But in this way thou treatest us :
> The least sadness thou givest us,
>   To departing
> From life fraught with melancholy,
> When misery perpetually
>   Is abounding.
> Of blessings devoid completely
> The beatitudes have left thee ;
>   We are toiling
> From thy birth—a tearful entrance,
> To thy end—a bitter severance,
>   Without sweetness ;
> Thus through life ever labouring—
> For longer years continuing,
>   Greater sadness—
> We die to find our happiness,
> After long strain and bitterness
>   To attain it.
> Evils here are long enduring,
> Come with swiftness, never ceasing,
>   To destroy us."

Such an attitude of elegant melancholia, of exquisite acquiescence, is characteristic of one of the most significant and beautiful

THE *DONCEL DE SIGUENZA.*

Part of the tomb of Don Martin Vázquez de Arce in the Chapel of St. Catherine, Cathedral of Siguenza, 1486.

(*See p. 13.*)

works of art of the last decade of the fifteenth century, the tomb
of Don Martin Vázquez de Arce in the Chapel of St. Catherine in
the Cathedral of Siguenza [2]. The inscription tells us that
the young knight of the Order of St. James was killed by the
Granadans in the Vega of Granada in 1486, while he was rushing
to the rescue of the Duque del Infantazgo. He was then twenty-
five years old. He lies in an attitude of abandon, half sitting,
leaning on a heap of laurels ; his hair is long and fringed over
the eyebrows ; he is armed, but holds in his hands with a tired
and precious gesture a book in which he is reading ; at his feet
is a little page, who passes his hand over his face in a gesture of
sadness. There is a delicate beauty about him. The body is
elongated and very thin, announcing already a typically Spanish
tendency, modelled with a feeling, almost a tenderness, for which
we would look in vain in the commercialised late Gothic sculpture
of France and Flanders. The spirit and the historical circumstances of the age seem to have entered into the creation of this
gentle masterpiece ; a secular fatigue which, after a brief spell
of renunciation, was producing a reaction of intense activity and
yet preserved a certain original quality of melancholy introspec-
tion ; a kind of dreamy refinement permitting the free play of
high ideals which at any moment may inspire unparalleled enterprise. We detect in his tomb a national spirit which appears at
the very end of the line of Gothic art. Neither the French nor
the Italian artists, who technically had already outdistanced all
others, could have expressed this peculiar spirit, so new and yet
so old, so entirely Gothic in its form and yet already imbued with
a new conception of life and death ; no longer, as in the middle
ages, the insistence on the perishable nature of the flesh, nor yet
the whole-hearted affirmation of life of the Italians, but a very
subtle and profoundly original adaptation of Gothic forms to the
expression of a new outlook. This tomb is the first in Europe to
represent the deceased as other than dead or asleep on his side,
as happens in Italy in the case of Sansovino's tombs of Santa Maria

del Popolo, which are in any case a few years later than the *Doncel de Siguenza*, to give the statue the name by which it is known in Spain.

The second attitude towards life, often contemporaneous with, but clearly distinguishable from, the first, leads on to the way of deliberate dreams. The world, as it is experienced directly, is unsatisfying, drab, prosaic, lamentable. Yet renunciation and austerity are difficult. At these moments—and the last quarter of the fifteenth century is pre-eminently one of them—the attempt is made to create another world, marvellous and beautiful. It is not art in the modern sense, a human activity with its own ends governed by its own laws, but, ultimately, an effort—often maintained with truly admirable discipline—to assert the free-will of man in adverse circumstances. Thus from the beginning of the fifteenth century onwards, well into the sixteenth, people tried deliberately to turn back to the knightly heroes of the past and re-live their existence in the unknightly present in which the individual ideal of justice of the knight had been superseded, or was about to be superseded, by the organised bureaucracy of Ferdinand and Isabella and the royal archers, the prototype of the modern police, who made acts of violence, regardless of the good intentions with which they were committed, into crimes effectively punished.

This shifting of values affected Spanish ideas not only more deeply than those of other countries in Europe but also differently. The projection of an Utopian ideal into the past was peculiarly difficult. Castile was imposing its political and cultural hegemony on all the Spains, and the Castilian temper, unlike that of French chivalry with its superb romanticism and tigerish ferocity, was realistic, restrained, almost classical, with *mesura*, " measure,' as the traditional ideal of which the Cid of the *Cantar* as well as the Cid of modern historical research [3] is the most complete embodiment. The Castilian genius loved concrete ideas and their immediate application to everyday life, and in Castile chivalry always preserved, more than elsewhere, its original meaning of "a body of horsemen equipped for battle [4]." These characteristics are noticeable even in mystical contemplation. Let us remember Teresa of Avila, one of the greatest explorers of spiritual continents, and at the same time so human and touching a figure, so admirably practical an administrator, tirelessly toiling over the dusty roads of Castile. She advised the women of Spain to seek God amongst the pots and pans of the kitchen, and it is no mere accident that the most universal of Spanish works of art should be a novel in which the tragic tension between ideas and practice has found its perfect expression.

The native common sense of the Castilian appears, thus, unfriendly to the elaborate confusion between a world of fantasy and the world of practical values. In Spain life never became a game of ceremony, as in France or Burgundy, and the Court of a Charles the Bold cannot even be conceived south of the Pyrenees. The increasing distance between the miserable and down-trodden life of the peasant and a knightly phantasmagoria never became a social or political problem. No athletic knights, consciously strutting in fancy-dress, breathed a subtle air altogether different from the one that filled the rotten lungs of the serf.

The ideal of knightly courtesy in its extreme form belongs to the later fourteenth century, but like all ideals, it took a long time to enter social practice. Before then Alfonso the Learned had dreamed of it, but had been severely checked by the rough soldiers of Castile, who, in spite of his admonitions, to be found in the *Siete Partidas*, continued to eat garlic and to laugh rudely at Court. After that, in the time of John II, the grandson of John of Gaunt, the Marquis of Santillana (1398–1458), the book-proud, semi-learned nobleman and great poet of the *Serranillas*, appeared *armado como francés*, "armed like a Frenchman," dedicated himself to the service of the Virgin, like his romantic French

15

models, and, although the first to write sonnets *al itálico modo*, he still preferred the French *Roman de la Rose* to these daring innovations, the advance-guard of the new Italian cultural forces. Yet he remained Castilian to the core, for, whenever he abandoned the pedantic conceits which so delighted him, he became the incomparable poet of popular song to whom we owe some of the most spring-like and charmingly simple lines in fifteenth-century poetry. The *Life of Don Pero Niño*, written by his Squire Gutierre Díaz de Gámez, reads like a fantastic romance [5], but it is interrupted by very accurate pictures of real things seen and heard, such as a most diverting impression of England. Mosen Diego de Valera visited France and Bohemia in search of adventure, which he found in abundance in the wars against the Hussites. In his old age he wrote often to the Catholic Sovereigns who thought much of the gallant knight, for he was an authority on duels, adventurous exploits, and pedigrees, about all of which subjects he composed several treatises.

There were few exceptions to the characteristic moderating power of Castilian traditional common sense, yet one of them at least reaches the limits of the pathological [6]. In the summer of 1439 a certain Suero de Quiñones undertook to defend a bridge near León against every challenger. Every Thursday he wore a necklet to show his devotion to his lady. Daily he and his companions heard Mass, and on Tuesdays Suero fasted in honour of the Blessed Virgin. For a month they battled against sixty-eight opponents, whom they entertained hospitably. The first was a German called Arnold von Rotwald. An Aragonese gentleman was killed, and another of the same nationality took an oath that, if he were victorious, he would never again make love to a nun. Seven hundred fights took place, and by the end of the month Suero and all his companions were wounded. Every lady who passed the place and whose escort did not fight had her right glove seized.

The attempts to impose on Castilian life, so simple and

FAÇADE OF THE UNIVERSITY OF SALAMANCA.

Lower portion of the principal façade of the University, an important example of the Plateresque style. The medallion contains portraits of Ferdinand and Isabella, and the influence of the new learning is seen in the employment of Greek for the dedicatory inscription:

ΟΙ ΒΑΣΙΛΕΙΣ ΤΗ ΕΓΚΥΚΛΟΠΑΙΔΕΙΑ ΑΥΤΗ ΤΟΙΣ ΒΑΣΙΛΕΙΣΙ

"The Sovereigns for the University, the University for the Sovereigns."

(See p. 25.)

possessing in the eleventh and twelfth centuries in all classes, and later in all but the highest, a patriarchal flavour which clearly separates it from the world of the French *Chansons de Geste*, are very old and not limited to those of Alfonso the Learned. Alfonso VII's Court was one of the most splendid in Europe. The contact with the Muhammadan Spaniards of Andalusia—essentially people of the same race as those inhabiting the north of the Peninsula, but separated from them by their religion and peculiar culture, equidistant from the civilisation of Damascus and that of Burgos and León—had profoundly affected the Homeric simplicity of earlier times.

The ultramontane tendencies of the Crown, which was in close contact with the Burgundian monks of Cluny, the abandonment of the Visigothic liturgy, which had separated the Spanish Christians not only from their Muhammadan compatriots but also from the Christian Occident generally, in favour of the Roman liturgy—one of the important victories of Gregory VII—the general French influence which gave to the kings of Castile not only French prelates but also French queens and mistresses, finally the cultural influence of those States within the Peninsula—Galicia with its sentimental and erotic poetry, Catalonia a great vehicle of Provençal influences—all worked together in producing a change of taste if not of character. This taste was becoming romantic, at first that of an aristocratic minority ; later it spread until its last and most debased manifestations reached the illiterate in the late fifteenth and early sixteenth centuries, when social circumstances made the gap between reality and the world of dreams unbridgeable and the imagination could soar untrammelled by any relation to experience. The heroes of chivalrous romanticism, Lancelot, Amadís of Gaul, Palmerín and the rest, filled the imagination of young and old, of Emperor and kitchen-maid, of hardy Conquistadores and great saints, of Charles V, who challenged Francis I to single combat, but certainly would have been very surprised if the King

C

of France had confused dreams with hard blows and had insisted on a duel in the flesh, of an old soldier like Gonzalo Fernández de Oviedo (1478–1557), companion of Hernán Cortés, the conqueror of Mexico and author of the most entertaining collection of early " Americana " that exists, who wrote a dreadful novel of chivalry, entitled Don Claribalte, of Saint Teresa who in her early youth was given to profane reading and of Ignatius Loyola who all his life through thought of himself as a knight-errant of Christ.

The destinies of the romances of chivalry in Spain—stretching, in so far as popularity and their innumerable editions are concerned, in unbroken line from El Caballero Cífar, the story of an Indian knight, which belongs to the first two or three years of the fourteenth century and is related to the famous Barlaam y Josafat, a Buddha story from the Sanskrit Lalita Vistara which wandered to Europe through Greek, Persian and Syriac versions and perhaps reached the unknown author, possibly a Toledan cleric, through some lost Andalusian adaptation, down to the atrocious Historia de Don Policisne de Beocia (1602) by Juan de Silva—are not only part of the history of literature but of an attitude to life, an index to secret thoughts and desires. These books had their roots in other much earlier works, and their antiquity shows how gradual and inevitable the unfolding of this world of romance was. The Amadís de Gaula, the oldest printed edition of which is that of Saragossa (1508), goes back to a subject-matter which is mentioned already in his Rimado de Palacio by the Chancellor of Castile, Don Pedro Lopez de Ayala (1332–1407), an historian who equals and, perhaps, from a purely literary point of view, surpasses Froissart and Fernam Lopez. The Chancellor was made a prisoner by the cavalry of the Black Prince in the battle of Nájera, and later again by the Portuguese in the battle of Aljubarrota, after which he was locked in an iron cage in the Castle of Oviedes until he was rescued. Tradition has it that in these uncomfortable surroundings he wrote the passages of self-depreciation and repentance in which the reference to the stories of Lancelot and Amadís occurs. Be that as it may, Don Pedro died in the year 1407, and the passage thus proves that the adventures of Amadís were known in the Peninsula before the end of the fourteenth century.

It is important to realise to what an extent the ideas and sentiments of this literature filled the imagination of the Isabellian age. The ultimate control of the great ventures of the age of discovery, the legislation that governed the new territories, was imbued with a modern spirit, new and original and not in any sense " reborn " out of classical antiquity ; but the execution of the designs, and especially the first all-important impetus, was steeped in a spirit of romance which belongs to this Rococo phase of the Gothic cycle, and is the outcome of an attitude to life which found the fantastic nature of the American enterprises, the conquest of vast empires by small bands of adventurers, the dream-like visions of dreamlike cities in Mexico and Peru, congenial in the extreme. Bernal Díaz del Castillo in his *Historia verdadera de la conquista de la Nueva España* [7] narrates that when the 400 Spaniards of Cōrtés, of whom he was one, first beheld the magnificence of the city of Mexico, " we were astounded and said that it seemed like those enchantments the book of *Amadís* tells about." When the Spaniards explored the Pacific sea-board, they called the most entrancing part of the Mexican coast-land " California," which is an Indian island of romance " near the earthly Paradise, very rich in gold and jewels," a most appropriate and prophetic name for these fantastic regions, borrowed from *Las Sergas de Esplandián,* by Garci Ordóñez de Montalvo, a shrewd magistrate of Medina del Campo, the favourite residence of Queen Isabella, who was herself devoted to romances of chivalry. It is to him that we owe the *Amadís* in its present form, the old original having been lost. When Columbus, who heard voices in his sleep and was so steeped in the spirit of the prophetic books of the Old Testament that some have thought him a Jew, wrote a letter to Ferdinand and Isabella in 1501 that he had been induced to undertake his voyages to the Indies not by any information derived from human sources—which is certainly quite untrue—but by a divine impulse, he added that the terrestrial Paradise would be found by him, and by him alone, in the southern regions of the Indies, and that the Orinoco was one of the mystical streams that flow from it.

All this means an escape from life generally into the world of art—not an art represented by the great masterpiece of the period, La Celestina, nor even less art in its modern connotation—but a kind of art with strong roots in wish-fulfilling motives, comparable perhaps, in this sense, to that of the modern cinema. The early Renaissance, still precariously perched on the dividing line between late Gothic melancholia and the constructive affirmations of the sixteenth century, adopted such an art enthusiastically. Literature did not reach its independence in this sense until the new century, when Garcilaso de la Vega (1501–36) found notes of piercing sweetness for his Eglogas, singing of " el dulce lamentar de dos pastores," and Jorge de Montemayor (1520–61), a Portuguese by birth but a Castilian writer, composed his " Seven Books of Diana,'' translated into English by Young in 1583.

The young Cervantes was still under the spell of the old enchantment when he wrote his first novel, La Galatea, now quite unreadable, but so beloved by its author, that on his deathbed he promised, if God should miraculously restore him to health, to write its continuation, preferring it to Don Quixote and the Exemplary Novels. It is in the mind of Cervantes that we can trace the great crisis of European literature, the change from extraverted fantasy to introverted analysis. When the two philosophical dogs, Cipion and Berganza, review their experiences, Berganza, quite incidentally, after the manner of Cervantes, describes the abyss that separates political from historical truth, the difference between " creation " and " representation," and he is struck by the difference of the lives of the shepherds in books from those he served. They had no names like Phyllis, Galatea, or Amaryllis, they did not sing with accomplished mastery, or promenade amidst a delicious and well-arranged landscape, but they were called Dominic or Paul, had rough and throaty voices, and spent most of their time repairing their boots and hunting for their fleas. Cervantes loved pure fiction, and yet his modern sensibility was bounded by intense feeling for what is probable.

The road to chivalry was thus, as in the case of Columbus, not the only avenue that was followed. The contrast between the artifice of the Court and the simplicity of a rural life began to be felt. It was eventually to be expressed in Guevara's *Menosprecio de Corte y alabanza de aldea* (1539), the catechism of that fashionable simplicity. There were the shepherds, at first real shepherds of rustic and often comic character such as those in the little plays (significantly called *Elegías*) of Juan del Encina (1469–1529), most of which the author wrote for private performances by the household of the Duke of Alba at Alba de Tormes. But later these rude yokels changed into polite and gentle bucolic poets. The desire for a beautiful life was dominant, regardless of all other values, in the years preceding the discovery of America. Almost at the very moment that Columbus sighted the low-lying shores of Guanahani (which he called San Salvador), Diego de San Pedro published the *Cárcel de Amor*, an allegorical, morbidly introspective yet entirely conventional story of adventure, suffering and suicide, which became almost as popular as the *Amadís*, was translated twenty times, and has been called the *Werthers Leiden* of that period.

The third attitude towards life—the one that specially distinguished the new era from the old—is one of belief in the destinies of the human race, belief in the possibility of powerfully affecting the material and spiritual surroundings of an age, and of doing so cumulatively and progressively in the sense that no individual effort is wasted. It embraces equally the romantic idea that in educating ourselves we act in a sense on the world around us in a manner not dissimilar from that of the practical politician and administrator. Underlying such an attitude is a certain cautious optimism, a belief in the possibilities of human nature, one of the characteristics—but by no means the only one—of what is commonly called the Renaissance. Such a belief was slow to be expressed and at first was limited to intellectual culture. Ulrich von Hutten's O saeculum, O literae, juvat vivere, has no other meaning, and Erasmus, the sceptical and worldly scholar, expressed nothing but a timid hope that soon there might arise a conspiracy of the élite ad restituendas optimas literas.

The influence of Erasmus in Spain is so considerable that without taking it into account no deeper understanding of sixteenth-century Spanish writers is possible. His corrosive spirit was, contrary to general belief, essentially congenial to that satirical and more particularly anti-clerical tendency of the Spanish soul which had been consistently expressed in the middle ages. From the Archpriest of Hita it ran on in unbroken line to the later Danzas de la Muerte and into the sixteenth century. Then the novels of roguery took it up in a very different strain, and so it ran down to the seventeenth century, when Cervantes, steeped, like Montaigne, in this subjective humanism to an extent which we are only gradually realising, made it the very core of his art [8]. Even in a personal sense Erasmus was closely related to the Spanish world ; he received a pension from the Emperor ; the Primate of Spain, the Archbishop of Toledo, Alonso de Fonseca, was his enthusiastic and generous admirer ; the Archbishop of Seville and Inquisitor-General, Alonso Manrique, was an almost fanatical follower of the great humanist of Rotterdam ; the brothers Valdés looked humbly in his direction, and thus it is not surprising that Erasmus should more than once have said that he owed more to Spain than to any other country. And Spain responded to his preference to such an extent that in 1527 Alonso Fernández of Madrid could write to the great man : " At Court, in the towns, in the churches, in the convents, even in the taverns and the highways, there is hardly anyone who does not possess your *Enquiridion* " [9].

Humanism in the narrow sense of direct knowledge of the classics became another, perhaps over-estimated but not unimportant, feature of the increasingly general affirmation of vital values. At first, as has been said, this knowledge was limited, specialised, and almost pedantically disciplined. But within two generations a polish of classical learning became a necessary starting-point for all who aspired to be gentlemen—and even ladies—for the Catholic Queen herself, under the intermittent tutorship of a notorious blue-stocking, Doña Beatriz Galindo, learned some Latin, and her daughters, the future Queen of England and the unfortunate Joan, were prepared for lives of misery by an iron training in spoken as well as written Latinity. This " social " and somewhat superficial interest in classical knowledge, comparable to the importance of French in the eighteenth century, was spread by Italian professors, two of them at least important figures in the cultural history of Europe—one a scholar, Lucius Marineus Siculus, who went to Spain with the Admiral Don Fadrique Enríquez in 1484 and whose address to Charles V is a kind of catalogue of the Peninsular humanists ; the other a man of great intelligence and wide interests, Pietro Martir d'Anghiera, brought to Spain by the Ambassador in Rome, the Count of Tendilla, who professed the humanities at Salamanca and became the first chronicler of the Indies, the importance of whose *Opus Epistolarum* and *Decades* as a source of information for early American history will be discussed later in the volume. He was completely identified with the Isabellian age, lived thirty-eight years in Spain, was a Canon of Granada at the conquest of which he had been present, an original member of the Council of the Indies, and one of the most prolific and " modern " letter writers of the age whose strongly journalistic Latin prose-style, deliberately remote from the great models he lectured on, is worthy to be classed with the greatest epistolary prose of any age in its vividness, power of observation, interest in " atmosphere," and feeling for sensational actuality.

Yet it is clear that if this aspect of the Renaissance had been limited to such visiting virtuosos it could never have become food for the minds of Spaniards to feed on, and an Hernán Cortes could not have consciously imitated the style of Caesar. The real mixture between the waters of the Tormes and those of the Pernessos was effected by Spaniards, the greatest amongst them Antonio de Nebrija, who " first set up a shop in Latin," more than ten years before Peter Martyr and Lucius Marineus. His great merit is to have put the teaching of languages on a sound basis. We can hardly conceive of the difficulties of learning Latin and especially Greek without rational grammars and dictionaries. Nebrija published his famous grammar in 1481, followed by the *Introductiones*, in which for the first time the rules are explained in a modern language and not in Latin " in order that all may learn easily." And not only did he thus give an original Spanish note to his humanism, but he became in a sense the father of Romance philology by the publication in the memorable year 1492 of his *Arte de la Lengua Castellana*, the first grammar (if I mistake not) of a modern language published in any country, thus showing that one of the two characteristic qualities of Peninsular humanism —interest in modern languages and literature, hellenism rather than latinism [10]—goes back to the beginnings of the movement and is doubtless due to temperamental causes.

Two circumstances are in differing degrees both causes and consequences of this humanism, the development of printing and the reform and foundation of universities. The art of printing entered the Peninsula rather late, precisely in the year of the accession of Isabella, was practised first in Valencia and Aragon, always more open to innovations—especially technical—than

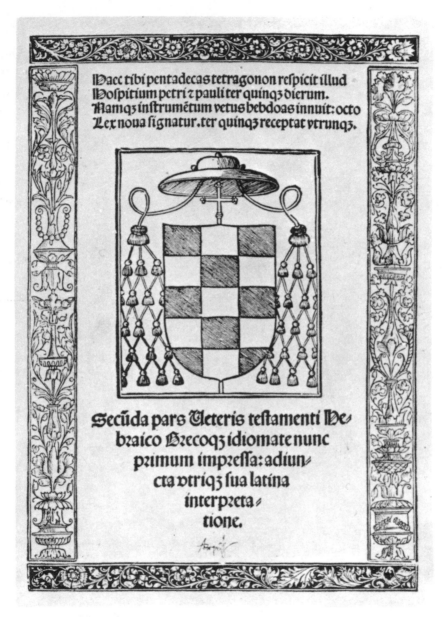

TITLE-PAGE OF THE COMPLUTENSIAN POLYGLOT BIBLE,
PRINTED BY ARNAO GUILLEU DE BROCAR, ALCALÁ
DE HENARES, 1514–1517.

The coat of arms is that of Cardinal Ximenez de Cisneros.

Castile, and then migrated to Seville, the most important centre, Salamanca, Barcelona and Saragossa in the north-east, Burgos in the north, and Toledo, less important, in the centre. Official protection was early and strong ; already in 1477 Theoderic the German who practised in Murcia was exempted from taxes, and there are many examples of such generous encouragement of the new art [11]. The new University of Alcalá was founded in 1508 by the Cardinal Ximénez de Cisneros, but printing had already been introduced there in 1502. It was to be a " modern " university, a centre of classical studies. Theology was to be cultivated not as a dogmatic and polemical discipline but based on the critical study of texts, Hebrew, Greek and Latin, the Greek being taught to some extent by Greeks, such as the Cretan Demetrios Dukas, and Hebrew by Spanish Jews who had preserved the Rabbinical tradition, amongst them the greatest authorities in Europe, such as Alfonso de Zamora and Pablo Coronel. Aristotle was vigorously attacked by Hernán Alfonso de Herrera, and a scholar like Pedro Ciruelo combined in a manner almost cantabrigiensian the study of mathematics with that of theology. Alcalá was, unlike Salamanca, a rich and intellectually aristocratic university [12]. The magnificent memorial which this school erected to its own glory and that of the Spanish printing-presses is the Complutensian Bible, printed by Arnao Guilleu de Brocar, one of the greatest printers of all time, a milestone on the road to modern philology. This Polyglot Bible, published in six volumes, consisted of juxtaposed Hebrew, Greek, and in parts Chaldean texts and the Vulgate version, together with interlinear translations into Latin of the Septuagint and Pentateuch. Pope Leo X lent the Vatican Greek manuscripts for the purpose, and even despatched them to Alcalá. The work was printed in five years amidst unbelievable difficulties, for the marvellously beautiful Greek, Hebrew and Chaldean type had, of course, to be specially cut at enormous expense. It was completed in 1517, although it was not put before the public till three years later. The Greek text of the New Testament, however, was published separately in 1514, and it is thus the epoch-making first, although imperfect, Greek text of the Gospels ever printed, the predecessor by two years of Erasmus's edition.

Plastic and pictorial art in the initial years of transition is allied rather to the medieval characteristics which we have assigned to the literature of the reign of Ferdinand and Isabella, than to this vital activity so rich in promise. The art of the second half of the fifteenth century is essentially northern and germanic, German and Flemish, to the point that the Andalusian cities that are carved in wood on the choir-stalls in Toledo Cathedral remind one of Augsburg or Nuremberg. The Isabellian style hails from Cologne, and only at the very end of the Catholic Queen's reign did Italian influences become important. Yet a transitional style was being evolved which is entirely Spanish and entirely original, the Plateresque, borrowing its name from the art of silversmiths—Plateros—such as the Arfe family, indicating by this comparison its detailed and intricate ornamentation of classical ancestry, typical of the work of Enrique de Egas, a his-panised member of the van der Eicken family from Brussels. Roman arches began to appear, though at first timidly and resting on very elongated columns. Even monuments of Roman anti-quity such as the Aqueduct of Segovia were restored, until architects like Fernán Ruiz, Covarrubias, Bustamante and others attempted, not always successfully, to adopt classical canons. But the characteristic feature remains the wealth of relief, a horror vacui, due, perhaps, to mudejar influences, contrasting with the sublime and stark energy of the later sixteenth century embodied in the Escorial. The Aragonese Damián Forment was creating his dynamic images, and in Gil de Siloe's alabaster work at Miraflores Gothic art was dying amidst a magnificent phantas-magoria of incredible richness. In Andalusia Bartolomé Ordóñez was about to model some of the greatest examples of Italianate art in the Peninsula, the tombs of the Catholic Sovereigns, of mad

SEVILLE CATHEDRAL.

Reja of the Choir.

(*See p. 27.*)

Joan and her beloved husband, resting in the Royal Chapel of Granada, still a largely Muhammadan city when they died. This is the age also of the great Spanish ironsmiths, whose craft is intensely national and unique in Europe. They were forging those magnificent *Rejas*, producing an art that was to culminate in work such as that of the Chapel of the Constable at Burgos by Cristóbal de Andino.

The work that looks towards the future, the most significant product of the Spanish mind, is to be found, however, not in plastic but in literary art. This work, *La Celestina*, the innermost substance of which is a final argument against those who desire a clearly defined Peninsular Renaissance, is neither a play nor a novel, but partakes of the qualities of both, a hybrid monster and yet most certainly the greatest composition in the Spanish language before Cervantes. This drama in twenty-one acts was written some time before 1499 by a converted Jew, the Bachelor Fernando de Rojas, held, in the largely Jewish city of Montalban, in high esteem by his fellow-citizens, whom he assisted as legal adviser when they got into trouble with the Inquisition, it being specially worth our notice that this legal practice did not affect his own position, for he became Alcalde Mayor of Talavera. The play, intensely dramatic in spite of its length, has been reprinted in Spanish as many as eighty times—sixty-two times in the sixteenth century—a number which leaves even the classic instance of *Don Quixote* far behind. Such success is not accidental. Here, it was felt, the essential rhythm of the new life was expressed in a vital tragedy of piercing sweetness. *La Celestina* was translated into Italian within a decade of its appearance, into German as early as 1520, into French shortly afterwards, and was not only the first Spanish book to be adapted into English—partially and most un-skilfully as it happens [13]—but also the one to find in its second English form (1631) the most perfect of translators in James Mabbe. And yet its fame has never spread to Printing House Square, for when the admirable M. Copeau produced in London not

27

long ago a free arrangement of Fernando de Rojas's masterpiece, neither *La Celestina* nor the excellent Don Diego Puedeser (as Mabbe called himself) was at all known, even by name, to the dramatic critic of *The Times*.

The play has many humanistic features. The final catastrophe, when Melibea commits suicide by throwing herself from a tower—suicide is a characteristic theme of this early Renaissance literature—was doubtless inspired by Musaeus' *Hero and Leander*, one of the first pieces of Greek poetry to be printed in the Peninsula [14]. Additional comedies of Plautus were made known during this period after the Cardinal of Cusa had discovered the famous codex in Germany, and were frequently performed, leaving their traces on Rojas. There is much in his work of the university or school-plays of which the oldest, the *Paulus* of Petrus Vergerius of Capodistria, goes back to the fourteenth century. But to say as much and no more is to ignore *La Celestina*'s transcendental significance. Like the scent of Castilian wild flowers (unlike any other in Europe, with the possible exception of those of Greece), the drama is redolent of Castilian quintessential substances, the wisdom of popular proverbs, and the spirit of that old worshipper of the senses, Juan Ruiz, Archpriest of Hita. Yet this is not a work of purely national significance ; on the contrary, it may well be described as the first universal book in Spanish literature with a multitude of themes ranging from classical antiquity and the great Italians, such as Boccaccio and Petrarca, to topical events, covering a vast world of human passions, and culminating in an uncompromising affirmation of spontaneous human life, autonomous within a universe the medieval unity of which had been broken, and expressed in a form which is the double origin of important features of the modern drama and the modern novel. The Renaissance is an age of dialogue, but no such dialogue had ever been written ; personality and therefore character were becoming the measure of things, but no such characters appeared before

28

Shakespeare. If underlying the late medieval flight from reality we detect a certain fatigue and melancholia, here a universal pessimism is expressed with a supreme sense of unsentimental tragedy. Love is not the great creator, love is death the destroyer, and the lover leaving his mistress is not ravished with delight, but laments the consequences of his irresistible passion. No revealed religion offers consolation, but this can only be found in art and beauty. Christianity has no place here. Calisto and Melibea never once speak of marriage, religion at the most supplies some metaphors for the voicing of nefarious purposes, and a disconsolate father, left in the presence of the mangled body of his beloved daughter, can only invoke hard earth : O tierra dura ! Como me sostienes ?

Almost at the same time as the lovely Melibea, created by the imagination of a Spanish Jew of the Renaissance, a prince of flesh and blood died tragically. In the autumn of 1497, at Salamanca, Don Juan, only son of the Catholic Sovereigns, ended his short life of nineteen years. With him ended all hope for a national dynasty that should have given permanence to the Hispanic policy of the great Queen, and, while the humanists of the Peninsula uttered subtle conceits in the pagan manner on this blow of destiny, the crown passed to a Flemish prince and the whole course of events was profoundly altered.

But this emancipation from old limitations is the road also towards social reform, it is the line that points ultimately towards the philosophers of the eighteenth century and the French Revolution. Virtue is no longer limited to the conquest of another world, but becomes external action primarily directed towards action on the world around one. Tradition and continuity are secondary considerations in this endeavour to live and expand. The place of despair is taken by energy and confidence. Divine Omnipotence acquires quite a new meaning. The ideal and the actual are far more closely interconnected than was thought. The wisdom of the great ages can be acquired directly from the original texts, unadulterated by the verbiage of the schools. In art the beauty of life—our life—is a sufficient theme without transcendental motifs. In politics the size of the world is shrinking, and the grandson of the Queen of one peninsular kingdom is on the point of becoming a universal monarch.

The process of the expansion of Spanish ideas from narrow insularity to world-wide comprehensiveness fills the years between the accession of Isabella and the middle of the reign of Charles I of Castile and fifth Holy Roman Emperor. Castile—for the Castilian characteristics and not the Aragonese predominated—became the centre of the far-flung Empire. In itself rigidly united after the expulsion of the Jews and the final destruction of the political power of the Muhammadan Andalusians, it became the centre of an immense American Empire. It always looked west ; its rivers flow in the direction of the setting sun, and all its ports are on the Atlantic. After the union of the two Crowns, Castile also gave its weight to Aragonese Mediterranean politics. The Catalans had widespread commercial interests, and had taken active part in the affairs of the Levant, as when Roger de Flor and Berenguer de Entenza had led 6,500 Catalans to fight the Turks. Their leaders had occupied the highest dignities Byzantium could offer. After the assassination of Roger, they had retreated through Macedonia and offered their services to the Duke of Athens. For generations their commercial establishments in the Near East were well known. In Italy the two Spains exercised a hegemony which began with the accession of Alfonso V of Aragon to the Crown of Naples, was re-established by the campaigns of the " Great Captain " in Southern Italy, and confirmed by the annexation of Naples in 1505.

In the reign of the Catholic Sovereigns such confident activity in the realm of political affairs co-existed with the medieval characteristics outlined previously. The marriage of the Infanta Isabella of Castile to Ferdinand, heir to the throne of Aragon, to which he succeeded in 1479, brought about the personal union of

PATIO OF THE ALCÁZAR OF TOLEDO.

The palace of the Emperor Charles V, rebuilt by Covarrubias, Vergara, Villalpando and Juan de Herrera, the greatest Spanish architect and creator of the Escorial.

A significant example of Renaissance-Imperial architecture, illustrating the change in feeling and outlook that took place after the Isabellian age.

(See p. 30.)

the two Crowns. It is true that this personal union did not obliterate frontiers : an Aragonese was a foreigner in Castile and a Valencian out of place in Galicia. But the union, such as it was, neutralised internal centrifugal forces. The Crown could devote itself entirely to the clearing up of the chaotic conditions which resulted from the civil wars and the frightful chaos left behind by Henry IV of Castile, the ignoble half-brother of Isabella, which Hernando del Pulgar describes so graphically in the twenty-fifth of his Letras (1473) addressed to the Bishop of Coria one year before the Catholic Sovereigns ascended the throne. In the year of the discovery of America the Doctor Francisco Ortiz, addressing the King and Queen in one of his Five Treatises, described the state of anarchy from which they had redeemed their people : " You received the royal sceptre from the Most High in very perturbed times, when all Spain was being shaken by dangerous tempests, when civil wars were at their height and the laws of the realm, already in abeyance, were about to be destroyed. None held his property fearlessly without danger to his life ; there was general distress, and everyone took refuge in the cities ; remoter parts were full of bloodshed by robbers. Arms were not prepared for the defence of Christian frontiers but in order to wound the vitals of our own country. The domestic foe gorged himself on the blood of fellow-citizens ; he who was strongest and most resourceful in malice was the most favoured and praised amongst us, and thus all things were outside the reign of justice, disordered, restless, and chaotic. . . . To whom did the highways offer safety ? To very few indeed ; the oxen were stolen from the plough, towns and cities were occupied by the more powerful. . . . Already the venerable majesty of the law had veiled its face ; all hope had departed."

The almost catastrophic change which took place in less than sixteen years made the Peninsula not only into the strongest monarchy in Europe but Castile into the centre of gravity of this monarchy, imposing Castilian characteristics in the first place on the other Peninsular kingdoms and in a wider sense on large parts of Europe and America. At the same time the Spanish and non-Spanish peoples subjected to Castilian hegemony did not lose their indigenous characteristics, but the immense whole formed a vast group of heterogeneous races with their own languages and traditions, and even their local government, bound together only by the beginnings of the first modern bureaucracy. The creation of this bureaucracy, devoted to the service of a system of decentralised despotism, which through this efficient instrument was able to act swiftly on the world around it, was the characteristic achievement of the Catholic Sovereigns. It gave permanence to their work and made their reign the vestibule of a new Europe. It is remarkable that in establishing a strong central power to save their people from anarchy they carefully avoided useless and dangerous innovations. Thus, the first great instrument of civil government, the Hermandad, a kind of gendarmerie with wide jurisdiction, was reorganised by the Cortes of Madrigal in 1476. But the institution in the new form, under the direction of a minister of the Crown who presided over the council of the brotherhood, was in name, and even to some extent in substance, but the continuation of the powerful Hermandad of 1465 and the previous ones which had been founded by the larger cities of Castile, León, Asturias and Galicia as bodies for municipal defence against the disorder round them. The new brotherhood consisted of picked men, mostly archers, of great efficiency. The pursuit of criminals was carried out methodically in the form of a relay race, for when one company reached the frontiers of its district it handed over the case to its colleagues in another. Nearly always the penalty was death, and the criminal died, like Saint Sebastian, in a volley of arrows.

These summary methods changed very quickly the gloomy picture which Hernando del Pulgar, Ortiz, Diego de Valera and others raise before us. The Queen was able to hand over the administration of justice to regular tribunals even before the

Hermandad was disbanded in 1498. The Sovereigns regularly attended the Council of Castile on the days when it disposed of judicial work. The methods were certainly severe, and the physician of Ferdinand and later of the Emperor Charles, Villalobos, speaks of the " frightful anatomies " of the Queen. When Isabella went to Seville in 1477 four thousand evil-doers left the city hurriedly, and two judges with their clerks who visited Galicia in 1481 did away with nearly fifteen hundred highwaymen and murderers. The Royal *Cancillería* or *Audiencia*, the principal court of justice, was reorganised. It had been a peripatetic body, but it was now permanently installed in Valladolid. In order to speed up accumulated business similar tribunals were set up at Ciudad Real and Granada with a subsidiary one in Galicia. They are the prototypes of the American *Audiencias* (although these differ slightly in their attributions) with their two *Salas*, *de lo criminal* and *de lo civil*, the *Oidores*, and, most important of all, the *Procurador fiscal*, the Public Prosecutor. Special lawyers were paid by the Crown for the defence of the poor, and when these were not to be found, any lawyer present was to give his services " without fee and for the love of God."

The reorganisation of the Council of Castile is above all other Isabellian reforms essential for an understanding of the internal politics of the Castile which forms the background of a young and fragmentary America. The *Consejo de Castilla* always retained its preponderance over the other Councils of State formed later. It was *Nuestro Consejo*, closely connected with the person of the Sovereign. It was the first to be constituted in a form which was to alter but little in three centuries, and although in the official hierarchy it ranked after the *Consejo de Estado*, in which the Grandees sat and whose chief domain was foreign affairs, yet the latter possessed no executive powers, partly, no doubt, because foreign affairs were directed by the Crown, more especially by Ferdinand, who nearly always presided at the meetings. The Council of Castile on the other hand normally worked under its

D

own president, the *Presidente de Castilla*, who after 1489 rapidly became the most important subject in the realm. In the *Consejos* the last and victorious battle against the feudal grandees of Henry IV's time was fought. Already their castles had been razed to the ground—forty-six in a relatively short time—they were deprived of their privileges and subjected to ordinary justice, duelling was prohibited, heraldic devices controlled, and while they were allowed to retain empty honours and shadowy rights, their place in the affairs of State was taken by a class, highly esteemed by the shrewd Aragonese Ferdinand, the *letrados*, or lawyers. The nobles were allowed to be present at sittings of the Council but not to vote, and thus they might enjoy the salutary spectacle of seeing plebeian specialists reduce still further their dwindling power.

The military orders, Santiago, Alcántara, Calatrava and Montesa, no longer formed a state within the State and a happy hunting-ground for turbulent noblemen, for they were doomed ever since in 1476 Isabella had ridden in a rain storm and through the night up to the Castle of Uclés, where the Knights of St. James were in conclave electing a new Grand Master. She announced her wish that her husband Ferdinand should be elected, and informed the amazed barons that she had already written to Rome for the Bull of Investiture. Eleven years later the King possessed himself of the Grand Mastership of Calatrava, seven years after that he became head of the Order of Alcántara, five years later he finally assumed office in the Order of Santiago, which, although controlled by the Crown, had elected its own Grand Master, who had been allowed to remain during the period of transition. Within a decade feudal barons like the Grand Master of Alcántara, Don Alonso de Monroy, " who always slept with a lance in his hand," the ferocious Archbishop of Toledo, Don Alonso Carrillo, the proud Master of St. James, Don Juan Pacheco, and the Marquis of Villena, who, from his castles of Chinchilla, Belmonte, Alarcón and Garci Muñoz,

MEDINA DEL CAMPO.

General view of the Castle of La Mota.

The Castle of La Mota, built by Fernando Carreño about 1440 for John II of Castile. Isabella enlarged it considerably in 1469, and it became one of her favourite residences. She died in the castle—quite near her birthplace, Madrigal de las Altas Torres—on 26th November, 1504. Peter Martyr, who was residing here at the time, wrote dramatically of the death of " this incomparable woman."

defied royal power, became anachronisms. Their wings were clipped and their successors and descendants were to be courtly prelates and Gentlemen-in-Waiting.

Although the Cortes of Castile, Aragon, Catalonia and Valencia were changing from a national assembly of the three orders into humble money-voting Councils, consisting of thirty-six *Procuradores* representing eighteen towns, and were in later years but rarely convoked, the Catholic Sovereigns used them at the beginning of their reign in order to confirm and establish the increasing power of the Crown. The most important of these Assemblies was the Cortes of Toledo in 1480. Here the great reform of *juros y mercedes* was given legal form, and slowly but steadily the Crown began to reclaim the immense alienations of rights and territories made in the reign of Henry IV. All claims were carefully examined ; wherever possible such grants were annulled, and later even grants made by Isabella herself were declared invalid. The most important contribution made to the constitutional history of Spain by that memorable Cortes was the consolidation, almost the re-creation, of the Council of Castile, which in its membership, place of meeting, procedure and powers is symbolical of all that the Catholic Sovereigns and their advisers strove for, the nucleus from which sprang the form of government of the Americas and for generations the most perfect political instrument in Europe. Of its thirteen (or twelve) members, nine (or eight) were *letrados,* three were nobles, and one an ecclesiastic. The meetings took place in the Royal Palace or as near to it as possible, and the councillors had access to the Sovereign. They were well paid, but much was expected from them, for they met every day except on Sundays and holidays, and the sessions, although in theory limited to four hours, were in practice to last until all the business had been transacted. The powers of the Council were very considerable and were much more than merely advisory. Its judicial functions, as the Supreme Court of Justice, have already been referred to. The

Council dealt independently with administrative matters, and its signatures were not necessarily countersigned by the Queen. After Isabella's death the Council summoned Cortes on its own authority.

It has been said with reference to Philip II that modern bureaucracy is one of the doubtful benefits conferred by Spain on Europe. The relative truth of this only a comparative analysis could prove. It is, however, certain that the vast and highly specialised bureaucracy of Spain of the sixteenth century is the immediate successor of the offices of State created or grafted on to older offices by the Catholic Sovereigns, and that it is this bureaucracy which made the incorporation of the Indies into the Spanish world in a social, economic and cultural sense possible. Although the Council of State, with foreign affairs as its main sphere of reference, did not appear as an independent organism until imperial times, its origin must be looked for in the several bureaux created by Ferdinand. Hernando del Pulgar speaks of five Councils, amongst them the embryo of the future Ministry of Finance, the *Consejo de Hacienda*. The affairs of Aragon, Catalonia, Valencia and Sicily were in the hands of an expert Committee which in 1494 was constituted as the *Consejo de Aragón*, the counterpart of the *Consejo de Castilla*. The *Consejo de Indias*, a body which has affected the destinies of the Americas to an incalculable extent, was not established as a Council till later, but who can doubt that its peculiar characteristics are to a large extent due to the original group of men who since 1492 had advised Ferdinand and Isabella on American affairs, of whom the best known is perhaps Juan Rodríguez de Fonseca, Archdeacon of Seville. The system of government by Council took root and became the essential feature of Spanish government down to the time of Napoleon.

Thus the Crown with its Councils retained practically all political initiative. The Grandees had been curbed, the Church was about to be reorganised, order reigned, and a prosperous and peaceful people were easily modelled by royal and conciliar omnipotence. Whether or not popular life and character suffered from this enlightened despotism is difficult to establish. The monarchy, especially as an anti-feudal force, rested on a broad democratic basis. On the other hand, local privileges were being curtailed and the process of municipal decadence accelerated, which led to the great revolt of the Communes under Charles V, and continued in Aragon into the reign of Philip II, who did away with most of the prerogatives of the eastern kingdom. Almost invariably these events are interpreted in a sense quite opposed to that of actual historical experience. The privileges of the towns were not ancient privileges guaranteeing the individual liberty of equal citizens, but privileges opposed to the privileges of the nobles, privileges, moreover, enjoyed only by a small minority, selfishly exploited by municipal aristocracies, who refused to share their advantages with the inhabitants of the countryside. It is thus that the *Fueros* were felt to be an intolerable nuisance, and that the levelling process visible in all departments of institutional life should at first reduce them and later destroy them altogether. Municipal government had for centuries been a hotbed of intrigue and violence. This view is perhaps contrary to the teaching of textbooks, but it is easy to establish. The *Fueros*, grants, and disproportionate privileges had divided and subdivided authority without creating a corresponding civic spirit, in any case in the fourteenth and fifteenth centuries. After the accession of the dynasty of Trastamara, royal influence had constantly transgressed the *Fueros*, and now the municipalities were ready to exchange privileges largely illusory for effective government. The Cortes of Toledo, already mentioned, regulated the appointment of civil magistrates. Hereditary offices were abolished, in theory at least ; town halls were to be built in all cities; and, most important of all, the office of *Corregidor* was made general. The College of *Corregidores* became the basis of municipal government throughout the Peninsula and the Americas, and through it the Crown indirectly and the Council of Castile directly exercised control over all urban matters. The *Corregidor* was a kind of Government Inspector. Neutral in local conflicts, he remained a valuable umpire; learned in the law, he could prevent feudal and ecclesiastical usurpations ; watchful, he was to denounce at once any attempt to erect castles or fortify buildings ; experienced in practical matters, he was the natural assessor of the local *Regidor* ; above bribes, he was a censor of morals, watching over gaming-houses and brothels. His integrity was guaranteed by a test, formidable for many years, that of the *Residencia*, when the outgoing magistrate, after handing over his office, had to remain in his district in order to undergo an enquiry into his conduct and answer charges against him. He was the last and perhaps strongest link in the chain that bound every subject either to the Crown of Castile or to that of Aragon.

The most important cause of the hispanisation of America, independent from the circumstances of the discovery, is doubtless the fact that the intensive colonisation took place at the very moment when conciliar government and bureaucratic organisation was reaching perfection. To this one other fundamental cause must be added. The penetration of the Americas was supported by a condition of prosperity in the Peninsula which would require considerable explanation to be fully understood. Spain never has been, and probably never will be, a rich country. A superficial examination reveals at once that the expulsion of the Jews and the hostility to the Muhammadan or former Muhammadan part of the population affected very seriously commerce and agriculture respectively. What, however, is specially significant amongst the consequences of the expulsion is the alteration in the balance of economic power. The Jews were specially influential in Aragon, Catalonia and Majorca, and therefore these countries, already weakened by social strife in the time of John II, suffered from the immediate economic results of the expulsion more than Castile, so that in a strangely indirect manner these great changes reacted favourably on the relative position of Castile, which alone, to the almost complete exclusion of Aragon, was to hispanicise the Americas, which owe precisely to this circumstance their impressive linguistic and cultural unity. Furthermore, industry, agriculture and cattle-raising profited enormously by the *Pax Catolica*, which followed on half a century of destruction and rapine, making up for the probably much over-estimated losses due to the transference of Jewish capital. The State regulated and protected ; weights and measures were standardised ; manufactures were revived, especially the cloth industries of Toledo and Seville ; the silk manufacturers of Andalusia were probably the most important in Europe ; communications were improved by the construction of highways, the abolition of feudal tolls, accompanied by rigidly enforced customs at the national frontiers. A great impetus was given to ship-building, an important factor not so much in the more or less accidental discovery of the Antilles as in the process of colonisation which required regular—if slow—communications with the mother country, and indeed the systematic regularity of the voyages is noticeable.

In agriculture it was the policy of the Sovereigns to encourage smallholders. A vigorous although not entirely successful step was taken towards the final abolition of serfdom, of *vasallos de parada* and *payeses*, a measure of great importance, especially in Aragon and Catalonia, where the *payeses* had revolted under John II and were living in abject misery. One pair of oxen belonging to each owner was in every case exempted from taxation. Agricultural implements could no longer be seized for debt, and the *Santa Hermandad* took the smallholder under its especial protection. By far the most important part of the national wealth was, however, derived from sheep-farming. Wool production was represented by a very powerful guild of sheep-owners, the *Mesta*, whose chief concern was to keep open the *cañadas* and regulate their use. Along these in rhythmic movement the vast flocks moved, grazing. The office of Alcalde of the *Mesta* had always been a very important one, and was conferred as early as 1454 on a member of the Royal Council. Ferdinand and Isabella now wished to strengthen it still further, and established for the purposes of taxation a close control over the sheep-farmers. They therefore created in 1500 the position of President of the *Mesta*, which was to be an appurtenance of the senior member of the Council of Castile. The sheep-owners flourished exceedingly. One-third of the wool produced was, in theory at least, sufficient to clothe the country, two-thirds being still exported after the importation of manufactured cloths had been forbidden. Thus the decline of agriculture in the sixteenth century must be considered in conjunction with the development of the *Mesta*. The decline did not mean in the larger portion of the Peninsula the decay of rural production, but the supremacy of pastoral over agricultural interests, for the *Mesta* was still increasing in wealth and power, proving incidentally that the hostile great landowners were powerless against it. The public revenues to which the American riches contributed but a small part increased steadily down to the accession of Philip II [15].

Within these manifold manifestations of a perfervid life, the discovery of America occupies a place of prominence but not of absorbing uniqueness. The Spaniard of the fifteen hundreds aspired to spiritual life with an intensity which is unparalleled in modern history. Hence the difficulty of interpretation and hence the fantastic injustice to Spanish culture in the past, for spiritual life can only be understood from within, and its immediate external consequences are often, from a social point of view, odious. The injustice has been perpetuated, even concerning the discovery itself, for it has been wholly attributed to the impulse of an Italian who had no scientific knowledge of geography, nor even the knowledge which was current among the educated men of his period, but accepted without question the wildest fables of the Baron Münchausen of medieval geography, the *soi-disant* " Sir John Mandeville " [16]. It was in reality the immediate result of his collaboration with an experienced Andalusian sailor, Martin Pinzon, who, to make irony even more pungent, was not interested in Antilia, but wished to go to Japan without clashing with the Portuguese, and identified Cuba with Cipango [17]. Pinzon died most opportunely for his colleague and rival and was never able to give his version of the events of the epoch-making first voyage, while Columbus, who had set out to find Antilles across the Atlantic whose existence had long been suspected, succeeded in his quest, but did not recognise it, and believed to his dying day that he had reached Asia by a back door and thus, in a subjective sense, never discovered a new world at all [18].

But the systematic Castilianisation of the Americas lies outside the paradoxical circle of accidents. The inference to be drawn from what has been said is that no other European country of the fifteenth century could have filled with its peculiar, perhaps limited, but intensely vital culture the vast spaces discovered and conquered. It is my belief that the strength of Spain lay in the circumstance that, more impervious to the logic of the historian than France, it held simultaneously the three attitudes to life about which I have spoken. Detached from life, Spaniards possessed a spirit of sacrifice and an endurance of which bands of adventurers inspired only by the lust for gold would never have been capable ; the flight from reality in Europe not only induced people to buy romances of chivalry at some book fair at Medina del Campo but also to take ship and revive the life of fantastic freedom of knight-errantry, conquering in reality the islands which Don Quixote conquered in imagination for his faithful squire ; the political authority of Spain in Europe, due to administrative ability and its instrument, a powerful and well-organised bureaucracy, turned the occupation and government of immense new territories from an Utopian task into a practical problem, capable of solution.

And yet when I review the different phases of the great drama no one even of these fundamental characteristics seems to me the most important from a purely human point of view, and I return to the Bishop of Chiapa, Bartolomé de las Casas, champion of the Indians, who presented in 1542 a pamphlet to the Emperor entitled *Brief Relation of the Destruction of the Indies* in which he outlined a policy—unpractical but redounding to his eternal fame —for the protection of his beloved American Indians. It was of him and of the magnificent humanitarian Spanish legislation in America, ignored by many English historians, that I was thinking when, not many months ago, I climbed the hill on which Trujillo is built, the site of the birthplace of a young swineherd, Pizarro, and of his tomb in the church of La Concepción, the native town of García de Paredes, one of the pioneers in Venezuela, son of that García de Paredes so famous for his strength and immense bulk, who could stop a windmill with one hand. It is no accident that there should be Trujillos in the Canary Islands, Cuba, Chile, Salvador, Santo Domingo, Mexico, Peru, Colombia, Puerto Rico, Venezuela, and that Columbus should have called the first point of the American continent where he raised the flag of Castile during his fourth voyage in the summer of 1502, Trujillo. This little town of Estremadura is not very far from a monastery, Guadalupe, the sanctuary of the Conquistadores, and, indeed, Estremadura is their cradle, for the great Hernán Cortes came from Medellín. They sallied forth, initiating a movement that, combined with the policy of the Hapsburgs in Europe, was to undo the constructive social work of the Catholic Sovereigns. In the end it was to reduce Spain, and especially Castile, to a condition which is graphically described in a lost work of Vasco Diaz Tanco of which only the argument survives :

" There are six Spanish adventurers ; one goes to the Indies, another to Italy, another to Flanders, another is imprisoned, another is involved in a lawsuit, and the sixth becomes a religious ; and in Spain there are no other people than these six."

NOTES TO CHAPTER II

1. Compare *passim* J. Huizinga, *Herfsttig der Middeleeuwen,* Haarlem, 1519; English translation, by F. Hopman, London, 1924.

2. See Ricardo de Orueta, *La escultura funeraria de España,* Madrid, 1919, p. 130.

3. See Menéndez Pidal, *La España del Cid,* Madrid, 1929.

4. Compare *Chivalry,* ed. E. Prestage, London, 1928, pp. 109–40.

5. *Ibid.,* pp. 134–5.

6. See Rodriguez de Lena, *Libro del Paso Honroso,* facsimile of the Salamanca edition of 1588, New York, 1902.

7. Ed. Jenaro García, Mexico, 1904–5, vol. i, p. 266. There is an English translation by A. Percival Maudsley, published by the Hakluyt Society, 1916.

8. The Erasmian attitude of Cervantes is the main point, as I conceive it, of Professor Américo Castro's masterly essay, *El Pensamiento de Cervantes,* Madrid, 1925; see especially pp. 281–3 and 309.

9. Américo Castro, *Recordando a Erasmo* in *Santa Teresa y otros ensayos,* Madrid, 1929, p. 157.

10. Compare *Cambridge Modern History,* vol. i, p. 578 : " Greek learning did *not* prosper in the Peninsula" !

11. See Dr. H. Thomas, *Short-title Catalogue of Spanish Books printed before 1601 now in the British Museum,* London, 1921 ; by the same author, in the series " Periods of Typography," *The Spanish Sixteenth Century,* London, 1926.

12. Srta. de Lara, Lecturer in Spanish at the University of Liverpool, has drawn my attention to the figures for a later period than the one under review. In 1551–2 there were on the registers of Salamanca 5,856 students, whereas there were only 2,109 at Alcalá. The annual income of Salamanca amounted about the same time to 6,000 ducats; Alcalá had 14,000, and its income increased during the sixteenth century to 42,000 ducats.

13. *An Interlude of Calisto and Melebea,* 1530 (?). See *Celestina,* trans. by James Mabbe, ed. H. Warner Allen. This edition contains a summary of modern research on the Tragi-Comedy. See pp. xxvi–xxviii and Appendix II, pp. 303–22.

14. Ποιημάτιον τα καθ' Ἡρὼ καὶ Λέανδρον, Alcalá de Henares, 1514. Printed by Brocar.

15. See for this section: *Colección de documentos de asunto económico correspondientes al reinado de los Reyes Católicos,* parte i, Madrid, 1917 ; Rafael Altamira, *Historia de España y de la civilización española,* vol. ii, Barcelona, 1913, pp. 369–549 ; T. H. Mariéjol, *L'Espagne sous Ferdinand et Isabelle,* Paris, 1892 ; R. B. Merriman, *The Rise of the Spanish Empire,* vol. ii, New York, 1918 ; M. Menéndez y Pelayo, *Antología de poetas líricos,* vol. vi, Madrid, 1911, pp. clxiii–cci ; A. L. Mayer, *Architecture and Applied Arts in Spain,* New York, 1921 ; M. S. and A. Byne, *Rejería of the Spanish Renaissance,* New York, 1924. The complete bibliography for the political history of the reigns of

Ferdinand and Isabella will be found in B. Sánchez Alonso, *Fuentes de la Historia de España,* Madrid, 1919. A useful bibliography for English students is appended to R. Altamira, *A History of Spanish Civilisation,* London, 1930.

16. Vignaud, H., *Toscanelli and Columbus,* London, 1902, p. 42, footnote 50.

17. The *Drang nach Osten* of the Pinzón family seems to have resisted the laws of probability and the action of time, for as late as the year 1499 Vicente Yáñez Pinzón, a brother of Columbus's late colleague Martín, cruising along the coast of Brazil for some two thousand miles, recognised the Amazon at once as the Ganges.

18. The name America was never used in Spanish documents and the New World remained *Las Indias* until the eighteenth century. See Gervasio de Artíñano, *El nombre América* in *Raza Española,* Año XII, Noviembre-Diciembre, 1930, pp. 1–22.

CHAPTER III

VASCO DA GAMA AND THE WAY TO THE INDIES

W H E N Prince Henry, the father of continuous maritime discovery, died in 1460, the Portuguese had reconnoitred and mapped the coasts of West Africa from Cape Bojador in Morocco to Sierra Leone or the River Roxo, a trifle farther ; in addition, the island groups of the Madeiras, the Azores and Cape Verdes had been visited and most of them colonised.

For more than forty years of effort, these results seem to us small, because with our incomparably better means of ocean travel, we can hardly appreciate the difficulties and dangers which the mariners of the fifteenth century had to face and conquer in penetrating unknown and uncharted seas. The caravels they used were little two-masted, half-decked boats of less than fifty tons burden, carrying lateen sails and dependent on wind and tide ; their crews did not generally exceed thirty men ; their nautical instruments, compass, quadrant and astrolabe, were very imperfect ; their salted provisions not infrequently ran short, and if the crews survived the hardships of a deadly climate, they often fell victims to the hostility of the savages on whose shores they landed. The raids they indulged in at first and the belief of the natives that the Portuguese were cannibals, like themselves, accounted for this. Duarte Pacheco in his *Esmeraldo*, the first accurate description of the African coastline, warns sailors of the " evil men " they are to beware of at various points ; he tells how in 1475 a Flemish ship went to trade at Mina, contravening the Papal prohibition against others than Portuguese sailing there, so that " God gave them a bad end, for it was wrecked and the niggers ate the crew of thirty-five."

The raids hindered the progress of discovery ; the temptation to recruit cheap labour led the mariners to disobey Henry's command to push on south, and if it had not been for the advances made by three or four men, but without the prospect of gain, whether from slaves or otherwise, the voyages might have ended with the Prince's life. At first they brought only disappointment, save to Henry and to those few whom he had inspired with his ideals ; it took twelve years before a man dared to pass Cape Bojador, and even then the explorers were merely skirting the bare and almost unpopulated fringe of the Sahara, from which no material profit, the chief incentive to human effort, could be obtained ; but when, in 1441, Cape Branco was reached and captives and gold dust began to reward their labours, critics were hushed, opposition turned into enthusiasm, companies were formed to exploit the wealth of the new-found parts, and whole fleets sailed thither.

The sequel we know ; one man by faith and persistency drove a nation to look for its prosperity overseas and launched it on a career of discovery and conquest, which in the sixteenth century took the flag, the Cross of Christ, into every ocean, so that the humanist George Buchanan, in his verses to John III, could truthfully tell the King that on his dominions the sun never set. But the aggrandisement of Portugal was not the main purpose of the Navigator, though his countrymen doubtless thought first of their personal interests, nor was it merely the increase of knowledge and still less pecuniary gain which governed his life and acts. Both by inclination and by duty as Governor of the Order of Christ, he was first a crusader, and sought to stem the advance of Islam ; his public life began and ended with a crusading expedition, Ceuta (1415) and Alcaçer (1460). In this respect as in personal piety he resembled St. Louis, to whose prayers he commended himself in his will ; he lived like a monk and died a virgin. In pursuit of his crusading purpose he did not hesitate to sacrifice himself, and his zeal for religion led him to rejoice when a company of adventurers brought back cargoes of natives, because of " the salvation of those souls that before were lost." He gave away those which fell to his share, for slavery was not in his design, though it was then and for centuries later considered lawful, and if he instructed his sailors to take captives, it was because he needed them as guides and interpreters. By his order raids on the so-called " Moors " ceased, at least from 1448, and peaceful trading took their place ; owing, no doubt, in part to his example, the captives were well treated, taught trades, and absorbed by the white population through intermarriage ; to their credit, be it said, the Portuguese as a whole have never known a colour line.

But Henry was also a scientist and a practical man, endowed with the power of organisation. He established his naval base at Lagos, the port most suited by its position for his explorations ; he invited foreign aid in the persons of the skilled cartographer, Jacome of Majorca (Jahuda Cresques), and experienced Venetian navigators, while he converted his own household into a school of sailors and pilots, and promoted trade by factories, joint-stock companies, and monopolies ; lastly he devised the caravel, a craft which Cadamosto called the best sailing vessel afloat.

After his death the progress of discovery suffered a temporary check. A country with a population of about one million had already scope for its energies on the mainland of Africa and in the islands. Private enterprise could not be expected to open a new way without encouragement from above, and the only individual voyages we hear of in the next ten years are the second venture of Diogo Gomes in 1460, and that of Pedro de Sintra to Cape Mesurado in 1462. All that the Infant Dom Fernando, Henry's heir, did was to complete the discovery of the Cape Verde Archipelago, for his uncle had left him heavy debts, the price of his services to Christianity and knowledge. State aid would have solved the difficulty if a capable director had existed, but neither Fernando nor Afonso V had Henry's personality, and both were bent on conquests in Morocco, where three fruitless attacks were made on Tangier from 1462 to 1464, and Anafé was occupied in 1468.   These costly enterprises and generous grants to the nobility kept the King ever impecunious, so that he took the best and cheapest course by leasing in 1469 the trade of the Guinea Coast to a wealthy citizen of Lisbon, Fernão Gomes, for five years, with the obligation of discovering one hundred leagues of coast annually, starting from Sierra Leone.   Gomes chose competent men, and a rapid advance was made : in 1470–1 João da Santarem and Pedro de Escolar, knights of the royal household, sailing along the Gold Coast, found Mina ; a year later Fernando Pó lighted on the island in the Gulf of Guinea which bears his name.   It was then seen that the coast turned south, which put another obstacle in the way to the Indies, but notwithstanding this disappointment, the mariners persisted, and about the same time Lopo Gonçalves crossed the Equator, while Ruy de Sequeira went on to Cape St. Catherine, two degrees south of the line.

Though the contract made with Gomes had been justified by the remarkable results, it was not renewed, and the disastrous war with Spain, 1475–9, which was not confined to the Peninsula, held up the work of discovery.

Notwithstanding the grants made by successive Popes to the Kings of Portugal of the exclusive right to the lands and seas they discovered to the south, the Kings of Castile persisted in laying claim to North-west Africa, on account of their descent from the old Gothic Sovereigns, and just before his death, John II of Castile was about to send an embassy to Afonso V to protest against the exercise of the monopoly.   His successor, Henry IV, allowed the dispute to lie dormant, and merely asked that his subjects should not be molested when they went to those parts to trade, provided they paid to the King of Portugal a part of their profits ; but Ferdinand and Isabella, who followed, were of stronger temper, and under their rule naval combats between the ships of the two powers took place, both in African and European waters.

The possession of the Canaries had been for over sixty years another bone of contention between Portugal and Spain. Though the former lost the war, she won the peace, for by the Treaties of Alcaçovas and Toledo, 1479–80, while the contested islands were allotted to Spain, the conquest of North-west Africa, Guinea and the islands to the south was exclusively reserved for Portugal. However, the latter found by experience that she could not rely altogether on written agreements, and in 1480, following the seizure of some Spanish ships, a decree of Afonso V ordered the crews of foreign vessels found in the sphere granted him by Papal bulls to be thrown into the sea after the savage medieval sea custom of dealing with pirates. The Cortes of 1481–2 protested against the intruders, and in 1482 John II had to send an embassy to Edward IV of England asking him to restrain his subjects from trading to Guinea and to prevent the sailing of a fleet then in preparation for that coast at Spanish instigation. In this connection it is well to remember that the doctrine of the *mare clausum*, maintained by the Portuguese, was subsequently adopted and enforced by the Dutch and English. Spanish rivalry had to be carefully watched, for, notwithstanding the peace, King Ferdinand of Aragon supported the conspiracy of the great nobles which broke out shortly after John's accession ; the Duke of Braganza, its leader, who ended his days on the scaffold in 1484, favoured the participation of Spain in the Guinea trade, and if John refused, he offered to help an invasion of Portugal.

When only Prince, in 1474, i.e. on the termination of the lease to Gomes, John had been entrusted by Afonso V with the administration of the conquests, and one of his first acts as King was to secure by effective occupation the rights which successive Popes had granted to his great-uncle and father over the lands and seas they discovered as far as the Indies. He gave orders for the reconstruction of the fort of Arguim, which had been built in his father's reign, and for the construction of another at São Jorge da

Mina, now Elmina Castle, which was raised in January 1482 by Diogo de Azambuja. He added to his titles that of Lord of Guinea and took up Henry's work with the like zeal, but with far more success. He had not the Infante's evangelical patience with his servants, and he could use all the resources of the Crown, including the large profits from the trade in gold dust at Mina, which amounted to 170,000 gold doubloons a year. With these he was enabled to create a maritime organisation with ships, pilots, cosmographers and cartographers far exceeding that of Henry, which led to the great discoveries of his reign and that of his successors. Henry by his crusading ideal belonged to the middle ages, though his critical mind and practical genius linked him up with the modern world. His nephew Afonso V was merely a medieval knight, but John II earned from his people the title of " the Perfect Prince," that is, after the model sketched by Machiavelli. Nevertheless, he sought as keenly as Henry to spread the Christian faith ; its value in facilitating Portuguese expansion and trade would not escape him.

Ruy de Pina describes him as a man " who sought after great and new achievements, and while his body inhabited the realm to rule it well, his mind was always abroad with the will to increase it." He was also " a very solicitous enquirer into the secrets of the world," that is, well versed in cosmography, and he set himself to overcome the difficulty which had hindered the progress of navigation ever since the Portuguese reached the Equator and were unable to see and determine their latitude by the polar star. Following the example of Henry, who had invoked the aid of Jacome of Majorca, he set up a commission of mathematicians, including the Jews Joseph Vizinho and Abraham Zacuto, and they invented a new method, which consisted in calculating the latitude from the height of the sun at midday, and prepared tables of declination which facilitated the work of the mariners.

These new aids to navigation were probably still incomplete when in 1482 the King sent out Diogo Cão to continue the task of exploration. In his first voyage of 1482–4 the latter found the mouth of the River Congo and went on to Seal Point, near Cape St. Augustine, setting up stone pillars at both points to take possession for his master. In the second voyage of 1485–6 he reached Cape Cross and Cape Negro, setting up similar pillars at each. Cape Cross lies 1,450 sea miles south of Cape Catherine, whence Cão's discoveries had begun, so that in four years he travelled almost as far as Henry's mariners had done in forty. But the first step is always the most difficult, and Cão had a driving force behind him in his master, John II, whom Isabella the Catholic, his old opponent, called admiringly " the Man."

His vessels took back the negro Caçuta as an ambassador from the King of Manicongo and the sons of some of his courtiers to be instructed in the Christian faith and taught to read and write ; the heathen King asked for priests to instruct his people and masons and carpenters to erect churches and houses, and in this and other ways desired that his kingdom should be like that of Portugal. The ceremonious baptism of Caçuta and his companions and the spread of Christianity in Manicongo are described by Pina in great detail in seven chapters of his Chronicle, yet he says next to nothing of the voyages, in accordance with the policy of secrecy already pursued of set intention by John II. This policy and the destruction of the records of the India House in the great Lisbon earthquake of 1755 are mainly responsible for our defective knowledge of early maritime exploration by the Portuguese.

In 1486 João Affonso d'Aveiro explored the coast beyond Mina, visited Benin, and brought back the first malaguette pepper, together with news of the existence of a King, Ogané, in the interior, who was identified with Prester John, with whom the Portuguese had first endeavoured to establish relations in Prince Henry's time. John II had already despatched ambassadors to him via Jerusalem and Egypt, but they got no farther than the Holy City, and in 1487 he resolved on two more expeditions, one by land, the other by sea, with the double object of reaching the Indies and of getting into touch with the Priest-King.

In May Pero de Covilhã and Afonso de Paiva were sent overland to Cairo and Aden, where they parted company ; the latter died, but the former travelled to India and then back to the coast of East Africa and returned to Cairo, whence he sent home a report of what he had learnt. This was the most important and fruitful of the land expeditions, but several more were despatched for the same purpose or to explore the interior of Africa for political, religious and commercial ends.

In August 1487 Bartolomeu Dias left Lisbon with two caravels of fifty tons each and a store vessel. Running down the coast past. the Congo and reaching Port Alexander, he landed some negroes who had been carried off by Cão and left there his store ship ; on 8th December he came to what is now Walfisch Bay, and on the 21st to another bay, which he named after the Apostle St. Thomas. Then, according to Barros, he met with a strong northerly wind before which he ran south for thirteen days, and a deadly fear took hold of the crews ; the distance they were from home, the smallness of their craft, and the cold, almost unendurable to men who had come through the tropics, would explain it. When the storm ended and Dias could hoist all his sails, he steered east, and as no land appeared for several days, he altered his course to north. After he had made 150 leagues, high mountains became visible, and on 3rd February, 1488, he anchored in Mossel Bay ; he had passed the southern extremity of Africa without knowing it. Following the new coast he had thus discovered, he got as far as the Great Fish River, and then, turning back, caught sight of the mountains of the Cape Peninsula in May.

In December 1488, after a voyage of sixteen months, he reached Lisbon again, having found 1,200 miles of new coast, which are shown on the map of Henricus Martellus Germanus. The discovery of the Cape of Good Hope and the reports on the

AFRICA FROM THE WORLD-MAP OF HENRICUS MARTELLUS
GERMANUS, DATED 1489.

(From British Museum, Add. MS. 15760.)

The map shows the discoveries of Diogo Cão and Bartolomeu Dias, which are referred
to in legends on the two scrolls in the lower part.

(See p. 52.)

Indian trade sent home by Covilhã showed the entire feasibility of the sea route and determined the voyage of Vasco da Gama.

This was delayed, however, for ten years by internal events and international complications. The marriage of the heir to the throne (1490) and his untimely death (1491) raised the question of the succession in an acute form, while the disputes with Spain that followed upon Columbus's return from his first voyage (1493) were only settled towards the end of John II's reign. Though he had for some time been preparing an expedition to complete the work of Dias, he did not live to win the prize, which fell to his successor, King Manuel, " the Fortunate."

As will be shown in the next chapter, Columbus first endeavoured to secure the support of John II for his enterprise, but he failed, and ultimately came to terms with the Catholic Kings, and with the help of Martin Pinzon he reached the Antilles. He owed his success to the qualities of imagination and persistency, while his misfortunes came from his defects of character. On his return, in March 1493, John II was advised that the new islands rightly belonged to him, because they were not far distant from the Azores, and it was decided to send a fleet there under D. Francisco de Almeida, afterwards first viceroy of India. This news caused alarm in Spain, and King Ferdinand requested the King of Portugal to delay his expedition until the ownership of the seas where the discovery had been made could be verified, and asked him to send ambassadors to discuss the matter. John complied, but Ferdinand secretly obtained from the Spanish Pope Alexander VI the bull of 4th May, 1493 [1], by which all lands already discovered, or to be discovered, west and south of the line drawn at 100 leagues from the Azores and Cape Verde Islands were to belong to Spain. Before this was published, the Portuguese embassy arrived at Valladolid and began negotiations, while Columbus hurried on the preparations for his second voyage to occupy in force the islands he had discovered.

On 5th September the Catholic Kings wrote to tell him that

after the interviews with the Portuguese it was thought that between the line of demarcation and the southern part of Africa islands or even a continent existed richer than all the others ; if he shared this view, he was to say so, that the bull might be modified.   Columbus's answer is not extant, but he no doubt replied in the affirmative, for he intended to pursue his discoveries to the very East which the Portuguese hoped soon to reach, and the Pope issued another bull, of 26th September, annulling the concessions made by his predecessors to the Portuguese (though they were not named) ; all the countries in the east which could be reached by sailing westward and southward were to belong to Spain, as well as those in the west and south, the object being to secure her access to India, and effective occupation was insisted on.   In view of this bull, John had to choose between a war with Spain and further negotiations ; he chose the latter, and by the Treaty of Tordesillas (7th June, 1494) secured an alteration in the dividing line, which was to run at 370 leagues west of the Cape Verde Islands.   His belief in, or possibly actual knowledge of, the existence of continental land to the south-west is sufficient to explain his willingness to compromise, and Robert Thorne, writing in 1527, dated the discovery of Brazil before 1494.   Thus the King yielded to Spain the route that Columbus claimed as leading to the Indies, rendered the Papal intervention nugatory, obtained control of the true route to the East, and got undisputed possession of Brazil.   We do not know by what means this great diplomatic victory was achieved, though we do know that John had leading Spanish officials in his pay, and thus learned and could counter Spanish plans ; apart from this we may attribute it to the superior scientific knowledge of the Portuguese delegates and to John himself, of whom Duarte Pacheco, one of the delegates, wrote : " His judgment and intelligence have been unequalled in our time."

The Treaty of Tordesillas was never put into execution, nor would it have been easy to do so ; the particular island of the

Cape Verde group from which the 370 leagues were to be calculated had not been set down, nor yet the measurement of a
league ; moreover, instruments did not exist of sufficient
accuracy to determine the line, and the fixing of longitude was an
unsolved problem until much later. So little was the treaty
observed, that according to a letter of Stephen Froes to King
Manuel of 30th July, 1514, the Equator was in practice considered
as the dividing line of the two spheres, that of Spain lying to the
north and that of Portugal to the south [2].

King Manuel succeeded to the throne of Portugal in October
1495, at the age of twenty-six, and since he inherited with the
realm the enterprise of the discovery of India, he caused the
question of its pursuance to be debated in the Royal Council in
the following year. Most of the members opposed the under-
taking because India was a distant country to conquer ; they
feared that the attempt would be beyond the strength of Portugal,
and foresaw that it would excite the jealousy and opposition of
other powers, whose commercial interests would be thereby
prejudiced. Some councillors, however, held a contrary opinion,
and as their arguments fitted in with the King's desire, he endorsed
them.

He conferred the leadership of the expedition on Vasco da
Gama, a gentleman of his household. Garcia de Resende, the
friend as well as the chronicler of John II, says that the King
trusted him because he had served in his fleets, and that in 1492
he had been employed to seize French vessels lying in the ports of
the Algarve as a reprisal for an act of piracy. Mariz asserts that
he had as good an acquaintance with navigation as the best pilots ;
and the story of his voyage makes it clear that he did not lack
technical knowledge. But this was not the only qualification
needed. Had it been so, Dias would doubtless have been chosen
to lead the expedition. But discovery was not the main business.

From the reports they had been collecting for years, the
Portuguese knew that when they reached the coast of India, they

would have to deal not with untutored savages, but with astute and capable Orientals and their old Muhammadan enemies. No mere sailor, however skilful, could handle the difficult negotiations that were inevitable. A first-rate man of affairs was needed, and da Gama was chosen for his experience as a soldier and diplomatist. He was to be the ambassador to establish relations between King Manuel and the important Asiatic potentate, the Samuri of Calicut, for the sake of Christianity and commerce. Contemporary writers describe the chosen leader of the expedition as a brave, tenacious, and authoritative man, proud and irascible ; a Venetian, who knew him, calls him violent. In spite of such natural defects, however, he showed patience as well as firmness in dealing with Orientals at Calicut and at the ports at which he touched, and these qualities enabled him to control and keep the confidence of his crews in a voyage of unheard of length through unknown seas.

The most authoritative account of the expedition is to be found in the *Roteiro*, or diary, kept by one of the sailors, probably Alvaro Velho. Da Gama's fleet consisted of four vessels : the flagship *St. Gabriel*, commanded by himself, the *St. Raphael* and *Berrio*, of which his brother Paulo and Nicolas Coelho were captains, and a store vessel. The first two were square-rigged ships of shallow draught, built for the voyage under the direction of Bartolomeu Dias ; the *Berrio* was a lateen-rigged caravel of the class used in the Henrician expeditions. The tonnage of the *St. Gabriel* and *St. Raphael* is stated by contemporary historians as being from 100 to 120 tons, that of the *Berrio* as fifty, while the store ship seems to have been of 200 tons ; but the " ton " at that time was a different measure from what it is now, and if we multiply the figures by two we shall not be exaggerating them.

The ships were provisioned for three years, D. Diogo Ortiz, the ablest geographer in the service of the Crown, supplied da Gama with maps, while Abraham Zacuto provided astronomical instruments, prepared tables of declination, and perhaps trained

MARTYRDOM OF ST. ANTA AND HER COMPANIONS, SHOWING
PORTUGUESE SHIPS OF THE EARLY SIXTEENTH CENTURY.

(From a painting attributed to Gregorio Lopes in the Museum of Ancient Art in Lisbon.)

(*See p. 56.*)

him to take observations. Lastly, stone pillars formed part of the cargo, and were set up at various points as a mark of discovery and overlordship, as they had been by Cão and Dias. The crews numbered 170 men, of whom over one-third died on the voyage. The vessels carried a priest, and convicts for employment on the more risky enterprises to be undertaken.

The expedition left the Tagus on 8th July, 1497, passed the Canaries on the 15th, and struck the African coast at Terra Alta. The vessels then parted company in a fog, and only came together at the Cape Verde Islands on the 26th ; the next day they anchored in the Bay of Santa Maria at S. Thiago, provisioned, and repaired the yards. Starting again on 3rd August, da Gama stood south-east until he was 200 leagues from S. Thiago, when he met with squalls and the *St. Gabriel* broke her mainyard. He then resolved to make a circular course through the South Atlantic to the Cape, and accordingly steered south-west into the ocean. Unless, as is probable, an earlier expedition had obtained a knowledge of the prevailing winds in the South Atlantic, it was an act of superlative audacity, for the experience gained by Dias would not have sufficed for the decision [3]. Save for the appearance of whales on two occasions, nothing of importance happened until 1st November, when signs of land appeared, and on the 4th it actually came in sight ; the mariners had been ninety-six days at sea since leaving the Cape Verdes. Six days later they discovered a broad bay, which they named St. Helena, and anchored there to clean the ships' bottoms, mend the sails, and take in wood. A native, probably a Bushman, but certainly not a negro, was captured and well entertained, with the result that others came, and at first friendly intercourse ensued between them and the Portuguese. One day a soldier, Fernão Velloso, obtained leave to return with them to find out how they lived, but some hours later he came running towards the shore, shouting to his comrades ; da Gama immediately ordered out a boat to take him off, but he was rescued with difficulty, because the natives followed him up, and, hurling their spears, they wounded the Captain-major and some others.

On the 22nd the Cape was doubled and a stay of thirteen days was made in the Bay of São Braz, where the store ship was broken up. The natives had shown hostility to Dias, but da Gama found them well disposed. Later on, however, a dispute arose; they accused the Portuguese of taking their water, and threatened an attack, but the discharge of two bombards sent them back helter-skelter into the bush. As the fleet was leaving, they were seen demolishing the cross and pillar that had been set up.

On 8th December da Gama set sail, and running with bare poles through a storm passed on the 16th the Rio do Infante, the farthest point reached by Dias. The Agulhas current bore the vessels back for a time, but on Christmas Day they came to a land which for that reason received the name of Natal; seventy leagues of fresh coast had been discovered. Da Gama now stood out from the land, but lack of drinking water soon drove him to seek a port, and putting in near the entrance of a small river, he was so well received by the negroes that he named it " the Land of Good Folk." Shortly after passing Cape Correntes, he came into contact with Muhammadan civilisation in the coast towns of East Africa; hitherto he had struggled with the forces of nature and with savages, now he was to meet the calculated hostility of members of a rival creed. At Quilimane, which he reached on 25th January, 1498, the people brought out their wares to sell, and a month was spent in careening the vessels, during which many of the crew fell ill, and some died of scurvy. After setting up a pillar, the fleet went on its way, and anchored before Mozambique at the beginning of March, and there its troubles from man commenced. Assuming the newcomers to be Muslims, the natives came on board freely and partook of the hospitality offered them, and da Gama heard that they traded with Arabs, four of whose vessels were then in port, that Prester John lived in the interior,

VASCO DA GAMA.

Reproduced from a painting of nearly contemporary date long preserved in the possession of his descendants. The portrait was presented by the Conde da Vidi-gueira to King Carlos of Portugal, and by him to the Lisbon Geographical Society.

(*See p.* 61.)

and that he held cities on the coast, tidings which made the Portuguese weep for joy.

The ruler of Mozambique had been forewarned of their creed, but he made a show of friendship by giving the two pilots he was asked for. The ships moved out to the island of St. George ; a pillar was set up, Mass was said, and, the season being Lent, the mariners confessed and received Holy Communion. The natives were now aware that they had to deal with Christians ; an attempt was made to induce da Gama to come nearer to the town, with a view of seizing his vessels, but he discovered the plot and, after watering by force, departed for Mombasa, where fresh treachery awaited him. The ruler invited him to enter the harbour, and he was actually doing so, when an unlucky manœuvre obliged the *St. Gabriel* to anchor ; thereupon the Muslims on board, thinking their design discovered, jumped into the sea, and at midnight armed swimmers tried to cut the cables. On Easter Sunday the Portuguese reached Melindi, and were welcomed as they had not been since they met the Muhammadans ; fear of their artillery probably accounted for this.

On the way from Mombasa some Moors had been taken off a boat, and da Gama despatched one of them to the Sultan to announce his desire for friendly relations and pilots for India. A favourable answer came, and an interview took place on the water ; da Gama would not land, saying that his master had forbidden him to do so until he reached India ; he had learned caution by his experiences at Mozambique and Mombasa.

The nine-days' stay was rendered agreeable by fêtes, but the promised pilot did not appear ; however, by detaining a confidential servant of the Sultan, a well-known pilot was obtained, and on the 24th the fleet sailed for Calicut.

After running up the African coast, it steered over the Indian Ocean, and in twenty-three days the Ghats came in view on 18th May. The *Roteiro* says nothing of the emotion which must have overtaken the navigators at the first sight of Asia, but Camões, who came the same way half a century later and used his own experiences in relating the voyage of da Gama, describes the scene, laying stress on their relief and on the Captain's gratitude to the Almighty. On the 22nd the fleet dropped anchor off Calicut ; the great enterprise was accomplished ; the Portuguese had reached the land of wealth abounding. From what we know of them at that time, we may believe the poet's assurance that in this supreme moment they did not forget Him, who had led them to their goal and protected them in their long journey.

Three months were spent in negotiations, which were rendered fruitless by the intrigues of Muslim merchants who feared to lose their monopoly of the transit of spices to Egypt, and then da Gama started on his homeward voyage on 29th August. Owing to calms and contrary winds, the re-crossing of the Arabian Sea occupied another three months ; thirty of the crew died of scurvy, and only seven or eight men in each ship were fit for duty. At last, however, da Gama caught a favouring wind, which brought him in sight of the African coast on 2nd January, 1499, and five days afterwards he reached Melindi. Finding, farther on, that he had not enough men to navigate the three vessels, he set fire to the *St. Raphael* and distributed the crew among the others. On 20th March the *St. Gabriel* and *Berrio* rounded the Cape together, but a month later a storm parted them ; Coelho held on his way, and entered the Tagus on 10th July, two years and two days after he had started, while the Captain-major proceeded to the island of S. Thiago. From there he is said to have despatched the flagship to Lisbon, while he took his sick brother in a hired caravel to Terceira, where he died ; Vasco reached Lisbon on 29th August or 9th September (the date is disputed), and made his triumphal entry into the city nine days later. The results of his voyage are shown in the maps of Juan de la Cosa, an anonymous one of 1502, and those of Cantino and Canerio, reproduced by Ravenstein in his excellent edition of the *Roteiro* [4].

Da Gama's diplomatic mission had been a failure, but he had found India, and brought back samples of its products ; what he had accomplished could be repeated, and fabulous wealth lay open to Portugal, if only she had the courage to seize it. His voyage out was the finest feat of seamanship recorded up to that time, and a greater one than that of Columbus ; for not only had the latter a much shorter distance to travel, but, favoured by the wind, he could proceed almost straight from the Canaries to his goal. In scientific knowledge da Gama proved himself the superior, the accuracy of his observations being in marked contrast to the errors made by the Genoese ; surely few will deny that he was cast in the heroic mould, when they consider the achievement by which he realised one of the dreams of Prince Henry the Navigator by uniting East to West ; it was the first meeting of the two civilisations since the days of the Antonines.

King Manuel added to his previous titles that of " Lord of the Conquest, Navigation and Commerce of Ethiopia, Arabia, Persia and India." In thanksgiving to God he built the Jeronymos Church at Belem on the Tagus near Lisbon and rewarded liberally the man who was the first to take a ship from Europe to India. He granted him the title of Dom, a large pension, the post of Admiral of the Indian Seas, and the right to import merchandise from the East to the value of 200 *cruzados* a year.

The King announced the discovery in letters to the King and Queen of Castile and to the Cardinal Protector, and three letters from Girolamo Sernigi, a Florentine merchant in Lisbon, supplement the *Roteiro*, and give an account of the East, its inhabitants, and their dress and religion, trade, shipping, precious stones, animals, etc. ; they are translated in Ravenstein's book, and the information Sernigi gives was derived from the members of the expedition.

Few of the great pioneers have had the good fortune of da Gama, for he lived to see the wonderful results of his discovery, died Viceroy of India in 15 24, and thanks to the genius of Camões, became an epic figure in poetry ; the Lusiads is woven round his voyage, and the route he found to the East continued to be used for nearly four centuries, that is, until the opening of the Suez Canal.

The immediate material results of his voyage far exceeded those of the discovery made by Columbus, which were disappointing to all concerned ; for instead of the precious metals he had dreamed of, the Genoese explorer found only savages. The India trade brought quick returns, the profits of the early expeditions were fabulous, and Lisbon superseded Venice as the European mart of Eastern spices, then worth more than their weight in gold.

It was natural that King Manuel should wish to ascertain what lay in the domain secured to his country by the treaty of Tordesillas, especially as Columbus had found islands in the Spanish sphere, and thus, while da Gama was still in the East, in 1498 he secretly despatched Duarte Pacheco to reconnoitre the Western Ocean, and as a result of his report Pedro Alvarez Cabral took a similar direction in 1500. To this year also belongs the first of the three expeditions of Gaspar and Miguel Corte-Real to the north-west. In Cantino's map of 1502 there appears in the North Atlantic, within the limits assigned to Portugal by the Treaty of Tordesillas, a land whose eastern coast alone is clearly defined. To the westward it is conventional, and as it is marked "Land of the King of Portugal," it unmistakably represents the discovery of the first Corte-Real voyage.[1] The brothers themselves never returned, and had we details of their end, these would probably add a chapter to that prose epic of shipwrecks, the Historia Tragico-Maritima, but as we find from a letter of Pietro Pascualigo to the Venetian Senate [5], the net result of all these voyages was to convince the Portuguese, as early as 1501, not only that they had found a new continent, for they never believed with

---

[1] See further, below, Chapter V.

THE BELEM MONSTRANCE.

Made by Gil Vicente to the order of King Manuel I for the Church of the Jeronymos at Belem, Lisbon. The gold used was that paid as tribute by the Sultan of Kilwa, East Africa, and brought to Lisbon by Vasco da Gama in 1503.

(*See p.* 61.)

Columbus that it formed part of Asia, but that it ran continuously from the land found by the Corte-Reals in the north to that discovered by Cabral to the southward.

On da Gama's return, the King at once began to profit by his discovery, and on 9th March, 1500, Cabral left Lisbon with a large fleet of thirteen ships, carrying the best cosmographers and pilots of the day, Bartolomeu Dias, Duarte Pacheco and Nicolas Coelho, and provided with everything needed for an absence of eighteen months ; on the 22nd they were off the Cape Verde Islands, and next day lost sight of the ship of Vasco de Ataide, though we are told that there was no bad weather to account for it, and after seeking it in vain, they held on their course. On 21st April, signs of land appeared, and the ships were then at a distance of about 660 leagues from the islands already mentioned, as the pilots said. On the 22nd they descried a high mountain and a stretch of low-lying coast to the south covered with trees ; as the season was Easter, they named the mountain Pascoal, and to the land they gave the name of Vera Cruz, a designation afterwards changed to Brazil, because of the red dye-wood it produced. They anchored the next day near the mouth of a river, and saw a number of brown men with long hair, entirely naked, carrying bows and arrows, but could not understand their language ; at night a strong south-west wind got up, accompanied by heavy rain, and they were compelled to run up the coast in search of a shelter where they could take in water and wood. They found a good port (Porto Seguro), and on Sunday, the 26th, the first Mass on the South American continent was said on an islet by Frei Henrique de Coimbra, afterwards Bishop of Ceuta, in the presence of the captains and crews. The natives seemed well disposed : they danced and played their musical instruments and helped the Portuguese to take in water ; some of the latter went to a village three miles inland, and in exchange for bells and pieces of paper, obtained a root called *inhame*, which served as bread, and parrots, which were so plentiful that the country was later on described on some maps as the " Land of Parrots." A stay of five or six days enabled the newcomers to observe the Brazilians more fully ; they were painted, had large protruding lower lips, and were expert fishermen. Like the people found by the Corte-Reals, they possessed no metals, but cut wood with a sharpened stone ; the hammocks they used for sleeping seem to have impressed the Portuguese, and these and other things are described in accounts of the voyage by an anonymous pilot [6] and others. Cabral ordered a cross to be set up bearing the arms of King Manuel, sent one of his ships home with news of what he had found, put two convicts on shore, who wept at being left behind, but were consoled by the savages, and then went on his way to India.

In letters to the King of Spain written in 1501 and 1505 [7], King Manuel spoke of the arrival of Cabral in Brazil as a new dis-covery, presumably because the previous knowledge of it had been kept secret ; Portuguese historians recorded it as such, and until recently it was believed to be so. Barros, for instance, following the official version says that Cabral, to escape from the Guinea coast, the calms of which might have impeded his journey,[1] sailed far out into the ocean so as to make sure of being able to double the Cape of Good Hope, and after following that course for a month, he lighted, on 24th April, on another continental coast, which most of the pilots took to be a great island. The anony-mous pilot does not attempt to explain the course taken ; he only says that they could not find out if the land was an island or a continent, but inclined to the latter belief on account of its size.

The instructions given to Cabral, of which only a part has been preserved [8], are supposed to have been dictated by da Gama, and, as we have seen, the former described a curve after passing the Cape Verde Islands, as his predecessor had done, but a wider one ; it is almost certain that he had orders to touch at Brazil, though these must have been confidential, and we must

---

[1] Ships were sometimes detained off the Guinea coast for more than a month ; John de Empoli, sailing with Albuquerque in 1503, was becalmed for fifty-seven days.

remember that Duarte Pacheco, who had already been there, accompanied him. In spite of what Barros says, everyone was not in doubt of the existence of land to the south-west, for Master John, the surgeon, wrote to the King from Brazil : " As to the position of this land, let your Highness have a *mappa mundi* belonging to Pero Vaz Bisagudo brought to you, and there you can see it " ; and he added that the map was an old one. Neither he nor the pilot, Pero Vaz de Caminha,[1] who also wrote to the King about the country, expressed surprise at having met with it. Since Cabral went farther out of his course than he need have done if he only wanted to avoid the doldrums of the Gulf of Guinea and catch a wind to round the Cape, some modern writers have suggested that he was driven westward by a storm or currents, while others have invented an error of navigation, but there is nothing in the letters of Master John and Caminha to warrant the first two hypotheses, while the third is most unlikely, seeing that Cabral had with him such experienced mariners as Dias and Coelho as well as Duarte Pacheco.

The Brazilian coast-line was further explored by Gonçalo Coelho in 1501 and 1502, when Fernão de Noronha found the island named after him ; Amerigo Vespucci sailed in these expeditions, though he is not mentioned by Portuguese historians, probably because he did not hold a leading position in them. Voyages to the newly discovered lands in the west soon became frequent, and a flourishing trade in dye-wood was established, but none of them are related by the chroniclers, the reason being that they were entirely absorbed with the military exploits in the East and, like their countrymen in general, had a disdain for mere trade, though King Manuel had different ideas, for he was the first merchant in his dominions. Finally, in 1519, the greatest of all navigators, Magellan, a Portuguese in the service of Spain, came the same way, leading the expedition which first circum-

[1] Pero Vaz da Cunha, called *o Bisagudo,* had returned in 1488 from a voyage to Guinea.

navigated the globe ; planned by Portuguese cosmographers and cartographers, and guided by Portuguese pilots, it was the logical consequence of the efforts put forth and the experience accumulated since the time of Prince Henry, and proved their superiority in the art of navigation.

On his way across the Atlantic to the Cape of Good Hope, Cabral was met by a sudden squall near the islands of Tristão da Cunha, in which four of his vessels foundered with all aboard, including that of Dias ; farther on the weather was very bad, and when, on 16th July, he arrived off Sofala with the remaining six, these were so damaged that they were " fitter to return to the Kingdom, if it had been near, than to conquer others." At length, however, he reached Calicut on 13th September, after a passage of six months, which was afterwards the usual length of an Indian voyage, even when no call was made at Brazil and neither storms nor accidents were encountered. Cabral's doings in the East do not concern us, as we are dealing with exploration and not with military achievements ; suffice it to say that, though by the intrigues of Moorish (i.e. Arab) merchants he could get no spices at Calicut, he was able to load pepper at Cochin and ginger at Cananor, and that after discovering the island of St. Helena on the way home, he reached Lisbon on 23rd June, 1501, with a cargo which amply repaid the cost of his whole fleet. His political action at Calicut has been severely criticised by some writers, but he has the distinction of having been the first man to make a voyage from South America to India.

King Manuel had previously determined that a fleet should sail yearly to the East in the month of March, the proper time to catch a favourable wind in the Indian Ocean, and in 1501, before Cabral returned, he sent out João da Nova with four vessels, which came back in September 1502 with a cargo of spices. In the same year Vasco da Gama went again to India, this time with a large force of twenty ships, because trade was no longer the only object. It was realised that if Portugal were to establish her power in the Indian

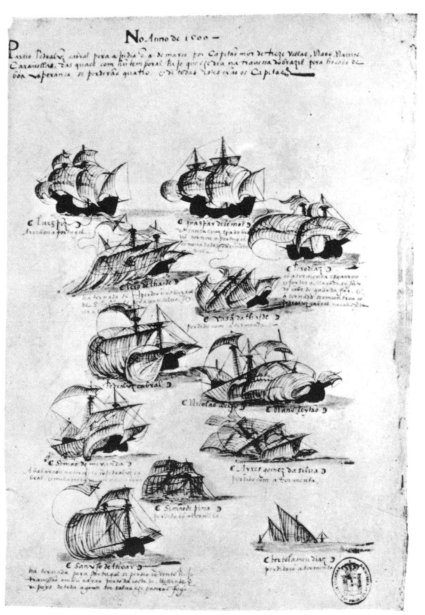

THE FLEET OF PEDRO ALVAREZ CABRAL, 1500.

(From an illuminated MS. of the sixteenth century known as the *Livro das Armadas*.
In the library of the Lisbon Academy of Science.)

(*See* p. 64.)

seas, she must beat down the opposition of her jealous enemies ;
a squadron was to remain to protect the factories already
established at Cananor and Cochin, and to close the mouth of the
Red Sea to Muhammadan merchantmen.   The King had assumed
the new title of "Lord of the Conquest, Navigation and Commerce
of Ethiopia, Arabia, Persia and India," and da Gama proceeded to
enforce the claim ; he took a cruel vengeance by land and sea on
the Moors,[1] the hereditary foes of the Portuguese, for their
hostility on his first visit, and for the massacre of the factor and
men left by Cabral at Calicut, and extracted from the Sultan of
Kilwa, on the African coast, a tribute of 2,000 *miticals* of gold, out
of which King Manuel had a monstrance made for the church of
the Jeronymos, which is a monument of the goldsmiths' art.

The Portuguese sought to divert round the Cape of Good
Hope for their own benefit the trade in spices and other Eastern
products which had enriched the Sultan of Egypt and the republic
of Venice, and to secure it they proceeded to compel the rulers
of the East African and the Malabar coast to accept the suzerainty
of King Manuel or become his allies.   This policy, initiated by
da Gama, was carried farther by D. Francisco de Almeida, who
went out in 1505, and it led to the formation of a Muslim league
against the newcomers.   The loss of revenue suffered by the
Sultan of Egypt caused him to despatch a naval expedition in aid
of his co-religionists which defeated a squadron of the Viceroy's
son at Chaul, but D. Francisco destroyed the combined fleets at
the battle of Diu on 2nd February, 1509, and thenceforth for a
century the dominion of the Indian Ocean and therefore of its
traffic remained in Portuguese hands.   Already in 1506–7 Tristão
da Cunha had sailed up the coast of Madagascar and reduced
Socotra, while Affonso de Albuquerque with a separate squadron
had conquered Ormuz, the key of the Persian Gulf, in 1507, and
two years later he succeeded Almeida as governor of India.   In the
six years of his rule he established Portuguese supremacy on a

[1] All Muslims were called Moors by the Portuguese.

firm footing, basing it on the command of the sea and on fortresses stretching from East Africa to Malacca : in 1510 he took Goa and made it his capital ; in 1511 he won Malacca, which controlled the narrow straits by which the traffic of the Far East reached the West. From there he opened up communications with Siam, Pegu and other neighbouring states, and exchanged embassies with the Shah Ismael of Persia, while Queen Helena of Abyssinia sought his friendship. Albuquerque failed to reduce Aden, by the ownership of which he hoped to close the Red Sea to Muslim shipping, but he put such fear into the Sultan of Egypt that the latter made no further attempts to interfere in Indian waters.

After his occupation of Malacca, Albuquerque sent a squadron to the Moluccas under Antonio de Abreu and Francisco Serrão, a friend of Magellan [1] ; the first-named reached Amboina, the home of the nutmeg, while the second was wrecked on an uninhabited island, but rescued by a native boat and taken to Ternate, where he became a power by helping the Sultan in his wars against the rival ruler of Tidor.

As early as 1508 Diogo Lopes de Sequeira had been sent out by Almeida to find Malacca, the essential fortress that commanded the Straits through which all the trade with the Far East must pass. He carried elaborate instructions, and was to enquire about the Chinese, their country, religion, trade, ships, wealth, arms and dress. On arrival he found some junks in the harbour, but owing to the hostility of the Malays he was obliged to return to Portugal without the desired information. When Albuquerque reached the city in July 1511, he also met with some junks, and established such good relations with the owners that these not only offered to help in his military operations, but conveyed his ambassadors to Siam and, more important still, they took home such a good impression of the Portuguese that when the deposed King of Malacca went to China to solicit aid against the European intruders, he failed to obtain it. After Albuquerque returned to

[1] See below, Chapter VII.

India, the governor he had left at Malacca was too busied with repelling native hostility to think of extending Portuguese influence and trade, but in 1514 he sent a mission to China, which, although not allowed to land, sold the goods it carried at a profit ; this mission is mentioned in the letters of two Italians, Andrew Corsali and John de Empoli, and alluded to by Barros. The next European to visit China was Raphael Perestrello, like Empoli an Italian in the Portuguese service ; when his brother was appointed factor of Malacca in 1514, he had accompanied him with orders to discover China. He carried out this commission in the following year, travelling in a junk with a number of Portuguese, and returned with a rich cargo and the news that the Chinese desired peace and friendship with Portugal, and that they were " good people."

These expeditions were of a tentative nature, and the first official embassy ordered from home was conducted by Fernão Peres de Andrade, who went to the East in 1515 with Lopo Soares de Albergaria, Albuquerque's successor in the governorship of India. The ambassador, selected by Lopo Soares, was named Thomas Peres, a man who had served with success on various missions in the time of Albuquerque ; by profession he was an apothecary, and it was apparently hoped that he would bring back useful plants. Andrade left Cochin in April 1516 ; at Pasai in Sumatra he met Empoli, who was also bound for the Celestial Empire on a trading venture, and in July he reached Malacca, but did not hasten to his goal, because he was more inclined to proceed to Bengal, the discovery of which was also included in the instructions he had received from King Manuel. However, when Perestrello returned to Malacca from his successful voyage, Andrade resolved to postpone his visit to Bengal, and in December 1516 he went to Pasai to take in a cargo of pepper and left for China in June 1517. His fleet consisted of his own vessel, the *Esphera*, of 800 tons, and seven others, Portuguese and native : all were armed and had Chinese pilots. They arrived at Tamau at the mouth of the Canton river, and applied for leave to go up to the city, but as this was delayed, Andrade left part of the fleet at Tamau under Simon d'Alcaçova, and himself went over to Lantau, whence he sent Empoli to press for the desired permission. This was given, and in September he sailed up the Canton river and anchored before the city. His artillery salute frightened the Chinese, and he had to apologise for having shown ignorance of local customs ; and he then sent Empoli to explain the object of the mission. The officials allowed the ambassador to land, assigned him a residence, and promised to write to the Emperor about him ; Andrade was also invited on shore, but refused to leave his vessels, alleging royal orders ; however, he obtained the use of a house for the sale of his goods, and supplied men for the purpose, instructing them to see as much of the city as they could and bring back information. Later on, the news that Alcaçova had been attacked by pirates, and an outbreak of fever which carried off Empoli and eight others, probably decided him to return to Tamau, and when after some months he heard that the Emperor had agreed to receive the ambassador, he left for Malacca in September 1518. The tact and ability he had displayed in dealing with the Chinese had given them a good impression of the Portuguese, and enabled him to take back a valuable cargo ; unfortunately, his work was ruined by the behaviour of the leader of the next expedition, his brother Simon, and many years passed before the relations of the two countries were re-established on a friendly footing, and it was not until 1557 that the Portuguese could settle at Macau, which they still hold as a colony. The unfortunate Thomas Peres never succeeded in obtaining an audience of the Emperor, but was imprisoned at Canton, where he died, and the presents he had bought from the King of Portugal were confiscated [9].

Though the Portuguese were now forbidden to trade with China, the profits obtainable were so large that some could not resist the temptation, and in 1542 three men, Antonio da Mota,

Francisco Zeimoto and Antonio Peixoto, started from Siam with a cargo of skins for Chincheu. On the way they encountered a typhoon lasting twenty-four hours, and after it had passed, their battered junk was carried by the winds in fifteen days to islands unknown to them. Boats came out from the land containing men whiter than the Chinese, but with small eyes and scanty hair, who said that those islands were called Nippon. They received the Portuguese well, and after bartering their merchandise for silver and repairing their vessel, the latter returned to Malacca. This was the first visit of Europeans to Japan.

Exploration was also carried on by land, and for the sake of knowledge and not of trade, and in this the Jesuits won the palm : Anselm de Andrade was the first to enter Tibet, Benedict de Goes undertook a five-years' journey from India to China and identified it with Cathay, while Peter Paes and Jerome Lobo sought to discover the sources of the Nile ; these travellers deserve even more credit than their successors, because they lacked their advantages. Camões did not exaggerate when he said of his countrymen :

" E se mais mundo houvera, lá chegára." [1]

NOTES TO CHAPTER III

1. For a definitive account of these bulls and their date see H.Vander Linden , "Alexander VI and the Demarcation of the Maritime and Colonial Domains of Spain and Portugal, 1493–1494," *American Historical Review*, October 1916, vol. xxii, pp. 1–20.

2. The Treaty stipulated that while Papal confirmation was to be sought, no Papal *motu proprio* should dispense the parties from observing the convention.

3. Admiral Gago Continho, in an address to the Lisbon Academy of Sciences in December 1929, stated his conviction that da Gama acted on the experience of former voyages.

4. *A Journal of the First Voyage of Vasco da Gama, 1497–1499.* Translated and edited by E. G. Ravenstein, Hakluyt Society, 1898.

5. The letter was written from Lisbon on 18th November, 1501, and with another from Albert Cantino of 17th October to Hercules d'Este, Duke of Ferrara, contains an account of the land and people found by the Corte-Reals. We are told that King Manuel

[1] And if there had been more of the world they would have reached it.

was delighted at hearing of the quantity of trees suitable for ships' masts and of the large population which would provide slaves.

6. First published in Ramusio's *Viaggi,* and subsequently translated back into Portuguese and issued by the Lisbon Academy of Sciences in 1867.

7. An inscription on the Cantino map also speaks of Cabral as having discovered Brazil.

8. An English translation will be found in J. R. McClymont, *Pedralvarez Cabral,* London, 1914.

9. *Vide* Donald Ferguson, *Letters from Portuguese Captives in Canton written in 1534 and 1536,* Bombay, 1902. The letters give most interesting information about China, and are preceded by a well-documented introduction on Portuguese intercourse with the country in the first half of the sixteenth century.

CHAPTER IV

CHRISTOPHER COLUMBUS AND HIS FIRST VOYAGE

W E have pursued the story of Portuguese enterprise far down into the sixteenth century without a break, because its development was essentially a continuous and self-contained movement little affected by outside influence. But we must now return to take up the consideration of what was in its early beginnings an offshoot from the work of discovery initiated by Prince Henry the Navigator, though later it pursued an independent course, and produced results which both in the spheres of thought and of material progress equalled, if they did not surpass, those of the opening of the sea route to the East Indies. The beginnings of this vastly important movement are bound up with the romantic career of Christopher Columbus, the central figure of the period of transition from medieval to modern times.

In the history of the world few names are more familiar or more celebrated. Nearly four and a half centuries have passed since his first discovery, and many great and proud nations have arisen in the new lands who acclaim him as their earliest hero. Each has vied with the others in commemorating him, and this has led to a stream of uncritical eulogies that have often borne little relation to historical fact. A Columbian legend has been accepted that is regarded almost as sacrosanct, and when scientific enquiry into the facts supported by documentary evidence began, it revealed so many debatable problems and aroused such controversy among the critics that the non-critical public assumed that the rival theories cancelled out. The Columbian tradition in the eyes of many continued to hold the field, and the most romantic versions of it have continued to attract their readers by the thousand, while the wrangles of the scholars have remained neglected. It is not our intention here to enter into those tangled controversial thickets, nor on the other hand to add one more to the innumerable recapitulations of the Columbian romance. It is rather to attempt to construct, as far as possible, an account of the work of the great discover based upon those results of documentary research which seem to command some measure of general agreement among scholars. Though it will be impossible to avoid all those points upon which doubt still prevails, and without the unlikely discovery of fresh evidence must still continue, we will attempt to distinguish such matters from others that are certain. We can best take our departure by briefly recapitulating the legendary story before replacing it with the results of modern research.

In the second half of the fifteenth century, according to the traditional story, Cristoforo Colombo, a Genoese of noble birth, descended from a family whose ancestry could be traced back to the great days of Rome, received a thorough training in geography and cosmogony in the University of Pavia, and became an expert sea captain who was employed by King René of Provence and sailed in every sea. He not only knew the Mediterranean, but voyaged to England and up into the Arctic. After many years of seafaring he determined to take up his residence in Portugal, in order to learn at first hand of the explorations of the Portuguese to find a sea-route to India. He married the daughter of an illustrious noble house, and voyaged to the Portuguese island colonies and to the Guinea coast, where he made astronomical observations. By scientific reasoning, by the consultation of the works of ancient authors, and by correspondence with the celebrated Florentine geographer, Toscanelli, he became convinced that it is possible to reach the shores of Asia direct by sailing to the west. He applied to the King of Portugal for his support of an expedition to accomplish the discovery, but his

74

proposition was peremptorily refused. However, the King determined to investigate its possibility, and treacherously despatched his servants to voyage out along the course indicated by Columbus, but they returned without having made any of the promised discoveries. Indignant at this treachery, Columbus resolved to leave Portugal and seek help in Spain, where, after seven years' petitioning, he at last secured the support of Queen Isabella.

He sailed on his quest in 1492, found what he thought were the outlying islands of the Indies, and returned to claim the great rewards that had been promised to him. Despite the machinations of his enemies, of whom the most vindictive was Bishop Fonseca, he was advanced to great honour, but after some years they brought about his disgrace, and he was ungratefully deprived of his government of the Indies he had won for Spain, and sent home as a prisoner. He was cast off and neglected by the monarchs he had served so well, but he carried out further explorations at his own expense, and, though he failed to find the Indies that he sought, he alone gave to Castile a new world. He was allowed to die forgotten in poverty and obscurity, while others reaped the rewards that were his due.

Such, in bare outline, is the traditional story, and though it has been often embroidered with additional trappings of romance, we have here the essentials that alone need concern us. Almost the whole of it comes from the statements of the Admiral himself, either in his own published writings, or by the report of his son Ferdinand or his friend and apologist, Bishop Bartolomé de las Casas. In their eyes and his own, Columbus was the first and greatest of geographers and scientific explorers who was neglected and thwarted by his sovereigns, and deprived with base ingratitude of what they had promised him, so that his hard fate has been handed down to history as one of the classic examples of Fortune's inconstancy.

While the story could only be read as a whole in the *Historie* of his father by an admiring son, Ferdinand Columbus, and the other writers who had written of him were mostly forgotten, the Columbian legend held the field, but modern scholarship, from the days of Humboldt [1] to those of Henri Vignaud [2] and de Lollis [3], saw something of its inconsistencies, and began to scrutinise the independent evidence with the microscope of historical criticism. Gradually a different story was revealed which proved the falsity or undependability of many of Columbus's own claims, and placed much of the interpretation of admitted facts in a wholly new light. It is with this new synthesis of the discoverer's life and work that we must concern ourselves if we are to place him in his true position as an essential link in the transition from medieval to modern ideas.

The name Colombo is common in Liguria and Northern Italy, and most of those bearing it had no connection with the noble families of the name. Cristoforo was born in 1451 as the eldest child of Domenico Colombo, sprung from a family of weavers of Terra Rossa near Genoa. Domenico practised his trade as a master-weaver at Genoa for many years, but later moved to Savona, where he was a tavern-keeper. But he did not succeed in his new trade, and fell into acute financial difficulties from which his eldest son tried in vain to rescue him. He was imprisoned for debt, and during the later years of his life lived sometimes in Genoa and sometimes in Savona, but he never recovered from his financial embarrassments, and died, leaving his debts unpaid, probably in 1499. Domenico and his wife, Susanna Fontanarossa, had three other sons and a daughter besides Cristoforo, of whom only the second, Bartolomeo, won celebrity. These facts have been proved unmistakably from legal documents remaining in the archives of the city of Genoa. A Genoese contemporary writer was therefore accurate when he stated that "the brothers Bartholomew and Christopher Colombo were Ligurians, and born at Genoa of a plebeian family, who lived by the trade in wool. Their father was a weaver, and his children, who were for some time wool-carders, have attained at this time [1506] to great celebrity by their bold daring, and by a discovery memorable in human affairs" (ANTONIO GALLO, chancellor of the Bank of St. George in Genoa, in De Navigatione Columbi per inaccessum antea Oceanum comentariolus) [4].

The youth of Columbus was passed with his parents in Genoa, and he took up his father's trade as a weaver, and later helped him in keeping his tavern. He received nothing but the education common among boys of his class, probably in a school belonging to the Corporation of Weavers which was established at Genoa in a little street known as the Vico di Pavia. He took to the sea at fourteen years of age, and rose to the command of a royal galley under King René of Provence, according to his own statements, but it is impossible to accept their truth, for he can be traced at frequent intervals either at Genoa or Savona until he was turned nineteen years of age, and he was always described as a weaver or wool-worker. His associates were either weavers, tailors or boot-makers, and there is no mention in the documents of his contact with sailors or travellers. But in a maritime and trading city like Genoa, there was every opportunity to learn of distant lands from those who had visited them. The latest dates at which he is found in Savona are August 1472 and August 1473, and after those years his name does not appear in the notarial documents for six years. This appears to indicate that his maritime career began at that period, and it is probable that one of his earliest voyages was to the island of Scio in the Greek Archipelago, which was then a Genoese possession. This may have been in a voyage that began at the end of May 1474. He undoubtedly visited the island once, and possibly twice, for in September 1475 another expedition was sent out by the Republic under the command of Giovanni Antonio di Negro and Nicolas Spinola, who were certainly known to Columbus in later years, and whose families were mentioned in his will. There were weavers and other artisans from Savona on board, and it may have been in some commercial capacity that he was employed. We do not know when he returned from the Levant, but in 1476 he was taking part in a voyage to the West that marked the beginning of his historical career.

According to the Portuguese historian Barros, [5] whose evidence, derived from contemporaries of the discoverer, we shall often have occasion to cite, Columbus " following the custom of his country and his own inclination, went to navigate the Levant until at length he came into these parts of Spain [viz. Portugal], and took up the navigation of the Ocean sea following the career he had previously adopted." Oviedo, who knew him personally, says much the same : " As his thoughts were bent upon the wide seas and high imaginings, he looked out towards the very great Ocean sea and betook himself into Portugal " [6]. According to Ferdinand Columbus and Las Casas, it was chance that took him there when he was saved by the intervention of Providence from death in an attack by French pirates. We can now identify this engagement as that fought in 1476 by the corsair Coullon off Cape St. Vincent against the Genoese ships of di Negro and Spinola, which were on their way to England. The survivors were compelled to take refuge in the harbour of Lisbon, and this gives us dates of Columbus's first arrival in that city.

After some stay in the Tagus the remaining vessels of the fleet proceeded with their voyage to England, and there is every reason to accept the explorer's statement that he visited Bristol and to date his stay there as early in the year 1477. At that time we know from independent sources [7] that Englishmen were coveting the profits derived by the Portuguese from the Guinea trade and were preparing to try for a share for themselves.[1] This may have further increased Columbus's interest in the African voyages of which he must already have heard. In later years he boasted of his knowledge of Bristol, Galway and the northern seas, and claimed to have sailed to Iceland and beyond it far into the Arctic,

[1] See above, p. 49.

but his story is so inconsistent with well-known facts that it provides means for its own refutation.

From his deposition before a notary in Genoa on 25th August, 1479, [8] we learn that he was then upon the eve of departure for Lisbon, and had been charged by Paolo di Negro with the purchase of a parcel of Madeira sugar. This is not only the first direct mention of his travels, but it also enables us to place the date of his settlement in Portugal before the end of 1479, which gives an important point of departure.

His brother Bartholomew was probably already resident in Lisbon, and may have begun his employment there as a maker of seamen's charts. The two brothers had ample opportunity of close association with the men engaged in the trade with the islands and with Guinea who thronged the quays of Lisbon, and this started them on their maritime career. Not long after he had settled in Portugal, Christopher became more closely connected with the Atlantic islands by his marriage in 1480 with Felipa Moniz Perestrello, daughter of Bartolomeu Perestrello who, in November 1446, had been appointed by Prince Henry the Navigator as hereditary captain of the island of Porto Santo near Madeira. Bartolomeu the first died about 1457, leaving his young children under the guardianship of their mother, Isabel Moniz, who was related to the noble Portuguese family of that name. She sold the captaincy of Porto Santo to her brother-in-law Pedro de Correa da Cunha, and returned to live in Lisbon, where she placed her daughter Felipa to be educated in the convent of Os Santos. When Bartolomeu the second reached his majority, he repudiated the sale made by his mother, and in 1473 was appointed to the captaincy and assumed the government of the island. Columbus by his marriage came into contact with persons of higher rank than he had known before, and as they were closely associated with Portugal's expansion oversea, he was able to gratify his growing interest in geography and glean knowledge of the ocean at first hand.

We have very little definite information concerning the discoverer's life in the Portuguese dominions, but he appears, from
the document mentioned above, to have had interests in Madeira,
where many of his wife's connections were settled. It is entirely
probable that Ferdinand Columbus is correct when he tells us
that his father at this time " commenced to conjecture if, seeing
that the Portuguese were voyaging so far to the south, one could
not do as much in the west, and if it were not probable that one
would find new lands in that direction. . . . He informed himself concerning the voyages and navigations that the Portuguese
were then making to El Mina and the coast of Guinea, and he took
pleasure in conversing with those who made the voyages. . . .
He noted all the indications [of undiscovered lands] of which he
heard certain persons speak and those of the sailors which he
hoped to be able to make use of" [9]. Ferdinand tells us
that Columbus also made use of the papers of his late father-in-
law, but he would be unlikely to obtain much information there,
for Bartolomeu Perestrello I had never carried out any maritime
enterprises. However, " from all the information he obtained,
he came to believe without a doubt that to the west of the Canary
Islands and the west of Cape Verde there was much land, and that
it was possible to navigate thither and to make discoveries " [10].
Thus, what Las Casas says seems to be true when he writes :
" We seem to have here the means and the occasion of the coming
of Columbus to Spain and the first origin of the discovery of this
great [new] world."

We have no independent information concerning the voyages
that Columbus made at this period, but there are reasons to
believe that he made at least one voyage to Guinea, and this may
have been with the expedition of Diogo d'Azambuja which
established the fortress of El Mina on the Gold Coast in 1482.
He stated definitely in later years that he had visited El Mina, and
the many incidental references in his writings to things seen in
Guinea have all the appearance of personal acquaintance with that

coast.   Unfortunately, however, at other times he made assertions about his travels to Africa that are manifestly false.   He stated that he had made observations which showed that El Mina lay below the Equator, whereas its true position $5°$ north of the line was well known to the Portuguese ; he also stated that he had made astronomical measurements which proved that an equatorial degree was equal to $56\frac{2}{3}$ miles.   Now not merely have we no reason to believe that he possessed the considerable astronomical skill necessary for so difficult a measurement, but the result given is impossibly far from the truth.   The claim must be classed with other examples of his boastfulness and lack of dependability when describing his own accomplishments.

By his travels to Africa Columbus's interest in discovery became an over-mastering passion, and at last he was moved to make proposals to King John II for permission to undertake an exploring voyage out into the Atlantic.   It is at this point that the Columbian controversy becomes most acute, and unfortunately it cannot be said that any measure of general agreement has yet been reached as to the object of his projected enterprise.   On the one side it is maintained that his only purpose was to discover new lands across the ocean, on the other that he designed, as he later claimed, to find a route to Asia and the realms of the Grand Khan, of which Marco Polo had told, by sailing westward over the Atlantic.

Those who hold this latter view maintain, following Ferdinand Columbus and Las Casas, that he had been confirmed in this idea by correspondence with one who was, perhaps, the most celebrated geographer of his time, Paolo Toscanelli of Florence. They point to two letters of Toscanelli, the first in reply to an enquiry from Columbus, who had heard of certain advice that he had given to King Afonso V touching the voyage to the Indies. Toscanelli replied, sending a copy of a letter which he had addressed in 1474 to a certain Canon of Lisbon, one Fernam Martins, for submission to the King.   In a second letter the Florentine geographer repeated this advice to Columbus, suggesting that the best route to the Indies was westward, and that the shores of Asia were not far removed across the Atlantic from those of Europe. With his letter of 1474 Toscanelli is also said to have included a map illustrating his ideas. Ferdinand Columbus, in his Historie, gives an Italian translation of these letters and Las Casas a Spanish one, but there is in a copy of the Historia Rerum of Pius II, which belonged to Columbus, what purports to be a copy in the explorer's own hand of the original Latin sent to Fernam Martins in 1474. It is round the authenticity of this correspondence that controversy has raged.

No generally agreed conclusion has yet been reached, but the balance of probability certainly appears to be against the story told by Ferdinand and Las Casas. Columbus himself never mentioned Toscanelli in all his many citations of ancient and modern authors, and he always claimed most emphatically that his ideas were wholly his own, derived from study and reasoning. Afonso V, as was stated in our previous chapter, was not interested in the route to the Indies, the quest which the Portuguese did not take up again vigorously until the time of John II. It is very unlikely, therefore, that he would make enquiries of an Italian geographer concerning it. There is no trace to be found of a canon of Lisbon named Fernam Martins in the time of Afonso or later, and the only mention of his existence is in the disputed letter. There are no traces in the letters and authentic works of Toscanelli of any correspondence with Columbus or of any particular interest in the Portuguese explorations. The disputed letters appear to contain many anachronisms, and the geographical ideas set forth bear a close and very suspicious resemblance to those that were expounded by Columbus in the period after his discovery, when he was attempting to prove to the sceptics the identity of the islands with those of Asia. Neither Ferdinand Columbus nor Las Casas seems to have attached as much importance to the letters as modern writers have done, but they both supported Columbus in his claim to originality of reasoning. Fortified with this great weight of negative evidence, we may allow Columbus to have conceived his own erroneous geographical system and proceed to trace something of its development.

On his return from his last voyage to Guinea, which probably occurred in 1482, Columbus determined to seek the approval of John II for an expedition to search for new lands in the Atlantic. We have no documentary evidence concerning his proposition, but such applications were not unprecedented in Portugal at the time. The air was full of projects of discovery under a king who was known to be sympathetic. In 1452 one, Diego Teive, received a licence from Prince Henry the Navigator to sail out into the Atlantic for the discovery of the island of Antilha. In the course of a voyage out from Fayal in the Azores he found the island of Flores and received the donation of it. Teive later ceded the rights of discovery under his patent to Fernão Telles, who in 1474 secured from Afonso V the exclusive right to explore westward in the Atlantic and to govern any lands he found. Telles made unsuccessful attempts to reach the " Isle of Seven Cities," and ultimately his exclusive privilege lapsed. In June 1484 John II granted to Fernão Domingo de Arco of Madeira permission to seek and occupy an island that he believed to lie to the west, and at about the same time Fernão Dulmo, a colonist of the Azores, petitioned for permission to search for the islands of Antilha and the Seven Cities. When the patent for a distant voyage of discovery was granted in 1486 he entered into partnership with a Madeiran, one João Affonso de Estreito, and with the German Martin Behaim, who was then resident in the Azores. To the significance of this connection we will return later. Dulmo had not sailed on his voyage by 1487, and possibly he never did so, but it is clear that the movement for oceanic discovery had reached such proportions that before long the secrets of the Atlantic must be revealed.

Columbus was but one of various projectors moving in the

same direction, and there was no particular reason why he, a Genoese, should receive preference over a native-born subject of the Crown. His petition was presented in 1483 or the early part of 1484, but there is nothing more than a casual reference to it in the contemporary chroniclers, Ruy de Pina or Garcia de Resende, in connection with his later success. In 1505 Columbus stated that he pressed the King for fourteen years to accept his project, but like many other of his assertions, this is inadmissible. The matter is involved in controversy into which we cannot enter, but a consideration of the evidence appears to confirm the substantial accuracy of the account of the matter given by João de Barros, the historian of the Portuguese discoveries in Africa and Asia. He tells us that Columbus, being curious of geographical knowledge, had read what Marco Polo had written of the Orient, of the kingdom of Cathay, and of the Isle of Cypangu. From this he came to fancy that one could arrive at that island and other unknown lands by way of the western sea. He said to himself that the discovery of the Terceiras Islands [i.e. the Azores] made one believe that by sailing farther west other islands and lands might be found, because it was unlikely that Nature had given the liquid element a preponderance over the terrestrial which was principally destined to receive life and see its development. " With which imaginations, suggested to him by his navigations and by the practical knowledge of men of that calling of whom the Kingdom [of Portugal] had the most expert in the discoveries of past times, he came to seek of the King Dom João that he would give him certain ships to discover the Isle of Cypangu by way of that western sea " [11].

By dint of his constant importunity the King was persuaded to take his application into consideration, and, as seems only natural, he referred it to his advisers in geographical matters for their opinion. Their verdict, however, was adverse to the project. That its main object was the discovery of unknown lands inhabited by primitive people and not of rich and civilised lands in Asia appears from the list of articles given by Las Casas as Columbus's demands for the cargo of the three caravels he desired. " Collars of beads, glassware of divers colours, little mirrors, scissors, knives, needles, pins, . . . and other like objects all of which are of slight value, but which are much esteemed among men who do not know them " [12]. These were the sort of things that the Portuguese explorers had found useful in trafficking with savages, and the application of Columbus to be appointed governor of any lands he might discover where such things might be disposed of was quite according to precedent. That he used theoretical arguments to support his plan and mentioned that it might open a new route to Asia is not impossible, but new lands stood in the forefront of his proposals, and his theories could only prejudice their acceptance by skilled geographers. Their adverse report only confirmed the King in his own opinion, for, as Barros says, seeing that Columbus " was a vain boaster, making a parade of his abilities, and more fantastic with his Isle of Cypangu than certain of what he said, he accorded him little credit " [13].

This was the end of the explorer's career in Portugal, and towards the end of 1484 or early in 1485 he left the country secretly for reasons that have not been explained, and determined to try to find support elsewhere. His wife was dead, and he took with him his only son Diego, then a little boy of four or five years old, to place in the charge of his maternal aunt at Huelva, not far from the little port of Palos. From hence onwards there is much more information concerning his proceedings, and documentary means of checking its accuracy can be found. It is unnecessary, therefore, to recapitulate the well-known story, and we must rapidly summarise the principal events of the next seven years.

On his way to Huelva Columbus came to a convent of Franciscans known as La Rabida, a little way out of Palos, and this chance call had momentous consequences, for it brought him into touch with Fr. Juan Perez, an able and saintly priest who was greatly interested in his guest, and having been the confessor of Queen Isabella had access to her ear. Columbus's enthusiastic belief in his divinely appointed mission to bring fresh souls to the knowledge of God and Holy Church commended him at once to the devout fathers of a missionary order, and they were much less critical of his ideas and reasoning than cautious and experienced Portuguese geographers had been. Thenceforward the Franciscans, and especially Fr. Juan Perez, became his invaluable allies and supporters. A description of his personal appearance by his contemporaries may serve to show wherein his undoubted personal attraction lay.

Andrés Bernaldez, parish priest of Los Palacios, near Seville, who saw a great deal of the explorer after his return in 1496, tells us : " There was a man from the country of Genoa called Christobal. Colon, a dealer in printed books who traded in the country of Andalusia, a man of very great natural intelligence without having much learning. . . . He came to Castile in the month of June 1496, clothed in robes of the colour of the habit of the brotherhood of St. Francis of the observance. In its cut it was almost like a habit and with a cord of St. Francis to show his devotion " [14]. Las Casas enters into more detail : " He was tall, above middle height ; his face long and with a look of authority ; his nose aquiline ; his eyes clear blue ; his colour blonde which inclined to a decidedly ruddy tint ; his beard and hair were red when he was young, but much care had early turned them white." He spoke with extraordinary fluency and vigour, and his conviction in his divinely guided purpose impressed all who met him.

Leaving Diego with the monks at La Rabida, Columbus proceeded to Seville to lay his proposals before the great Andalusian nobles, the Dukes of Medina Sidonia and Medina Celi. He was favourably received, but they thought that such important matters were properly the affair of the Crown and therefore sent him to

THE EARLIEST OR JOVIAN PORTRAIT OF CHRISTOPHER COLUMBUS, 1575.

(From the folio edition of Paulus Jovius' *Elogia Virorum Bellica Virtute Illustrium*, published by Petrus Perna at Basle in 1575.)

There is certainly no authentic portrait of Columbus extant, and this, the earliest that can be accurately dated, is undoubtedly imaginative. Paolo Giovio, Bishop of Nocera, began about 1521 to collect portraits of famous men for his villa on the Lake of Como, and that of Columbus was probably among the last included about 1551. In October 1556 Cristofano dell'Altissimo, working for the Uffizi Gallery in Florence, copied this portrait among many others from the Jovian collection.

The portrait was engraved by Tobias Stimmer, who worked in Basle from 1570 onwards, but it is uncertain whether he ever saw the Jovian pictures. His borders were undoubtedly of his own invention. The block was used again by Theobald Müller for his *Musaei Joviani Imagines*, published at Basle in 1577.

(See p. 86.)

Court. With such influential support he found it easy to obtain access to the highest authorities, and in April 1486 he was received in audience by Ferdinand and Isabella and allowed to expound his project before them. This was an extraordinary advance for an unknown Italian and is a tribute to the persuasive power of his arguments. Cosmogony was in fashion, and Columbus's fervour made him eloquent, as all his contemporaries tell us. But when his proposals were submitted to a commission of experts for examination, there was an interval of nearly five years before it reached a conclusion. We have no exact information as to what were the proposals they considered or the reasons advanced by the explorer to support them, but there is no doubt about their decision, in 1490, that his promises and offers were impossible and vain and rested upon such uncertain foundations that they were unworthy of acceptance. This was a bitter disappointment, and Columbus retired from Court to Seville and La Rabida to arrange for his departure from Spain. He determined to go to France to seek help, while he sent his brother Bartholomew to England to petition Henry VII.

But his Franciscan friends at La Rabida persuaded him not to abandon hope, and while Juan Perez tried to induce the Queen to recall him, they put Columbus in touch with certain experienced seamen in Palos, who were themselves anxious to engage in Atlantic exploration and might assist him with their practical knowledge. Many of them, as we learn from their evidence in later legal proceedings, believed in the existence of undiscovered lands across the Atlantic, and some had been employed in voyages to search for it and knew the marine conditions beyond the Canaries.

" Amid the inhabitants [of Palos] there were three brothers of the name of Pinzon. They were rich seamen and persons of condition. One of them was called Martin Alonzo, who was the richest and most considered of the three ; the second was called Vicente Yanez and the third Francisco Martinez. Almost all the inhabitants of the town were under their influence, for they were the richest and the best connected people there " (LAS CASAS). Columbus had met Martin Pinzon on his previous visits to Palos, but now in 1491 he was anxious to meet him again to discuss the possibilities of a route to the west. At the time Pinzon was absent on a voyage to Rome with a cargo of sardines, but on his return he reported a find of great interest. One of his friends who was a servant in the Papal Court had shown him in the Pope's library a book or writing setting forth the possibility of reaching the very rich Isle of Cypangu by sailing westward across the Atlantic. He had also shown him a *mappa mundi* on which the island was marked with its distance in degrees from the coast of Europe. Columbus was overjoyed at this. Many years afterwards the Pinzon family brought an action to share in the great rewards that came to Columbus. They maintained that there had been an agreement with Martin Alonzo to share profits, but the judges decided that their contention could not be accepted. But undoubtedly the information of the Pinzons was of great assistance to Columbus in renewing his petitions to the Court of Castile and, owing to the direct intervention of Queen Isabella, he was recalled to Court.

His propositions were referred to a new commission for examination, but again they were rejected as chimerical. However, the final stage of victory of the Cross over the Crescent in the Peninsula was at hand, and Queen Isabella, exalted in her belief in a divine mission, was peculiarly ready to listen to an enthusiast who promised to find for her the opportunity of bringing millions of new souls to Christ. In its very inception, as all through Spain's long colonial history, the missionary spirit of the Church played a compelling part. The extraordinary conditions demanded by this persistent projector from which nothing could persuade or drive him, his visionary harangues, and his proclaimed intention of devoting his profits to the re-conquest of the Holy Sepulchre—all this caused hard-headed statesmen or officials to look at him askance ; but they were extraordinarily attractive to the Catholic Queen and her spiritual advisers.   At the Court of John II exploration was treated as a matter of hard business and considered in a very modern fashion, but here in Spain, at the culminating point of victory in the last crusade, medieval motives and the ideas of the ages of faith were supreme.   To those ideas the missionary promises of Columbus's plan made irresistible appeal.   If there are any turning-points in history where age meets age, was not this spring of 1492 one of them, where the same scribes were recording the fall of the last fragment of the Western Caliphate and drafting the conditions of the discoverer of the New World ?

Strange though it may seem, we have no contemporary evidence of the plan proposed by Columbus to the Catholic Kings or his precise objective.   All is inference and conjecture, for we certainly cannot place implicit trust in what he or his apologists said about it after his return.   Those who hold the traditional view maintain that his primary proposal was to forestall the Portuguese and reach Asia and the lands of the Spiceries by sailing west.   Henri Vignaud and those who follow him hold that this was an after-thought, and that his primary, if not his sole, object before he sailed was to discover new lands in the Atlantic, as, in fact, he did.   But he certainly took with him a formal letter of commendation from Ferdinand and Isabella to the Grand Khan of Cathay, and Pinzon, if not Columbus, was dreaming of reaching the Isle of Cypangu which Polo had described as lying off the farthest coast of Asia.   There is no agreement among those who have engaged in the controversy, but many now believe that the true answer to the question need exclude neither of these objectives.   May it not be that Columbus, before he started, had both in view, and that he sought both Antilia and Cypangu on his way to the Spiceries of Asia ?   Both to that age were vague and uncertain islands in the Ocean Sea, and both awaited discovery by those who would sail to the west.   What no man knew before 1492, and for years afterwards, was that across the Atlantic there lay the immense mass of an unknown continent.

Before we turn to trace how that knowledge was gradually attained, we may note the geographical notions of the Atlantic that another projector, one Martin Behaim, was advancing while Columbus was a suitor at the Court of Castile. We stated earlier that in 1486 Fernão Dulmo of the Azores and João Affonso do Estreito obtained from King John II letters patent for an expedition to discover " a great island, islands or mainland beyond the coast that are believed to be the Isle of Seven Cities." With the proposed expedition it was arranged that a German resident of the Azores should sail, and this is supposed to be Martin Behaim, who had some reputation in Portugal as a cosmographer and pretended to prophetic powers as an astrologer. He was a native of Nuremberg and claimed to have been a pupil of the celebrated astronomer Regiomontanus, who did a great deal to advance the science of navigation by his improved astronomical instruments. Behaim arrived in Portugal on a commercial mission in 1482 or 1484, and probably got his reputation as a cosmographer by the sale of Nuremberg instruments, which were the finest astrolabes and quadrants of the time. He probably accompanied the expedition of Affonso d'Aveiro to Guinea in 1485–6, but this statement depends only on his own authority, and the voyage may have been with the second expedition of Diogo Cão. Behaim married and settled in Fayal in the Azores, and it was there that he was concerned with the project of Estreito. It has been suggested that it inspired its promoters with the idea of finding a route to Asia across the Atlantic, but this is quite uncertain. In 1490 Behaim returned to Nuremberg for a stay of two years, and while there he was employed by the civic authorities in the construction of a globe to exhibit the state of geographical knowledge, and it is upon this that his fame is based.

We are uncertain of the geographical ideas of Columbus before 1492, but there is no doubt about those of Behaim, for

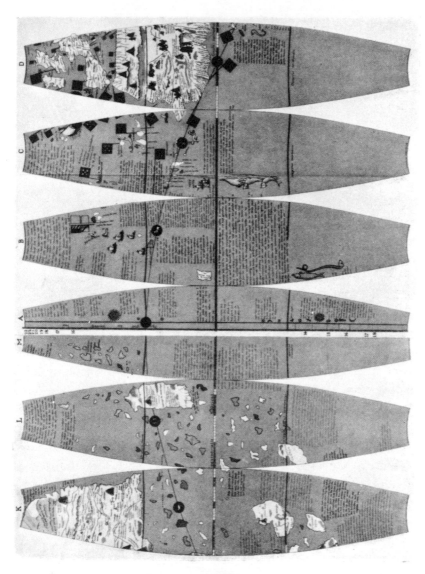

THE ATLANTIC OCEAN ACCORDING TO MARTIN BEHAIM,
1492.

(Gores from his globe, made at Nuremberg 1490–1492, as reproduced by E. G. Ravenstein, *Martin Behaim*, London, 1908.

The Western Ocean as portrayed on the oldest globe extant, uninfluenced by the discoveries of Columbus. The Asiatic sector reveals the influence of Marco Polo, and itself influenced later cartography. Cypangu is shown as attainable by sailing westwards from Europe, and in accordance with traditional belief the distance involved is greatly underestimated.

(*See p.* 91.)

they are fully set forth upon his globe. The two men were certainly in Lisbon at the same time and mixing in the same circles, and it is highly probable that they met. Bartholomew Columbus must certainly have known Behaim, for he remained in Lisbon longer than his brother and was probably there as late as 1488. There is an extraordinary similarity between the erroneous geographical ideas of Behaim, as set out upon his globe of 1492, and those of Columbus which he expounded fully in 1498 but undoubtedly held earlier. It is impossible to say whether they were independent or which had the priority, but the essential feature of both was the idea of the comparative narrowness of the Ocean Sea and the possibility of reaching the Far East by sailing to the west.

In July 1493 a cosmographer of Nuremberg, Dr. Hieronymus Müntzer, wrote to King John II of Portugal urging him to employ Behaim for the discovery of a shorter sea-route to the Spiceries by the west than that round the Cape of Good Hope. He maintained that it was possible to cross the Ocean Sea in a few days and reach the lands of Eastern Cathay, and supported his views by reference to the same ancient authors that later were quoted by Columbus in support of his theories [15]. But when the letter was written the explorer had returned to Europe from his great voyage, and therefore his discoveries may already have been known in Nuremberg, as they were in Lisbon, where he had arrived in March, though this is improbable. In any case King John was better informed upon the matter than was Müntzer, and no notice was taken of the suggestion. The matter had passed on to a different plane, and Behaim was never employed again as a cosmographer. He fell upon evil days and died in obscurity in Lisbon in 1507.

With the indispensable co-operation of Martin Alonzo Pinzon and his brothers, Columbus spent the summer of 1492 in Palos making ready his ships, and he left that port on the passage to the Canaries on 3rd August, 1492. He had with him three caravels,

91

of which the *Santa Maria,* commanded by its owner, the celebrated pilot Juan de la Cosa, had a burthen of about 220 tons, while the *Pinta,* commanded by Martin Alonzo Pinzon, and the *Nina,* by Vicente Yanez Pinzon, were only a little smaller. There were from 90 to 120 persons on board, and with its surgeon, its secretary and other accessory officers, the expedition was certainly well organised. Gomera, the last of the Canaries, was left on 6th September, and the course was set to the westward along the twenty-eighth parallel. After a variety of incidents, which are minutely described by his biographers, but what was in reality a prosperous and uneventful voyage, land was seen at two o'clock in the morning of 12th October, 1492, and at daybreak Columbus landed upon a small island, Guanahani, an outlier of the modern Bahamas, which he solemnly annexed to Spain by the name " San Salvador."

Before we discuss what were his ideas as to his discovery, we may rapidly summarise the rest of the voyage. [Leaving Guanahani after two days' stay, a week was spent among the islands of the Bahama Archipelago, and the ships passed on to the discovery of Cuba, which Columbus first described to his crews as Cypangu. But by the beginning of November it was clear that this could not be, for none of the features of that land as described by Marco Polo could be found. The search was resumed, and on 5th December another great island was discovered, which he was certain was Cypangu, though in annexing it he gave it the name of Española.] The Cuban coast he now considered must be an outlying promontory of the Asiatic continent, and this he expounded to his company. It seems extraordinary that one who had set out to find islands in the Atlantic should not have realised that he had discovered new lands and should have deluded himself into the error of believing that what he had found was but the extremity of the ancient world. Columbus was, above all, no ordinary explorer but a visionary and mystic who, having once formed a belief, held to it with extraordinary mental obstinacy and persistently sought in his pseudo-scientific knowledge of medieval geography and the Scriptures for reasons to support the delusion. It may be that the superficial resemblance to Asiatics of the natives he met first put the idea in his mind, but having once adopted it, he maintained it to the very day of his death.

Thirty-seven men of his company were established in a small fort called "La Navidad" constructed on the north coast of Española, and on 4th January, 1493, Columbus sailed away north-eastwards on his return voyage. A recent writer [16] has suggested that in setting his course he was guided by a profound scientific knowledge of the winds and currents of the North Atlantic, but that is clearly impossible. The course set was the most direct to Palos, his objective, and it was his lucky chance to have found favouring south-westerly winds all the way, as is common in those latitudes. The Gulf Stream drift helped him, though he does not seem to have known it, and the current was not described until some twenty years later. By 15th February the ships were off the Azores, and there Columbus landed on the 18th, proclaiming that he was returning from the discovery of "las Indias." Setting sail once more on the 24th, he was driven by heavy weather to shelter in the Tagus, and there, on 4th March, all Lisbon was astonished to hear that Portugal had been forestalled in the quest in which she had been engaged since the days of Prince Henry, and that a captain in the employ of their Castilian rival was about to reach in the west the goal that had been sought so long in the opposite direction. Five days after his arrival, King John II summoned the discoverer to attend him and gave a courteous hearing to his story. But John was an expert cosmographer, as were many of his courtiers, who were thoroughly experienced in matters of oceanic navigation, and they do not appear to have been much impressed by Columbus's description of what he had found. Among those present at the interview was the chronicler Ruy de Pina, and he tells us that the King only summoned Columbus with repugnance, for he knew the vainglorious character of the man, and he accused himself of negligence for attaching so little credit or authority to the words of the Genoese when he first came to offer him his plan of discovery.

De Pina's description of the results of the voyage contains no mention of Cathay or the islands of the Spiceries, and Columbus's boasts that he would shortly reach them are passed over in silence. The complete fact was recorded by the statement that Columbus came " from the discovery of the islands of Antilha and Cipango which he had carried to a successful end by order of the Kings of Castile ; he brought from that land as the first evidence of his discovery some native people and some gold and other things that are to be found there " [17]. The experienced Portuguese, in fact, were sceptical about Italian exaggerations from the beginning. What King John feared was not that he would be anticipated at the spice marts on the coast of Malabar, about which Covilhã was sending home reports, but that he might have renewed difficulties with Spanish interlopers in the waters near to his preserve of Guinea. It was this very practical fear that led to the negotiations for the Treaty of Tordesillas, as we have seen elsewhere.

Immediately upon his arrival at Lisbon, Columbus sent off letters to his Sovereigns enclosed in one to Luis de Santangel, chancellor and comptroller of Aragon, who had supervised the preparations of the expedition on behalf of the Crown. He was the proper official channel of approach, and the covering letter addressed to him, which is the only part of the correspondence extant, is of great importance, as we shall see in a moment. After a stay of a little over a week Columbus left Lisbon and arrived in the harbour of Palos on 15th March, 1493, just over seven months after he had left it.

He now emerges from the comparative obscurity which has given rise to so much controversy, for we are able henceforward to trace the gradual spread of the knowledge of his discoveries in contemporary documents. Since the terms of these earliest documents show in what light the discoveries appeared to the men of the time, some of their actual phrases are of interest. The first is the letter of the Duke of Medina Celi to Cardinal Mendoza, Archbishop of Toledo, the first minister of Castile. It is dated 19th March, 1493, four days after the arrival of the two surviving ships, the Pinta and the Nina, at Palos. The Duke asked to be granted a share in the profits of the enterprise, because it was he who sent Columbus to the Queen when he was proposing to seek the aid of the King of France in his design " of the discovery of the Indies." Her Highness received him and sent him forth in search of the Indies, " and now he has returned after eight months and has found what he searched for and that very completely." Medina Celi learned of this while Columbus was in Lisbon, and now wrote to ask that he might be allowed to send forth caravels annually to the lands that had been discovered [18].

The next evidence is the letter written by the Sovereigns to Columbus at Seville immediately after the receipt of his letters from Lisbon. It was dated from the Court at Barcelona on 30th March, 1493, and ordered the discoverer to come at once and make his personal report of what he had achieved. The Sovereigns addressed Columbus by the honourable titles that had been promised to him if he were successful, and in this, their first letter after the discovery, they explicitly accepted the truth of his description of what he had found. " Don Christobal Colon," they wrote, " our Admiral of the Ocean Sea and Viceroy and Governor of the islands that have been discovered in the Indies : We have seen your letters and we have much pleasure in knowing what you write to us by them and that God has given so good an issue to your enterprise."

Clearly in Barcelona at that date men were certain that the Indies of Asia had been reached by the west, and this belief is put definitely in a letter written by an agent of the Duke of Ferrara a week later. Writing on 9th April, 1493,[1] Hannibal Januarius is

[1] The letter is dated 9th March, but this seems impossible as not affording time for the transport of letters from Lisbon. Harrisse emends it to 9th April.

quite explicit on the point. He says : " In the month of August last, this lord King at the petition of one named Collomba caused four little ships to be equipped to navigate, as the afore-named assured him, upon the Ocean in a straight line towards the west in order to reach the east. The earth being round, he necessarily reached the eastern parts. For this purpose, the said caravels were armed and directed beyond the strait in the direction of the west according to the letter which he has written and which I have seen. In thirty-four days he came to a great island inhabited by men of an olive tint, completely naked, not at all inclined to fight and very timid. . . . From that island he passed into the neighbouring islands of which two are each greater than England and Scotland and another is more extensive than the whole of Spain. Collomba has left a part of his men there. . . . The said Collomba having retraced his route has arrived at Lisbon and he has written to the lord King who has commanded him to come here [i.e. to Barcelona] as soon as possible. I think I shall be able to procure a copy of the letter such as he himself has written and I will send it to you. When it comes, if I learn of anything else, I will write to inform you . . ." [19].

Soon after the beginning of April, therefore, the news was current in Barcelona that a new route to India had been discovered, and before the end of the month it was generally announced to the Spanish public by the printing of a carefully edited version of the covering letter sent by Columbus to Santangel with his despatches from Lisbon. Minute research has proved that this original version was in Spanish and that it now exists only in a single copy in the Lenox Collection of the New York Public Library. It is a semi-official résumé of the information given by Columbus, but it could not have been written by him, for its Castilian is purer and more fluent than any of his extant writings. On certain of the copies of the letter that were circulated in manuscript the addressee was given as Gabriel Sanchez, treasurer of Aragon, who was better known than

Santangel and whose name would therefore give more weight, but otherwise the letter was the same.

One of the printed tracts or, more probably, a manuscript copy of the letter, must have been sent to Italy at once, and it was there translated into Latin by one Leonardo de Cosco, an Aragonese, and published from the press of Stephen Plannck at Rome soon after the end of April 1493. It consists of four leaves of Gothic type with thirty-three lines to the page, and before the end of the year 1493 seven other Latin editions of this translation were published with only slight alterations. This shows the widespread interest excited by the news of the discoveries, but it resulted in the permanent intrenchment of Columbus's error in the identification of the new-found lands with those of Asia. The title may be translated thus : *A letter of Cristoforus Colom : to whom our age owes much : concerning the Islands of India beyond the Ganges lately discovered.* . . . Three Latin editions were published at Paris, Basle, and Antwerp in the course of 1493–4, and a metrical version in Italian was made by Giuliano Dati, one of the most popular Tuscan poets of the day, which was circulated in very rough and cheaply printed editions that show how not only the learned but also the general public were interested in the momentous news that lands beyond the old world had been found. Thus the Antilles became firmly associated with the idea of " the Indies," and their strange aboriginal inhabitants, whose manners and customs excited so much wonder and interest, have ever since been known as " Indians."

It was not long, however, before the identification of the new lands with India came to be sceptically regarded by men of affairs. It is doubtful if the Catholic Kings and their ministers believed in the identification for more than a few months, or at any rate long after the receipt of news concerning Columbus's second voyage in 1494. The growth of this scepticism can be followed most tellingly in the writings of the author, to whom more than all others the world for thirty years looked for knowledge of the discoveries. Columbus's letter to Santangel or Sanchez had a very wide circulation; but it was the only part of his writings that achieved this, and the progress of geographical knowledge was almost entirely due to the Latin letters of Peter Martyr of Anghiera, the apostle of the learning of the Renaissance in Spain.

Though Peter Martyr never crossed the Atlantic or made discoveries, his part in the work was of prime importance, and no account of the period could be complete without some notice of it. The achievements of the men of action could only produce their full effect when they were correlated and knit together by the thinkers and the cosmogonists. Peter Martyr served to provide a channel of accurate and critically reported information from the Spanish explorers to the intellectual world, and for two generations or more his letters were almost the only source from which the new knowledge was distributed. Born at Arona on the shores of Lago Maggiore in 1457, the future scholar, whose family name is unknown, was baptised under the name of a Dominican saint of the thirteenth century, St. Peter Martyr, and has always been called after him. As a youth he received some training at the Court of his native Duchy of Milan, but at twenty he moved to Rome and became an associate of the best humanists of the time in the celebrated Academy of Pomponius Laetus. There his great natural abilities and his shrewd judgment were trained in the soundest methods of intellectual criticism. He obtained a secretarial appointment under the Papal government and began to write the first of the series of letters to his patrons and friends upon which his fame securely rests. His interest was especially directed to the geography of the ancients, and he was recognised in the very critical world of scholars as a first-rate authority in the subject. This is a point of considerable importance, for Martyr was no mere dilettante or amateur but one who was equipped with ample knowledge and the best means of the age for criticising any new facts that came before him.

In September 1487 Peter Martyr decided to take an appointment in Spain under the patronage of the Count of Tendilla, who had come as the ambassador of the Catholic Kings to the Papal Court and was then returning home. When his friends and patrons in Italy were unable to dissuade him from his intention, they obtained his promise that he would write regular letters to give them news of the events that came to his notice, for they were intensely interested in the progress of the crusade against the Moors that was then entering upon its final phase. It is to his fortunate observance of this promise that we owe the invaluable series of letters that until his death in 1526, nearly forty years later, poured regularly from his pen and are perhaps the best contemporary source for the history of Spain in her greatest age. The letters, written in a clear, free Latin style, were not mere private correspondence but intended to keep his friends *au courant* with accurate information of the events of a momentous time. Like many of the letters of that day, they were widely circulated among intellectual circles in Italy and fulfilled a purpose similar to that of the foreign correspondence of a great newspaper of to-day. They were in the best sense news-letters written as events proceeded and not in the fashion of a historian criticising all the available evidence long afterwards. They were strictly contemporary and allow us to see how events were viewed while they were in train. Thus they necessarily are sometimes wrong in the interpretation of the facts with which they deal, but they are invaluable as a source in which to trace the growth of the ideas of a sound scholar who was in a particularly favourable position to learn of what was happening and endowed with a naturally shrewd and highly trained judgment.

The first letter of Peter Martyr in which the new discoveries were mentioned was addressed from Barcelona on 14th May, 1493, to his patron John Borromeo, of the great Milanese family of that name. His reference to the discoverer is somewhat casual, for at that early date it was impossible to appreciate the momentous importance of the news. There is no mention of Columbus's claim to have reached the Indies. " A few days ago there returned *from the western antipodes* a certain Cristoforus Colonus, a Ligurian, who, because they thought that what he said was fabulous, only got three ships from my Sovereigns and that with difficulty. But he has brought back proofs of many precious things but especially of gold which those regions produce of their own special nature." During the course of the summer the letters, or at any rate those that were collected, were scanty, and we have to wait until September for any further mention of the discoveries. Meanwhile the preparations for a new expedition were going on in Spain, and great care was being exercised to avoid a clash with the acknowledged rights of Portugal. When orders were issued at the end of May 1493 for the equipment of the ships, it was no longer said, as in March, that the new lands were " en las Indias," but only that they were " en la parte de las Indias," which may be freely translated " in the portion of the world where the Indias are," which is quite non-committal.

The first serious geographical interpretation of the discoveries is given by Peter Martyr in writing to his patron Cardinal Sforza on 13th September, 1493 [20] :

" It is a strange thing not at all unknown to thee that of this globe of the earth about which the sun circles in the space of four and twenty hours, only the half part up to our time has been travelled and known—from the Golden Chersonese to our own Spanish Gades, and the remainder was left by cosmographers as unknown. And if mention was made of it, it was scanty and uncertain. . . . But now . . . a certain Cristoforus Colonus, a Ligurian, has followed the setting sun from Gades provided with three ships by my sovereigns and has come to the antipodes above five thousand miles away. Blest by weather and sea they voyaged for three and thirty days."

In his next letter, that of 1st October, 1493, to the Archbishop of Braga, Martyr is a little more explicit. " A certain Colonus has sailed to the western antipodes—even to the Indian coast, as he himself believes." Note the somewhat incredulous phrasing : " He has found several islands. These they think to be those whereof mention is made among cosmographers as lying outside [or beyond] the eastern Ocean and adjacent to India. Although the size of the globe seems to suggest otherwise, I do not wholly deny this, for there are not wanting those who think that the Indian coast is distant from the ends of Spain but by a little stretch. . . . [Be that as it may] it is enough for us that the hidden half of the globe comes into the light, while the Portuguese daily push themselves farther and farther under the equinoctial circle " [21]. The cool scientific tone of this comment, so different from medieval credulity for the fabulous and the tendency to obscure knowledge by recourse to speculation, is striking. It shows how in Peter Martyr we may rightly see the first of the Renaissance as distinct from the medieval cosmographers and appreciate something of the keen intellectual pleasure with which his fascinatingly novel letters were read by his friends in Italy. The romance of adventure can still attract the blasé moderns after four hundred years, but its exciting appeal to those so long imprisoned in the rigid and limited world of medieval thought can never recur. The arrival of his letters was eagerly awaited in Italy, and they passed from hand to hand to provide inexhaustible subjects of conversation in the most cultivated circles. In 1493 their mines of interest had hardly yet been opened, but for thirty-three years, until almost the day of his death in 1526, Peter Martyr was the sole comprehensive chronicler of the discoveries and the only easily accessible source for descriptions of the wonders of the new lands.

On 1st November, 1493, he devoted a whole letter to the subject of Columbus's discoveries, in place of the merely incidental references in earlier letters. Writing to Cardinal Ascanio Sforza, he narrated the principal events of the momentous voyage at some length, but paid special attention to the natural history of the new lands which he knew would interest his reader most. At the beginning of his letter he described the purpose of the voyage in a phrase that seems to indicate that Columbus must have mentioned the Indies of Asia as his objective before sailing : " A certain Christopher Columbus, a Genoese, proposed to the Catholic King and Queen, Ferdinand and Isabella, to discover the islands which touch the Indies by sailing from the western extremity of this country. He asked for ships and whatever was necessary to navigation, promising not only to propagate the Christian religion, but also certainly to bring back pearls, spices and gold beyond anything ever imagined " [22].

Towards the end Peter Martyr allowed himself to indulge in some speculation as to whether the explorer had really accomplished this purpose as he claimed to have done.

" Although the opinion of Columbus seems to be contrary to the theories of the ancients concerning the size of the globe and its circumnavigation, the birds and many other objects brought thence seem to indicate that these islands do belong, be it by proximity or by their products, to India, particularly when one recalls what Aristotle, at the end of his treatise De Coelo et Mundo, and Seneca and other learned cosmographers have always affirmed, that India was only separated from the west coast of Spain by a very small expanse of sea. . . . Happy at having discovered this unknown land, and to have found indications of a hitherto unknown continent, Columbus resolved to take advantage of favouring winds and the approach of spring to return to Europe " [23].

NOTES TO CHAPTER IV

1. See Humboldt, Alexander von, *Examen critique de l'histoire de la géographie du Nouveau Continent,* Paris, 1836–9, 5 t.

2. See Vignaud, H., *Etudes critiques sur la vie de Colomb avant ses découvertes,* Paris, 1905 ; and *Histoire critique de la grande entreprise de Christophe Colomb,* Paris, 1911, 2 t.

3. See Lollis, Cesare de, *Scritti di Cristoforo Colombo,* Rome, 1892, 2 vols.

NOTES

4. Gallo, Antonio, Chancellor of the Bank of St. George, *De Navigatione Columbi per inaccessum antea Oceanum comentariolus* in *Raccolta Colombiana*, vol. ii, no. 76.

5. Barros, João de, *Da Asia*, Lisbon, 1778–88, 24 vols. in-12.

6. Oviedo, Gonzalo Fernandez de, *Historia General y natural de las Indias*, Seville, 1535.

7. Hakluyt, R., *Principal Voyages* (Everyman Edⁿ.) vol. iv, p. 21. See also Chapter III, p. 49.

8. See Assereto, Ugo, in *Giornale storico e litterario della Liguria*, January 1904.

9. Columbus, Ferdinand, *Historie del S. D. Fernando Colombo*, Venice, 1571, translated in Kerr, R., *Collection of Voyages*, Edinburgh, 1811, vol. iii, p. 19.

10. *Ibid.*

11. Pina, Ruy de, *Chronica d'el Rei Dom João II*, in *Colleçao de libros ineditos*, Lisbon, 1792, vol. ii, pp. 177–8.

12. Las Casas, Bartolomé de, *Historia de las Indias*, Madrid, 1875, 5 vols. Bk. i, ch. 28; vol. i, p. 218.

13. Barros, João de, *Da Asia*, Dec. I, liv. iii, ch. xi.

14. Bernaldez, A., *Historia de los Reyes Catalicos*, chap. 118.

15. Müntzer, Dr. Hieronymus, Letter to John II, Nuremberg, 14th July, 1493. Reproduced in Vignaud, *Histoire critique de la grande entreprise*, vol. ii, p. 620.

16. Nunn, G. E., *Geographical Conceptions of Columbus*, New York, 1924, p. 50.

17. Pina, Ruy de, *Chronica*, vol. ii, pp. 177–8.

18. Reproduced in Harrisse, H., *Christophe Colomb*, Paris, 1884, 2 t., vol. i, pp. 349–50.

19. *Ibid.*, vol. ii, pp. 7–9.

20. Martyr, Peter, d'Anghiera (Anglerius, P. M.), *Opus epistolarum Petri Martyris Anglerii Mediolanensis*, Alcalá, 1530. Letter cxxxv.

21. *Ibid.*, Letter cxxxvi.

22. Martyr, Peter, *De Orbe Novo*, English translation ed. MacNutt, F. A., New York, 1912, 2 v., vol. i, p. 57.

23. *Ibid.*, vol. i, p. 65.

CHAPTER V

ASIA OR MUNDUS NOVUS?

AFTER five months of preparation Columbus set sail on his second voyage on 25th September, 1493. The main purposes of the new expedition were two : to establish the Spanish power firmly in Española, and to complete the search for Mangi and Cathay. It was to the first that Columbus's main attention was directed for the next three years, but unfortunately with very little success. His greatness lay in his capacity as an explorer, and not as a coloniser or governor. But that side of the story does not concern us, and we need only note the results of the voyage in revealing the great extent of the Antilles chain. The fleet of seventeen caravels left Cadiz on 25th September, but it was not until 13th October, 1493, that it took its final departure from the Canaries and steered westward. Twenty days later, after a prosperous voyage, Columbus saw for the first time a little island without a harbour, which he named La Desirada (the Desired), and on Sunday, November 3rd, the large island of Dominica, which thenceforth until the days of steam was to be the usual landfall of ships from Europe. In his first voyage he had heard in Española of the dreaded Caraibes, the eaters of human flesh, *anthropophagi*, or *cannibali*,[1] whose fierceness and horrid practices caused so much sensation among those who read of the discoveries. In Guadeloupe, the next island discovered, the Spaniards came into contact with them for the first time, and thence onwards throughout the Lesser Antilles, which were traced and successively named from Madanina (Martinique) to the

---

[1] This word, which was first used by Peter Martyr, is a corruption or another form of *Caraibes*, or, as we now say, " Caribs."

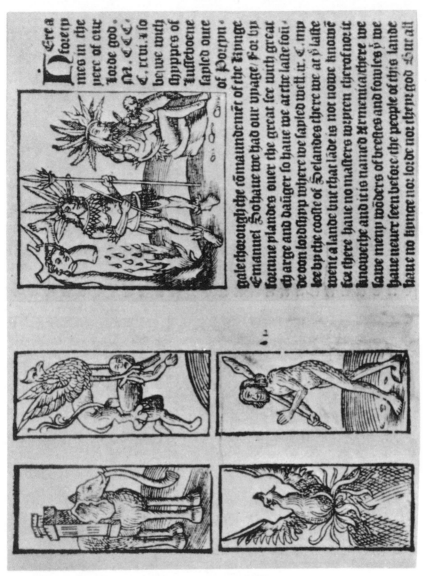

THE FIRST BOOK IN ENGLISH CONCERNING THE DISCOVERIES

(The first page with wood-cuts from the tract printed by Jan van Doesborgh in Antwerp about 1519.)

The elephant has a trunk and howdah but the legs and hoofs of a horse. The other illustrations on the left represent (1) a hippogriff carrying off a man as its prey, (2) the phœnix rising from the flames, and (3) a cyclops with a single eye in the middle of his forehead. The wood-cut on the right represents a cannibal with his wife and two children by a fire over which severed human limbs are cooking. (See R. Proctor, *Jan van Doesborgh*, Bibliographical Society Publications, London, 1894.)

Virgin Islands, they constantly saw their war canoes. The larger island of San Juan (de Porto Rico) was found to be inhabited by less savage tribes of the Arawak race, and amicable relations with them were possible.

The expedition arrived in Española on 22nd November, and from thence onwards for the next few months Columbus worked to establish a colony in a sound state of defence, and to procure the gold that he had promised. In February 1494 he sent back home twelve of the seventeen ships that had come out from Europe with him, and it was from Antonio Torres, their commander, that Peter Martyr learned the mass of interesting details about the islands and their natural history that he forwarded to Cardinal Sforza in May 1494 [1] :

"The eve of the nones of April, this commander of the squadron, who was the brother of the nurse of the eldest royal princes, arrived at Medina del Campo, being sent by Columbus. I questioned him and other trustworthy witnesses, and shall now repeat what they told me, hoping by so doing to render myself agreeable to you. What I learned from their mouths you shall now in turn learn from me."

Thus Peter Martyr indicates the first-hand sources of his information and shows its authenticity. The particulars he gleaned were of such extraordinary interest that he came in the course of the summer to the momentous decision to constitute himself the recorder of the events in the discovery of what he was now convinced was a wholly new world. His first use of this term was rather in a metaphorical sense :

"The Admiral selected an elevation near the port [of Isabela in Española] as the site for a town : and within a few days, some houses and a church were built, as well as could be done in so short a time. And there on the feast of the Three Kings (for when treating of this country one must speak of a *new world*, so distant is it and so devoid of civilisation and religion) the Holy Sacrifice was celebrated by thirteen priests " [2].

It was to the revelation of this new world and its wonders that he determined to devote his pen, as he tells us in his letter to Count John Borromeo on 20th October, 1494 [3].

" Day by day more and more marvellous things are reported *from the new world* (*ab orbe novo*), through that Colonus the Ligurian who has been created as Admiral of the Ocean on account of good services. . . . He declares that he has pushed his way from Española so far toward the West that he has reached the Golden Chersonese which is the farthest extremity of the East. The Admiral thinks that there remains for him to discover only the space covered by two of those four and twenty hours consumed by the encircling sun in his daily passage. . . . I have begun to write a work concerning this great discovery. If I am suffered to live, I shall omit nothing worthy of being recorded, and whatever portions of this work shall come out of the press, a copy shall be sent to you. At all events, I shall supply the learned men who are accustomed to write of great things with a vast and new sea of material."

But Peter Martyr was not content to be merely a recorder ; he applied his scientific powers of reasoning to place the information he acquired in its proper relation to the content of knowledge. A sentence or two from his letter of April 1494 [4] may illustrate his work as a geographer :

" Melchior [an important officer in Columbus's second voyage] has told me that amongst the cannibals the days of the month of December are equal to the nights, but knowledge contradicts this observation. . . . When I enquired particularly concerning the elevation of the north star above the horizon, he answered me that in the land of the cannibals the Great Bear entirely disappeared beneath the arctic pole. There is nobody who came back from this second voyage whose testimony you may more safely accept than his ; but had he possessed knowledge of astronomy, he would have limited himself to saying that the day is about as long as the night. For in no place in the world does the night during the solstice precisely equal the day : and it is certain that on this voyage the Spaniards never reached the equator, for they constantly beheld on the horizon the polar star which served them as guide. As for Melchior's companions, they were without knowledge or experience, therefore I offer you few particulars, and those only casually, as I have been able to collect them."

As a shrewd collector of evidence with unique opportunities of access to the sources, as a scientific cosmogonist who was capable of arranging the data collected and as a practised writer who could set forth his results in clear and interesting fashion, his accomplishments gave Peter Martyr an unique position among the writers of his period. His letters were not mere sketchy fragments like Cosco's tract, but serious and connected contributions to knowledge, and since no other writer was performing a similar task, it is to Peter Martyr that we may attribute above all the glory of revealing the new knowledge to the world and thus bringing in the new age.

It is surprising to note the contrast between the great public interest in Columbus's first voyage and the indifference with which the news of the results of his second expedition was received. New editions of Cosco's tract poured from the printing press in the first half of 1494, but the only contemporary printed account of the first part of the second voyage as brought home by Antonio Torres in March 1494 appeared in a little tract published at Pavia by Nicolo Syllacio at the end of the year or early in 1495. This contained a somewhat confused summary of the news Syllacio had received in letters from an Italian gentleman, one Guglielmo Coloma, who had accompanied Columbus and returned with Torres' fleet. The tract [5] seems to have had but a small circulation, and it was not re-printed, which shows that the public sensation had waned and that there was little call for fresh news. Outside Spain it was only in the learned world that continued interest in the discoveries was maintained, though there curiosity was all on the alert. Expectations ran high, for

Peter Martyr wrote on 31st January, 1494 [6], before any news had arrived: "Great things are promised as about to be discovered in the western and antarctic antipodes."

Henceforward for the next six years the only accessible source of information as to what was happening was to be found in the letters that were passed from hand to hand in cultivated circles in Italy. Modern research has discovered a few other sources of information as to the second voyage, but these were concealed in official papers and private correspondence, and they were inaccessible to the general reader, for none of them were published for many years. The full account in Ferdinand Columbus's *Historie* was not written until after 1530, and it remained unpublished until 1571. For the second part of the voyage we are even now largely dependent upon what was written by Peter Martyr, and this illustrates his vital importance as the sole interpreter of the new geographical knowledge to his own age. On 5th December, 1494, he wrote from Alcalá to his old friend, Pomponius Laetus, in Rome [7] : " Spain spreads her wings more and more over the Indies, and stretches her glory and name to the antipodes." It was of this progress that he was now firmly resolved to be the chronicler and interpreter.

On 24th April, 1494, Columbus set sail from Isabela with three caravels to search for the kingdom of Mangi along the southern coast of what he firmly believed was a great Asiatic peninsula, but was in reality the island of Cuba. Sailing westward along that coast until the middle of May, he then turned due south and found the island of Jamaica, but that was clearly not what he was searching for, and he returned north to continue his exploration, as he thought, of the continental coast. He persisted in his quest amidst immense difficulties until at the end of June he arrived at the Isle of Pines, which he named Evangelista. The results were a terrible disappointment, for he found nothing in the least resembling what Marco Polo had described as characteristic of eastern Asia. But his persistence and powers of self-deception were such that he was convinced that he was correct in his identification, and before he would consent to the return that the exhaustion of his stores necessitated, he compelled or persuaded his subordinates to attach their signatures to an extraordinary document by which they proclaimed their adhesion to his beliefs. It is uncertain how much they really shared in the delusion, but when they struggled back to Isabela at the end of September, their discontent with the results of his leadership came to a head. Throughout 1495 he was compelled to struggle against faction in the colony and serious revolts amongst the Indian tribes, and finally, in March 1496, he set sail for Spain to justify his proceedings to his Sovereigns and to maintain his privileges against the many enemies at Court whom his failure to fulfil his promises had encouraged.

Not merely were there negligible results to show for the great expenditure of money and effort, but more and more doubt was aroused in the minds of shrewd observers as to whether the neighbourhood of Asia had been reached at all. As Columbus encountered this growing scepticism, he became ever more determined to maintain the truth of his assertions, and he embarked upon a campaign of pseudo-scientific argument which resulted in nothing but the loss among skilled cosmographers of all credit in his capacity for accurate thought. It is to the period between his arrival in Spain in June 1496 and his departure on his third voyage in May 1498 that we must date the collection of the extraordinary mass of erroneous cosmographical data that thenceforward for the rest of his life he expounded with less and less judgment and restraint. Peter Martyr succinctly summarised his beliefs when he wrote in 1501 [8] : "The Admiral . . . named the first coast he touched [in Cuba] Alpha and Omega, because he thought that there our East ended when the sun set in that island, and our West began when the sun rose. . . . He expected to arrive in the part of the world underneath us near the Golden Chersonese, which is situated to the east of Persia. He thought, as a matter of fact, that of the twelve hours of the sun's course of which we are ignorant he would have only lost two."

Into the unprofitable mazes of the controversy that arose it is unnecessary for us to enter. Columbus's star was on the wane, and though he had still great discoveries to make, the interpretation of the discoveries was passing to others. Before the turn of the century the skilled cosmographers of the time had come to a large measure of agreement that the newly discovered lands really belonged to a hemisphere that had previously been wholly unknown. Peter Martyr, writing as early as 31st October, 1494, to the Archbishop of Braga [9], introduces a new phrase into literature : " Hear what things have lately been discovered at the antipodes in the ' Western Hemisphere ' (ab occidente hemisperii antipodum) " ; while the term " the new world," which at first was used only metaphorically about the Antilles, with their strange new fauna and flora, was by 1500 beginning to be employed in its accurate sense. Cosmographers were coming to believe that a new habitable world had been discovered at the antipodes to balance the οἰκουμένη, or habitable world of the ancients.

Meanwhile Columbus was incessant in his complaints to the Crown against the infringement of his rights involved in the royal order throwing open the navigation to the lands of his discovery to all Spaniards, and early in 1496 he succeeded in securing its cancellation. It was, however, not until early in 1498 that he obtained permission to sail in command of a new expedition. He left San Lucar with six caravels on 30th May, 1498, and on 21st June, off the island of Ferro in the Canaries, he divided his fleet into two, sending three caravels direct to Española while with the other three he steered south to the Cape Verde Islands, for he believed that by taking a more southerly course across the Ocean he might find a direct route to the rich kingdoms for which he was searching. He left the island of S. Thiago on 4th July and steered south-west. The steady trade winds that had helped him on his previous passages were replaced by baffling airs and

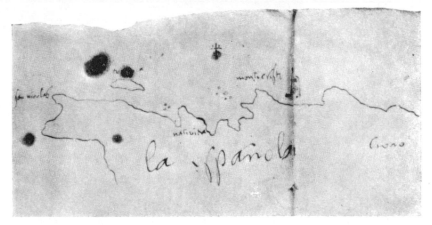

(a) SKETCH-MAP OF THE NORTHERN COAST OF ESPAÑOLA, DRAWN BY CHRISTOPHER COLUMBUS, POSSIBLY DURING HIS FIRST VOYAGE.

(From the Duchess of Berwick and Alba's *Nuevos Autografos de Cristobal Colon*.)

This is probably the first map of any portion of the new discoveries. It is preserved in the Alba Collection.

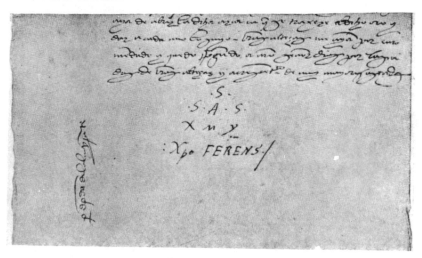

(b) SIGNATURE AND HANDWRITING OF CHRISTOPHER COLUMBUS.

(From a holograph letter addressed to the Catholic Kings in April 1493. Preserved in the National Archives at Madrid.)

The meaning of the curious anagram has been much disputed. It possibly may be read thus:

.S.[alva]   Save[me]
.S.   A   .S.
 ↑   ↑   ↑
X[ristos] M[aria] Y[osephus]   Christ, Mary, Joseph:

: Xр̄о FERENS.   [I come] bearing Christ

This subject of St. Christopher bearing Christ over water is a favourite one for wall paintings in medieval churches. *See also p. 148.*

calms, and his provisions were running low when after twenty-six days land was at last seen. Three high mountains were first observed, and this led him to give to the new land the name of Trinidad, by which it has ever since been known. When he noted the enormous volumes of fresh water that were pouring across his course as he gradually steered from the island towards the high mountains that he saw farther west, he felt certain that he had come at last to a mainland of infinite extent (*Este rio procede de tierra infinita*) [10]. So, in fact, he had, and when on 5th August, 1498, he or some of his men set foot on the coast below the lofty mountain chain of what we now call Venezuela, it was probably the first landing of Europeans on the southern continental mass of the new world.

In some measure Columbus recognised the true character of his new discovery, and he was right when he wrote in his report, " I believe that it is a very great continent " (*Yo estoy creido que esta es tierra ferme grandisima*) [11]. But he was hopelessly involved in his interpretation of the discovery, and his mystical imaginings and wild theories destroyed any possibility that the discovery might restore his credit at Court. From Paria he sailed out through the Boca del Drago and traced the coast westward as far as the island of Margarita, whence he sailed direct to Española, arriving at the new port of Santo Domingo on the southern coast on 31st August, 1498. Thence he wrote describing his discoveries to his Sovereigns, and it is in this letter that we have his geographical ideas first set forth at length. The letter was intended solely for the Sovereigns, and was quite unknown to the public, and remained unpublished until the nineteenth century. In fact, nothing was available to his contemporaries about this third voyage save what was written by Peter Martyr to his correspondents or included in Books VI and VII of the First Decade of his *De Orbe Novo*. Thus the first discovery of the mainland by Columbus remained unknown, with important consequences that will appear in a moment.

It is hardly worth while to devote much space to Columbus's geographical fictions, for they were entirely without influence in moulding opinion, but a phrase or two will indicate how essentially medieval were his conceptions, and how far removed from the matter-of-fact realism of the Portuguese.   In his letter of 1500 to Doña Juana de la Torres describing his third voyage, he wrote [12] : " God made me the messenger of the new heaven and the new earth of which He spoke in the Apocalypse by St. John, after having spoken of it by the mouth of Isaiah ; and He showed me the spot where to find it."   His mystic belief in his Divinely appointed mission mingles strangely with wild legends of the middle ages and impossible scientific guesses to make a mixture from which it is hard to disinter the serious facts of the voyage.   Two extracts alone must suffice to illustrate this : " I have always read that the world comprising the land and the water was spherical, and the recorded experiences of Ptolemy and all others have proved this by the eclipses of the moon and other observations made from east to west, as well as by the elevation of the pole from north to south.   But I have now seen so much irregularity, that I have come to another conclusion respecting the earth, namely that it is not round as they describe, but of the form of a pear . . . or like a round ball, upon one part of which is a prominence like a woman's nipple, this protrusion being the highest and nearest the sky, situated under the equinoctial line, and at the eastern extremity of this sea where the land and the islands end. . . . I affirm that the globe is not spherical, but that there is this difference in form the which is to be found in this hemisphere at the point where the Indies meet the ocean, the extremity of the hemisphere being below the equinoctial line. . . . [The ancients] had no certain knowledge respecting this hemisphere, but merely vague suppositions, for no one has ever gone or been sent to investigate the matter until now that Your Highnesses have sent me to explore both the sea and the land " [13].

Columbus then goes on to associate this strange conception with a typical idea of the medieval cosmographers : " The Holy Scriptures record that our Lord made the earthly paradise, and planted in it the tree of life, and thence springs a fountain from which the four principal rivers in the world take their source. . . . I do not find, nor ever have found, any account by the Romans or Greeks which fixes in a positive manner the site of the terrestrial paradise, neither have I seen it in any *mappa mundi* laid down from authentic sources . . . [but] I have no doubt that if I could pass below the equinoctial line, after reaching the highest point of which I have spoken, I should find a much milder temperature and a variation in the stars and in the water. Not that I suppose that elevated point to be navigable, nor even that there is water there ; indeed, I believe it is impossible to ascend thither, because I am convinced that it is the spot of the earthly paradise whither no one can go but by God's permission. . . . I do not suppose that the earthly paradise is in the form of a rugged mountain, as the descriptions of it have made it appear, but that it is on the summit of the spot which I have described. . . . I think also that the water I have described [i.e. the waters of the Orinoco] may proceed from it, though it be far off, and that stopping at the place which I have just left, it forms this lake. There are great indications of this being the terrestrial paradise, for its site coincides with the opinion of holy and wise theologians, and, moreover, the other evidences agree with the supposition, for I have never either read or heard of fresh water coming in so large a quantity in close conjunction with the water of the sea. The idea is also corroborated by the blandness of the temperature ; and if the water of which I speak does not proceed from the earthly paradise, it seems to be a still greater wonder, for I do not believe that there is any river in the world so large or so deep " [14].

Fantastic ideas such as these, added to the complete failure of Columbus to justify his identification of the new lands with the Indies of Asia, demonstrated unmistakably to the Sovereigns his incapacity as a cosmographer. The disorders in Española similarly demonstrated his deficiencies as the governor of a colony, and henceforward the Crown ceased to employ him. When he was sent home as a prisoner by Bobadilla and reached Cadiz in chains in November 1500, the Sovereigns released him from confinement and treated him with courtesy, but they never again gave him any responsibility.

For the next two years he was entirely neglected, and the news of the triumphant return of Vasco da Gama with his fleet richly laden with the undoubted products of India must have been a bitter blow. Other sailors of Spain, as we shall see later, were voyaging for profit to coasts that he had discovered while he was lingering in Spain in comparative poverty and enforced idleness. At last, however, he was permitted to sail upon a fourth voyage of discovery, but it was only as a private individual and under prohibition from landing in Española. He left Cadiz with three caravels on 11th April, 1502, and Ferro on 26th May. Thence he sailed direct to Matinino and Dominica, which he saw on 11th June. He was refused permission to land at Santo Domingo and passed on to Jamaica and the southern coast of Cuba, whence he steered south into unknown waters. At the end of July he discovered the little island of Guanaja off the coast of Honduras, and turned east hoping to find a passage that would lead to the south. It was not until 12th September that he found the coast at last trending southwards at the Cape that he named Gracias à Dios, but his hopes were bitterly disappointed, for after many weeks of difficult navigation he came again to the definitely eastward trend of the coast of Veragua. He believed that he was now only nineteen days' sail from the mouth of the Ganges, but he could find no strait through the land, and he does not seem to have realised how narrow was the isthmus at this point, though the Indians certainly told him of the sea on the other side.

For several months Columbus remained upon the coast of Veragua making short expeditions into the interior in search of gold mines and in parley with the Indians for purchase of their gold. But at length, worn out by ill-health, disappointment, and fatigue, he was compelled to sail for Española to get help to repair his worn-out vessels. His passage was impeded by terrible storms, and at length in May 1503 he made his landfall, not near Santo Domingo, as he hoped, but on the southern coast of Cuba. Despite all the evidence of his own voyages, he was still convinced that this was part of Asia and, as he wrote in an extraordinarily confused letter to the Sovereigns, that he had " reached the province of Mangi, which is contiguous to that of Cathay. . . . The nation of which Pope Pius writes [i.e. the Massagetae] has now been found, judging at least by the situation and other evidences, excepting the horses with the saddles and poitrels and bridles of gold ; but this is not to be wondered at, for the lands on the sea-coast are only inhabited by fishermen, and, moreover, I made no stay there, because I was in haste to proceed on my voyage " [15].

From Cuba Columbus struggled with difficulty across to Jamaica, which he reached in July 1503, and thence he wrote to the Sovereigns to beg for succour and assistance to conquer Veragua and the mines of Solomon described by the Jewish historian Josephus, of which, as he claimed, he alone knew the direction. The letter, as we have said, was so extraordinarily incoherent and its geography so clearly impossible that the explorer's claims were set aside as wild imaginings, and no reply was sent to his petitions for help. At length, after many months of waiting in Jamaica, he succeeded in obtaining assistance from some of his own friends in Española and thus in getting back to Spain, where he landed for the last time at the end of November 1504. He was still less than sixty years of age, but his fatigues and the spasms of mystical trance into which he now fell repeatedly had made him a very sick man. He remained in Seville until the spring of 1505, and then began to follow the Court in order to pursue his various financial claims on the Treasury. He was certainly regarded with disfavour and even contempt by the majority of Spaniards when they did not completely forget him, but the legends of his poverty are false, for we have many official papers showing his dealings with a considerable fortune. As in most of his other utterances, his complaints of royal ingratitude and injustice are wildly exaggerated, and cannot be taken at their face value, as so many of Columbus's panegyrists have done. In fact, he was treated fairly, and the Spanish monarchs abided by the letter of their agreements with him until they clearly became incompatible with the public interest. But as a scientific explorer or cosmographer he had become merely an object of contempt, which he had largely brought upon himself. Hence his death on 21st May, 1506, in Valladolid passed unnoticed, and even Peter Martyr made no direct mention of it in his letters, but merely referred to it casually much later.

The events of the fourth voyage were not recounted by Peter Martyr as those of the others had been, for after 1499 he devoted most of his attention to the explorations of others than Columbus. The only published description was that of Constantio Bayuera, of Brescia, who was travelling in Spain in 1504. There he saw a copy of the letter written by Columbus from Jamaica in July 1503, and being interested decided to translate it into Italian. This translation was published in Venice in May 1505, and it is now known as the Lettera Rarissima [16]. The account given only relates to the first part of the voyage, and it does not appear to have had any wide circulation or to have been much read. Columbus's later work, in fact, never excited much interest or attention among the reading public of the time, though the new lands of his discovery had become by the opening of the new century an object of universal interest. The encouragement of this interest arose from an entirely new quarter, and before we trace the work of the explorers who were contemporary with Columbus, it is well to show how that work became generally known.

Down to 1504 the interest in Italy in the discoveries was satisfied mainly by the circulation of manuscript copies of Peter

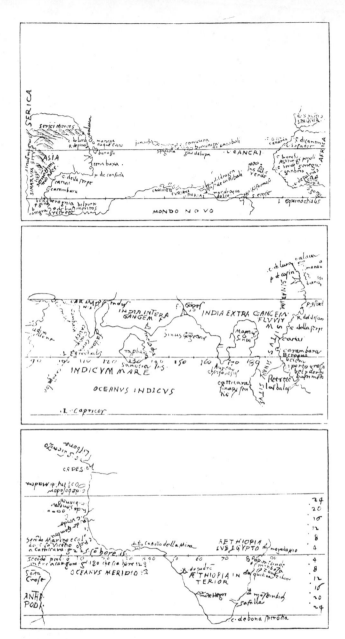

SKETCH-MAPS OF BARTHOLOMEW COLUMBUS TO ILLUSTRATE
THE DISCOVERY OF VERAGUA ON THE FOURTH VOYAGE OF
CHRISTOPHER COLUMBUS AND ITS RELATION TO THE
COASTS OF ASIA.

(From F. von Wieser, *Die Karte des Bartolomeo Colombo über die vierte Reise des Admirals.*
Innsbrück, 1893.)

The description of the voyage was given by Bartholomew Columbus in Rome in
1506 to his confessor, Fr. Hieronymus, of the canons of St. John Lateran, and by him
conveyed to a collector of accounts of voyages, Alessandro Zorzi. It is now preserved
in Zorzi's hand in the National Library of Florence with three illustrative sketch-maps
in the margin.

(*See p.* 79.)

Martyr's letters, but there was no printed compilation. Clients of Italian notabilities who visited Spain did what they could to satisfy their patrons' curiosity by sending them copies of such information as they could secure. Among them was one Angelo Trivigiano, secretary of the Venetian legation in Spain, who entered into personal communication both with Columbus and Peter Martyr. On 21st August, 1501, he forwarded to the celebrated Venetian admiral Domenico Malpiero a map of the voyages, which is now unfortunately lost, and an account of them, which he described thus [17] : " As for the voyage of the said Columbo, it has been composed by a man of merit and it is a very long history. I have copied it and possess the copy, but it is so voluminous that there are no means of sending it to you except by fragments. I send to-day to your Magnificence the first book which I have translated into the vulgar tongue for more facility. . . . The author of this work is the ambassador of these most Serene Kings who is proceeding to the Sultan [of Egypt] and who is leaving here with the intention of presenting it to our Serene Prince [the Doge], who, I think, will cause it to be printed."

This work was the First Decade of Peter Martyr's De Orbe Novo, which the author had only circulated in manuscript. But now he found himself forestalled in its publication. In 1504 Trivigiano's Italian translation was published in Venice under the title Libretto di tutta la navigazione del re di Spagna de le isole et terreni novamente trovati [18]. Three years later a further piracy took place, and collections of voyages containing extracts from the work were published in 1507 and 1508 in Vicenza, Milan, Basle and Paris under the title of Paesi novamente ritrovati et Novo Mundo da Alberico Vesputio florentino intitulato [19]. Thus, before Peter Martyr could publish his own authorised edition of his First Decade, as he did in 1511, pirated versions of it were circulating widely in which the discoveries were associated not so much with Columbus as with another traveller, Amerigo Vespucci. There are six sections in this

widely circulated work, the first three recounting the voyages of
Cadamosto, da Gama, and Cabral, the fourth reproducing the
Libretto pirated from Peter Martyr, the fifth the letter of Vespucci,
of which we have now to speak, and the sixth certain Portuguese
narratives of the East.

The fifth part of the Paesi published in 1507 contains what
purports to be the Italian version of a letter from a Florentine,
Amerigo Vespucci, to Lorenzo Pietro Francesco de Medici
describing a voyage that he had made in the service of the King
of Portugal for the discovery of lands in the south-west. In
reality it is an Italian translation of a Latin tract of four leaves
published at Florence in 1503. This was a Latin translation of the
original Italian letter from Lisbon, and it is known as the Mundus
Novus [20]. Many editions of this tract appeared in the three
years before it was translated in the Paesi, and it undoubtedly
did much to spread the idea that a new world had been revealed.

While the various Latin editions of the Mundus Novus were
pouring from the Italian presses and it was being translated and
printed also in German, Dutch and French, a new letter from
him appeared in 1505 in Florence under the title Lettera di Amerigo
Vespucci delle isole nuovamente trovate in quatro suoi viaggi [21].
This was ostensibly written from Lisbon on 4th September, 1504,
to an unnamed correspondent of high position in Florence, who
was undoubtedly Pier Soderini, Gonfaloniere of the republic.
In its Italian form the tract had but a small circulation, and it is
now very rare. But two years later it was translated into French
and thence into Latin, in which form it was included in a work
published at St. Dié in the Vosges by one Martin Waldseemüller,
who was known by the Latin pseudonym of Ilacomilus. The
work was the Cosmographiae Introductio, and six or seven editions
of it appeared at St. Dié in the single year 1507, which shows how
much interest it excited. The letter of Vespucci forms the
second part of the work under the title Quator Americi Vesputci
navigationes, and it was this book along with the Mundus Novus

describing the third voyage and the *Paesi novamente ritrovati* that above all brought a knowledge of the new world from the cabinets of the statesmen and the learned into the general current of human affairs.

Who was this Amerigo Vespucci whose fame in his own day and the next generation entirely eclipsed that of Columbus and caused his name to be given in perpetuity to the new continent ? This question has given rise to an immense amount of controversy, and some writers of repute have even believed that the accounts of his voyages were fictitious, and that he was nothing but a glib impostor with a facile pen. It is impossible here to enter into the mazes of this controversy or to attempt to find a solution. It is sufficient to summarise certain probabilities that modern research has revealed, for the essential fact in explaining the undoubted influence that his supposed voyages had on public opinion is not the way in which they were carried out, but the belief in their truth that was universal down to the middle of the sixteenth century, when Las Casas attacked them in order to re-habilitate the memory of Columbus.

As successive reports came back to Spain of the Admiral's failure to fulfil his promises of a rapid disclosure of the way to Mangi and Cathay, the doubts of the Catholic Kings and their expert advisers of the accuracy of his identification of the newly discovered islands with those of Eastern Asia rapidly increased. Many applications were made to them during 1494 by pilots, including some of those who had sailed with Columbus on his first voyage, for permission to undertake discoveries on their own account. In April 1495 Ferdinand and Isabella decided to send out a commissioner to Española to enquire into the accusations against the Admiral for mismanagement, and at the same time they issued a decree throwing open discovery to any Spanish subject who wished to undertake it. The equipment of the fleet to take out the commissioner, Juan Aguado, was entrusted to Juanoto Berardi, the representative in Seville of the great

Florentine commercial firm of the elder branch of the Medici. There had come to Seville in the employment of the firm early in 1492 a Florentine, one Amerigo Vespucci, who had long been interested in cosmography and had received some mathematical training. When Berardi died, in 1496, the carrying out of the royal contract was entrusted by the firm to Vespucci, and he had to see to the equipment of the second squadron, which was to follow up that of Aguado. The first section sailed in August 1495, and the second in February 1496, while the third and last of the squadrons arranged for was ready by May 1497.

According to Vespucci's own account in the *Lettera*, he set sail from Cadiz on 10th May, 1497, towards the Great Gulf of the Ocean Sea, and took eighteen months over the voyage, returning on 15th October, 1498, with little of value but a cargo of 222 slaves. Much discussion has centred round the discoveries made upon this voyage, largely owing to the divergences between the proper names as printed in the Italian and the Latin versions, the latter being the only one known for many years. The principal difficulty occurred over the name printed in the Latin edition as " Parias," which some scholars have claimed to indicate that Vespucci was plagiarising the discoveries made by Columbus in his third voyage. But in the earlier Italian edition the Indian name of the land discovered was given as " Lariab," and this seems to remove the point of the controversy. Other writers, however, accept the statements of Vespucci as indicating that his discoveries were made upon the coast of Honduras and in the Gulf of Mexico, which he left through the Florida Passage between Florida and Cuba. The objection that this was impossible, since the insular character of Cuba was unknown until Ocampo's voyage of 1508, has little weight, for on the celebrated Cantino map of 1502 the passage is clearly shown, and Cuba is marked as an island.[1] It is held by Vespucci's supporters that the information upon

---

[1] The western end of Cuba also appears in La Cosa's map of 1500 and does not seem to have been drawn merely from guesswork.

which this part of the map was constructed was derived from the results of this first voyage, for there is no other known discoverer who could have supplied it. It cannot be claimed that the matter has yet been settled.

There is less dispute concerning the second voyage, for we have the independent testimony of Alonso de Hojeda, its commander, who stated definitely in his deposition to the Crown on 7th December, 1512, that when he sailed in 1499 to follow up the discoveries made by the Admiral in his third voyage of 1498, he " took with him Juan de la Cosa and Morigo Vespuche and other pilots, and was despatched for this voyage by order of Don Juan de Fonseca, Bishop of Palencia, by order of their Highnesses " [22]. According to Vespucci the expedition first touched land in June 1499 somewhere near where the boundary between Brazil and French Guiana now runs. This has been disputed, for it would make Hojeda and Vespucci anticipate the separate discoveries of Pinzon and Cabral in the following year. But there is little importance in the matter, for the discoverers did not trace the coast to the east, since they knew that this would carry them into the forbidden Portuguese sphere. They steered instead along the coast in the opposite direction towards Paria and the great river mouth that had been discovered by Columbus. Vespucci's description of the Guiana coast, with its half-drowned lands, is recognisably accurate, and when they came at length to the high mountains of the coast of Paria, they passed on to explore it further. When Hojeda arrived in Santo Domingo in September 1499, he stated that he had explored 600 leagues of new coast (i.e. from Paria to Maracaibo and Cape de la Vela), and this is shown on the celebrated map constructed by Juan de la Cosa after his return. The explorers compared the Indian villages built on piles in the water to the city of Venice, and hence the country was given the name of Venezuela, which it still bears. With the exception of Vespucci's very generalised descriptions there is no detailed account of the voyage, for Peter Martyr makes no mention of it, though he knew Amerigo well. It is uncertain whether Vespucci returned to Spain with Hojeda or separately, but at any rate he was back at Cadiz by the autumn of 1500, and he then was recognised as a capable cosmographer and explorer.

Meanwhile the Spanish government had determined, after receiving the news of da Gama's successful voyage to Calicut, to ascertain whether there were not a passage southward and westward round the continental land discovered at Paria by Columbus. The command was entrusted to Vicente Yanez Pinzon, who had commanded the *Pinta* in the Admiral's first voyage of 1492. There is a probability that he was the commander of the voyage described by Vespucci in 1497–8, for Peter Martyr, writing before 1508, tells us that Pinzon had proved that Cuba was an island, and other witnesses speak of his voyage of 1499–1500 as being the second in which he held supreme command. At any rate, he was recognised as an expert navigator and leader, and he amply justified the trust placed in him. He started in December 1499 and steered directly to the south-west. His first landfall was near Cape San Roque in January 1500, so that he somewhat anticipated Cabral's discovery of the Brazilian coast. He turned north-west and traced the land across the Equator and the enormous estuary of the Marañon (i.e. the River of the Amazons), where he was astonished to find vast quantities of fresh water far out of sight of land. He entered the mouth of the river and explored it for some distance before he again steered north-west until he came to the Pearl Coast, and returned to Spain by way of Española. Diego Lepe, a sailor of Palos, like Pinzon, almost at the same time explored the coast of Brazil from Cape San Roque to 10° S., and recognised its south-westerly trend, so that before the end of 1500 the whole of the coast of the southern continent had been traced from Cape de la Vela to the lands that unmistakably lay within the Portuguese sphere and had been named by Cabral (22nd April, 1500) " Tierra de Vera Cruz," as we can see on the Cantino map of 1502.

None of the results of these voyages were made accessible to the public, but they caused concern to the King of Portugal, who feared that the Spaniards would infringe his undoubted rights to the land named by Cabral.   He therefore determined to explore its coast farther to the south, and for this purpose he engaged the services of Vespucci, sending him out as cosmographer of an expedition under the command of one Nuno Manoel.   Like all his other writings, the authenticity of Vespucci's account of this, his third and most celebrated voyage, has been disputed.   The strong balance of probability is in its favour, and since the story formed the material of the widely circulated *Mundus Novus*, it had more influence in moulding geographical ideas than any other single voyage, save the first of Columbus.

Three caravels set sail from Lisbon in May 1501 and dropped down the coast of Africa as far as Cape Verde, where they met the ships of Cabral returning from his successful voyage to India. Thence they steered across the Atlantic nearly along the Equator, and on 17th August, 1501, they came to a thickly peopled coast which they believed to be that of a continent.   They called the cape near which they landed in 5° S. "Cape San Rogue," and since the land abounded in parrots, the sailors came to speak familiarly of it as the "Land of the Parrots."   Thence they followed the coast southward and came, at the beginning of November, to a fine harbour which they called Bahia de Todos os Santos.   On 1st January, 1502, it seems probable that they discovered a large opening which they took for the mouth of a river, and called the Rio de Janeiro, in 22° S.   In February they left the Brazilian coast and steered south-west into icy waters, where they found nothing but an uninhabited island, possibly Tristan d'Acunha, on which it was impossible to land.   Ruysch's map of 1508 and other contemporary authorities state that the Portuguese had been as far south as 52°, and this probably marks the limit of the voyage.   Returning north via Sierra Leone and the Azores, the ships arrived in the Tagus in September 1502.

Despite the scepticism of certain writers and the impossibilities that are found in Vespucci's letters, there seems to be no doubt that the voyage took place as described, and that to it we owe much of the nomenclature of the southern continent. Independent authorities confirm this, and notably the maps of Cantino and Canerio, which we know date from 1502 and were based on Portuguese information.

In a fourth voyage, lasting from June 1503 to June 1504, and intended to search for a passage to the city of Malacca by the south-west, Vespucci again visited the coast of Brazil. The island of Fernando Noronha was discovered and a Portuguese colony established on the coast near Cape Frio, but otherwise the results of the voyage were negligible. In 1505 Amerigo left the service of King Manuel and passed back to Spain, where he met Columbus, who had now returned from his last voyage. In an extant letter of 5th February, 1505, to his son Diego, the explorer commended him as a worthy supporter. " I spoke with Amerigo Vespucci, the bearer of this letter, who is gone to Court on matters relating to navigation. He always showed a desire to please me and is a very respectable man. Fortune has been adverse to him, as to many others. His labours have not been so profitable to him as he might have expected. . . . I have told him all I can about my affairs and of the payments that have been made to me and are due " [23]. A similar good opinion of the Florentine and his capacity as a cosmographer was held by Peter Martyr. In the tenth book of his Second Decade, when he was discussing the configuration of the new continent, he wrote : " I addressed myself to the Bishop of Burgos [Juan Fonseca] to whom all navigators report. Seated in his room, we examined numerous reports of those expeditions, and we have likewise studied the terrestrial globe on which the discoveries are indicated, and also many parchments called by the explorers navigators' charts [i.e. portolani]. One of these maps had been drawn by the Portuguese, and it is claimed that Amerigo

OBSERVATION OF THE PASSAGE OF THE SUN WITH A PORTABLE
ASTROLABE AND A CROSS-STAFF ON A PORTUGUESE SHIP
OF THE SIXTEENTH CENTURY.

(Engraving from the original edition of the Travels of Hans Staden to Brazil, 1557.)

Vespucci of Florence assisted in its composition. He is very skilled in this art, and has himself gone many degrees beyond the equinoctial line, sailing in the service and at the expense of the Portuguese " [24].

Immediately after his return from Portugal, official documents show him engaged in the Spanish service until September 1506, in the preparation of an expedition to be commanded by Vicente Yanez Pinzon to search for the Moluccas, i.e. in all probability to seek for a strait through the new lands, for Spain had no intention of disputing the route round the Cape of Good Hope. But the protests of the Portuguese caused the abandonment of the scheme for the time being, though it was resumed in 1508 under the leadership of Vespucci, only to be dropped once more. He was then named pilot-in-chief of the India House or Casa de Contratacion, and entrusted with the task of preparing navigation charts and the examination of candidates for the office of pilot. His detractors are unable to deny the evidence of his reputation as an able cosmographer, but they account for it by making him out a supernaturally clever impostor. It seems impossible that such an one could have held so important an office with entire and lasting credit until his death in 1512, and it is improbable that no trace should have been left of contemporary attacks upon his veracity, if such there were. His *Mundus Novus* and his *Quator navigationes* were circulating all over Europe before his death, and there must have been many living who could have proved them to be a fraudulent imposture, if he, a respected person holding a high professional position, had not made the voyages as he pretended. It was not until Las Casas attacked him in 1552 as a detractor from the memory of Columbus that the authenticity of his adventures was disputed. Subsequent controversy has excited so much heat and divided scholars so sharply into opposing camps of pro-Columbians and pro-Vesputians that it has been forgotten that the antithesis is entirely unnecessary. To rate Vespucci's influence high, as we are driven perforce to do, and to hold that the evidence in his favour proves that he was not the boastful liar and plagiarist his detractors have painted, need not influence our estimate of Columbus and his work in the least. The two men were independent contributors to human knowledge. Most of Las Casas' strictures were ill-conceived on imperfect information and badly aimed, and we may safely put them aside.

The resolution of most men's doubts as to the accuracy of the identification of the new lands with Asia came very soon after the publication of the *Mundus Novus*. " It is lawful," Vespucci wrote, " to call [the new countries] *a new world*, because none of those countries were known to our ancestors, and to all who hear about them they will be entirely new. For the opinion of the ancients was that the greater part of the world beyond the equinoctial line to the south was not land, but only sea, which they called the Atlantic ; and if they affirmed that any continent was there, they gave many reasons for denying that it is inhabited. But this their opinion is false and entirely opposed to the truth. My last voyage has proved it, for I have found a continent in that southern part ; more populous and more full of animals than our Europe or Asia or Africa, and even more temperate and pleasant than any other region known to us " [25].

The form of this assertion was so positive and clear as to catch the imagination, while the interesting facts about natural history and cosmography could hold it and make the impression permanent.

Such was the effect upon the mind of Martin Waldseemüller when he read the text of the *Lettera*, and resolved to add it to his *Cosmographia* as the most significant work of the time. There are various passages in his book in which he refers to Vespucci's explorations, but we need only quote the most significant : " To-day these parts of the world (Europe, Africa and Asia) have been more fully explored, and a fourth part has been dis-covered by Americus Vesputius, as we shall see later [i.e. in the *Quator Navigationes* which formed the second part of the book].

Since Europa and Asia have received the names of women, I see no reason why we should not call this other part 'Amérigé,' that is to say, the land of Americus, or *America* after the sagacious discoverer Americus. We are exactly informed concerning its situation and the customs of its people by the four navigations of Americus " [26]. Just as the book took the public fancy, so did this suggestion. Within a very short while it became customary to speak of the southern continent of the new world as America, and later to extend the name to the whole continent of the western hemisphere. By 1520 the idea of its Asiatic connection was abandoned by almost all cosmographers, its true situation on the globe was established, and the problem became the finding of a strait by which to sail through it farther to the west.

NOTES TO CHAPTER V

1. Martyr, Peter, *De Orbe Novo*, Dec. I, bk. ii, ed. MacNutt, vol. i, p. 69.

2. *Ibid.*, vol. i, p. 83.

3. Martyr, Peter, *Opus epistolarum*, Letter cxliii.

4. *De Orbe Novo*, Dec. I, bk. ii, *ed. cit.*, vol. i, p. 82.

5. Syllacio, N., *De Insulis Meridiani atque Indici Maris nuper inuentis*, Pavia, 1494.

6. *Opus epistolarum*, Letter cxli.

7. *Ibid.*, Letter cxlvi.

8. *De Orbe Novo*, Dec. I, bk. iii, vol. i, pp. 92–3.

9. *Opus epistolarum*, Letter cxlv.

10. *Select Letters of Columbus*, ed. Major, R. H., Hakluyt Soc., 2nd edn., 1870, p. 147.

11. *Ibid.*

12. *Ibid.*, p. 153.

13. *Ibid.*, p. 134.

14. *Ibid.*, pp. 140–2.

15. *Ibid.*, pp. 194, 198–9.

16. *Copia de la lettera per Columbo mandata a li Sere^mo Re & Regina di Spagna de le insule et luoghi per lu triouate.* Venice, 7th May, 1505. Usually called the *Lettera Rarissima.* Venice, 1505. Translated by Major in *Select Letters*, pp. 175–211.

17. Harrisse, H., *Christophe Colomb*, vol. ii, p. 120.

18. Published by Albertino Vercelle, Venice, 1504.

19. For an account of the various editions, see Vignaud, H., *Améric Vespuce*, Paris, 1917, pp. 19–29.

20. *Ibid.*

21. *Ibid.*, pp. 31–57.

22. Navarrete, M. F., *Coleccion de viages y descubrimientos,* Madrid, 1825–37, vol. iii, p. 544.

23. *Ibid.*, p. 57. Translated in *Letters of Amerigo Vespucci,* ed. Markham, C. R., Hakluyt Soc., 1894, p. 31.

24. *De Orbe Novo,* Dec. II, bk. x, *ed. cit.,* vol. i, p. 271.

25. *Letters of Amerigo Vespucci,* p. 42.

26. See Vignaud, H., *Améric Vespuce,* p. 238, and editions there cited.

CHAPTER VI

THE FIRST EXPLORERS OF THE NORTH AMERICAN COAST

During the latter half of the middle ages the Italian republics were the recognised middlemen for the transport of the silks, spices and groceries of the East to the countries of Western Europe. In this traffic the rôle played by Venice was an important one. In the year 1317 that republic had established a regular service of galleys between the Adriatic and the Low Countries. "The track of the Flanders galleys," wrote Mr. Rawdon Brown, "seems with little variation to have taken the following course. In the first place they made for Capo d'Istria, then passed on to Corfu, Otranto, Syracuse, Messina, Naples, Majorca, the principal ports of Spain and Morocco and then Lisbon. On reaching our coasts they generally repaired to Camber before Rye, or the Downs, where they parted company ; those destined for England proceeded to Sandwich, Southampton, St. Catherine's point or London, creating in our English marts as great a sensation as ever did the arrival of the Indian fleet at Calcutta " [1]. By means of these galleys the ginger of Malabar and the cloves of Ternate, the cinnamon of Ceylon and the nutmegs of Malacca, the camphor of Borneo and the aloes of Socotra, not to mention the china-ware from China, found their way into English homes. In the *Libel of English Policy* of 1436 one reads how—

> " The grete galees of Venees and Florence
> Be wel ladene wyth thynges of complacence,
> Alle spicerye and of grocers ware,
> Wyth swete wynes, alle manere of chaffare,
> Apes, and japes, and marmusettes taylede " [2].

Among the Italians interested in this spice trade was Giovanni Caboto, who, though he had been born in Genoa, applied in the year 1461 for permission to settle in Venice [3]. At one time or another Venice had possessed factories in most of the principal cities of the eastern Mediterranean. Even at that date she owned important establishments at the two great termini of the routes from the East, at Alexandria and at La Tana. This latter, situated at the point where the Don enters the Sea of Azof, was in close communication via that river and the Volga with Astra-khan on the Caspian Sea, which was itself the terminus of the caravan route from China through Turkestan. By this route Venice received the glass and chinaware which she forwarded to Western Europe. Astrakhan also carried on a large trade with Persia, the silks of which country enjoyed an excellent reputa-tion. Here were also brought, via the Persian Gulf, the spices and precious stones of India. At La Tana therefore was centred a most important trade.

At Alexandria, in the latter half of the fifteenth century, Venice possessed two factories as well as a church and a public bath for the exclusive use of her citizens. The goods handled here were the precious stones and gems of India as well as the drugs and spices from the Moluccas. These goods were brought in native boats to Calicut, whence they were carried in Moorish vessels into the Red Sea. A caravan route led thence to the Nile, down which they were transported in dhows to Alexandria.

About the year 1421 Jiddeh, the port of Mecca, had taken the place of Aden as a place of transhipment in the Red Sea. In this way Mecca, in addition to being a great shrine for pilgrims, became one of the most important marts of Asia. Thither caravans made their way both from Cairo and Damascus as well as from Astrakhan and Persia.

As soon as Giovanni Caboto had become a citizen of Venice, which was accorded to him in 1476 after fifteen years' residence, he seems to have visited the two chief centres of Venetian trade in the Levant, La Tana and Alexandria. From the latter city he passed on to Mecca, but in what year we do not know.

Varthema, who visited it in 1503, tells us that he found there " a marveylous number of straungers and pylgryms, of the whiche some came from Syria, some from Persia and others from both the East Indies, that is to say, both India within the ryver of Ganges and also the other India without the same ryver," meaning our Siam and China. "I never sawe in anye place," he continues, " greater abundance and frequentation of people. From India the Greater they have pearles, precious stones and plentie of spyces, and especially from Bangalla they have a very large quantity of cotton and silks." In the lower part of the Temple were " fyve or sixe thousande men that sell none other thyng than sweete oyntmentes and from hence all manner of sweet savours are carried into the countreys of all the Mohumetans " [4].

Cabot's experience must have been somewhat similar. As he had " studied the sphere," he was anxious to find the country whence came the spices traded in Mecca. Having questioned those in charge of the caravans, he learned that they received the spices from other caravans that had brought them from a very long distance. These latter had received them in turn from others coming from still more remote regions. This was evidently the long caravan route from China via Turkestan, Astrakhan and Damascus. It occurred to Cabot that since the men in the East affirmed to the men who came to Mecca that the goods came from still farther to the east, the spices must grow on the very eastern confines of Asia. Would it be possible, he thought, in view of this, to bring them by ship from the extreme eastern coast of Asia across the Atlantic Ocean to Western Europe ? The idea seemed of sufficient importance, at any rate, to merit further reflection and investigation.

How many years Cabot debated this matter we do not know, but eventually, some time in the 'eighties of the fifteenth century, he made his way with his wife and three sons, Lewis, Sebastian and Sancio, in the Venetian galleys to London, living apparently in Blackfriars. The Italian colonies in England then were very numerous, and several statutes of the realm bear upon this trade. By an Act of 10th February, 1486, Henry VII took the merchants of Venice under his special protection.

Cabot found that in the matter of a route to Asia by the west attempts had already been made to find the islands placed upon medieval maps to the west of Ireland. In the middle of July 1480 two ships, one being of eighty tons, had sailed from Bristol in search of the island of Brasyl, which in Erse means the "land of the Blest." After nine months they had returned unsuccessful. Another island sought for was that of the Seven Cities, to which a Portuguese archbishop and six bishops were said to have fled with their flocks from the Moors in A.D. 741. Cabot moved, therefore, from London to Bristol, and under his directions sometimes two, sometimes three, and sometimes four vessels were despatched to try to find the island of Brasyl or that of the Seven Cities, which were to form stepping-stones along the route to Asia across the western ocean. In every case they returned home without having sighted land.

Matters were in this state when suddenly, in the spring of 1493, news reached England that another Genoese, Christopher Columbus, had sailed westward from Spain and had reached the Indies. The excitement everywhere was intense. At the Court of Henry VII this new discovery was pronounced to be a thing more divine than human. Cabot and his friends at Bristol were greatly impressed. They now had tangible proof that their own efforts had been in the right direction, and it was decided to continue them. It so happened that Henry VII passed the winter of 1495–6 at Bristol, and on 5th March, 1496, letters patent were issued to John Cabot, citizen of Venice, and to his sons Lewis, Sebastian and Sancio, giving them "full and free authority to sail to all parts, countries and seas of the East, West and North under our banners and ensigns upon their own proper costs and charges, to seek out, discover and find whatsoever isles, countries and regions which before this time have been unknown to all

Christians." They were bound to sail from and return to Bristol, and to pay to the King, after their expenses had been deducted, the fifth part of the capital gain in wares or money. All the goods brought home were to pass the customs at Bristol free of duty, and no one might visit the regions to be discovered without the licence of the said John and his sons [5].

For reasons unknown to us, possibly the protest of the Spanish ambassador in England, Cabot was unable to set sail until 1497. On Tuesday, 2nd May, of that year he finally left Bristol in a vessel called the *Mathew*, manned by eighteen men, mostly from Bristol. Rounding Ireland, they headed north and then west. As the prevailing winds are from that quarter, they probably had to sail fairly far to the south, for they would also be carried northwards by the Gulf Stream. The fact that they saw no icebergs shows that they kept to the south of the region where these are met with. At length, after being fifty-two days at sea, at 5 o'clock on Saturday morning, 24th June, they sighted what is usually considered to be the most westerly point of our Cape Breton Island. The royal banner was unfurled, and on stepping ashore John Cabot took possession of the land in solemn form in the name of King Henry VII. They saw no inhabitants, but found snares set for game and a needle for making nets. They also noticed notches in the trees, and so judged that the country was inhabited. The soil they thought excellent and the climate temperate. They also observed that the rise and fall of the tide was very slight. They were convinced they had reached the eastern coast of Asia, whence came the Brazil wood and the silks Cabot had seen at Mecca. To our present Cape Breton they gave the name of " Cape Discovery," and on it, as was then the custom, they set up a large cross with the arms both of England and of Venice. As the day was the festival of St. John the Baptist, our Scatari Island lying off this cape was named " the island of St. John."

Wood and water having been taken on board, they set sail to

the northward. Our Cape Ray seems to have been named " St. George's Cape," while our St. Pierre and Miquelon, which then, with Langlade, formed three separate islands, were called the " Trinity Group." Chapeau Rouge was possibly christened " Cape St. John," while Cape St. Mary, or Cape Race, was named not inappropriately " England's Cape." Along this coast they met great schools of cod which almost stayed their ship.

Setting sail thence early in July, Cabot reached Bristol safely on Sunday, 6th August. He hastened to Court, and on Thursday, 10th August, was granted a reward of ten pounds for having " founde the new Isle." He reported that 700 leagues to the west he had discovered the country of the Grand Khan. Although silk and Brazil wood were not to be found there, it was his intention on his return to proceed down that coast until he reached the rich island of Cipangu and the equatorial regions whence came the spices he had seen at Mecca. He would thus make London a greater centre for spices than was then Alexandria.

Henry VII was delighted and promised Cabot in the spring a fleet of ten ships. Meanwhile, he received a pension of twenty pounds a year for life. This would be worth, of course, a great deal more in those days. Fresh letters patent were issued of 3rd February, 1498, empowering Cabot to " take at his pleasure 6 English ships and them convey and lede to the londe and iles of late founde by the seid John." So interested was the King that he also advanced large sums to men " going towards the newe Ilande." Thomas Bradley had thirty pounds and Lancelot Thirkill forty.

Among the seamen engaged by Cabot for his second voyage was a Portuguese named João Fernandes, called " the Labrador," i.e. landowner. It appears that on a voyage he had made to the north in 1492 he had seen or heard of Greenland. As Cabot had proceeded so far south on his outward voyage, and as the course to Iceland, with which Bristol each year carried on a regular trade in cod-fish, was well known, it was decided on this second voyage to take the route by the north.

Early in May Cabot at length set sail in two ships provisioned for one year, while in his company " sailed also out of Bristowe three or four small ships fraught with sleight and grosse merchandizes as coarse cloths, caps, laces, points and other trifles which divers merchauntes as well of London as Bristowe aventurede " [6]. On leaving the Irish Sea they set their course north-west for Iceland, " not expecting," adds Sebastian Cabot, " to find any other land than that of Cathay and from thence to turn towards India." Soon they encountered a storm which drove one of the ships to seek refuge in Ireland. The rest of the fleet proceeded on its way, keeping as far as possible along the parallel of 58°. Day by day they were carried farther northward by the Gulf Stream. At length, early in June, they sighted the east coast of Greenland above Cape Farewell. As Fernandes had told them of this land, they named it " the Labrador's Land " [7].

Cabot and his men were much struck by the length of the daylight in these high latitudes, as well as by the clearness of the nights. At first they made their way north, noticing that only a few spots on the coast were free from ice and snow. The cold, however, steadily increased and the icebergs grew larger and larger. They were, in fact, in the very track of the largest ice-floes from the Arctic. They also had a strong current against them and their compass would not work. Finally, on 11th June, in latitude 67° 30', in the middle of Denmark Strait between Iceland and Greenland, the crews mutinied and refused to proceed farther, although the sea lay open before them. Cabot had no alternative but to turn about and to proceed in the opposite direction. In time they must reach the region explored in the previous summer and also Cipangu.

Several names were given to places on the east coast of Greenland, such as " the Round Bay," " the River of Melted Snow," " the Straight Coast," and " Mainland Cape," but it is difficult to identify these with their modern equivalents. The last was probably intended for Cape Farewell, the point where the coast turned

westward, just as " Cape of Shoals " would correspond to our
modern Cape Desolation, where the coast turns northward again.
Crossing Davis Strait, the crashing of the ice floes in a storm made
them think they were near islands full of demons, which figured
on the maps for a long time. Eventually they sighted our
Labrador in about 57° 30′, where there is a headland nearly 2,000
feet high.

Sailing down our modern Labrador they appear to have done
some bartering with the Indians, since three years later the Corte-
Reals found among the Nascopees a broken gilt sword and a pair
of earrings which had been made in Venice. Our Strait of Belle
Isle was mistaken for an ordinary bay and its importance not
realised until Cartier's exploration of it in 1534. Baccalieu
Island may have been named at this time, as it appears on Ruysch's
map. On reaching the southern parts of Newfoundland they
were again struck, as on their first voyage, with the immense
shoals of cod which according to Sebastian " sumtymes stayed his
shippes." The Cabots noticed also " the greate plentie of beares
in those regions, which use to eate fysshe, for plungeinge theym
selves into the water where they perceve a multitude of these
fysshes to lye, they fasten theyr clawes in theyr scales, and so
drawe them to lande and eate them " [8].

Proceeding along the coast already explored in the previous
summer, Cabot made his way steadily southward in search of
Cipangu. They were also impressed by the distance westward
they had come. The east coast of Greenland lies in 43° W.,
while the coast of Maine is in 70°, or 27° farther west. How far
they proceeded southward we do not know. Sebastian said they
reached the latitude of the Strait of Gibraltar, which is in 36° ;
other writers give 38°. In any event they saw no sign of Cipangu
nor of the spices of the Orient. As their provisions had now
begun to run low, they had no alternative but to come about and
to make the best of their way back to England.

Of the reception accorded to them on their return we know

nothing, but it is not difficult to understand that it was not enthusiastic. Instead of bringing spices and oriental gems, their ships were empty of everything, and those who had supplied money for the expedition realised that it was lost for good and all. Sebastian Cabot, when questioned some thirty years later, threw the responsibility for the complete cessation of further discovery upon the political state of the country on their return. It is true that Perkin Warbeck had escaped from the Tower and also that war had nearly broken out between England and Scotland, but the complete failure of the Cabots to discover Cipangu or even to find a trace of any spices is sufficient to explain everything.

João Fernandes, " the Labrador," seems to have returned to Portugal, and in October 1499 was granted by King Manuel the captaincy of any island or islands he might discover within the Portuguese sphere of influence [9]. This was limited to the region lying within the line of demarcation laid down by the Treaty of Tordesillas, viz. 370 leagues west of the islands of Cape Verde. Whether he took advantage of this we do not know, but no account of any further discoveries by him have come down to us.

On the island of Terceira, where Fernandes had his home, lived a noble Portuguese family called Corte-Real. The head of this family, Gaspar Corte-Real, was not only greatly interested in the discoveries then taking place but himself had already made several explorations. On 12th May, 1500, letters patent were issued to him at Cintra, near Lisbon, giving him the governorship of any islands or mainland he might discover within the Portuguese sphere of influence, with civil and criminal jurisdiction. If any trade was opened with these places, Corte-Real was to receive one-fourth of the proceeds. An expedition was at once fitted out, and with two ships Gaspar Corte-Real set sail from Lisbon in the summer of 1500. After touching at Terceira, he headed north and early in June reached the east coast of Greenland. Proceeding northward along this coast he seems to have been checked, about the end of June, as the Cabots had been, by the icebergs in Denmark Strait. Coming about, he proceeded southward as far as Cape Farewell, to which he gave the significant name of " Cape Get-sight-of-me-and-Leave-me." A point farther west was christened " the Coast of João Vaz," after Gaspar Corte-Real's father, while a fiord on the west coast was called " João Vaz's Bay."

Along the west coast Gaspar Corte-Real met with some Eskimos, whom he described as " very wild and barbarous, almost to the extent of the natives of Brazil except that these are white. By exposure to the cold, however, they lose this whiteness with age and become more or less brown. They are of medium height, very active and great archers. For javelins they make use of bits of wood burned at the ends which they throw as well as if they were tipped with fine steel. These natives clothe themselves in the skins of animals which are plentiful in that region " [10]. How far up this west coast he proceeded we do not know.

Heading once more to the south and passing in sight of Cape Desolation, Gaspar again set his course for Portugal, and reached Lisbon in safety some time in the autumn of 1500. He reported that the region they had explored, which they thought was part of Asia, was so inhospitable that they had been able to land only in a few places. It was covered with lofty mountains whose summits and sides were wrapped in ice and snow. He hoped, however, to return in the following year and to discover land of more importance.

Accordingly, three vessels were fitted out in the spring of 1501 by Gaspar and his brother Michael, and in these they set sail from Lisbon on 15th May. For four weeks they had no sight of land, but in the fifth week they fell in with some very large icebergs, from which they obtained fresh water. Still holding a course for Greenland, they met with an immense pack of field ice which forced them to alter their course towards the west. In their progress across Davis Strait they encountered a severe storm,

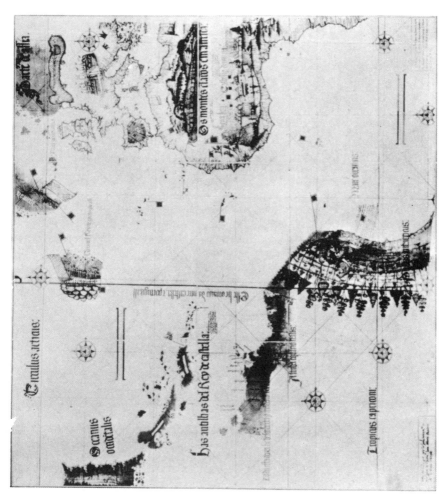

THE ATLANTIC OCEAN FROM THE MAP OF ALBERTO CANTINO,
1502.

(From the facsimile by A. and S. Pilinski in the British Museum.)

The new discoveries are depicted from the Portuguese point of view. Brazil and the northern lands explored by the Corte-Reals are shown to the east of the line of demarcation fixed by the Treaty of Tordesillas. The inscription attached to Newfoundland refers to its discovery by Corte-Real on behalf of the King of Portugal. The trees growing there are described as suitable for the making of ships' masts.

(See p. 62.)

during which they saw two imaginary islands called " Storm " and " Tempest Islands," which continued to figure on the maps of this region for many years. At length, after continuing westward, they sighted our present Labrador in about 58°. At this point the coast, which is 3,000 feet high, is visible a long way out to sea. They seem to have given the name of " Boundary Cape " to our modern Table Hill. Following the coast to the south, they named the modern Gull Island in 55° 30' the " Island of Birds." Cape Harrison, farther south, was called the " Beautiful Cape." On account of the reindeer which were formerly most numerous in these parts, Hamilton Inlet was named the " Bay of Does." As the coast now began to improve in appearance, they named Cape North, on the south side of Sandwich Bay, " Good Luck Cape," and Wolfe Island, " Good Luck Island."

From the size of the rivers along this coast they realised that this coast was that of a mainland. They were also struck with the profusion and size of the pine-trees which covered the country, which would supply masts for the largest ships then made. Up one of these openings they came upon a band of Nascopee Indians, of whom they seized some sixty men and women. Being in appearance a hardy, active race, it was thought they would make excellent slaves, such as Portugal was receiving from the west coast of Africa.

Our Strait of Belle Isle was mistaken for an ordinary bay, which they named the " Bay of Roses," then common thereabouts. Our Belle Isle was likewise christened, perhaps on 25th August, " the Island of Fray Luis," while to our Cape Freels they gave the name of " Cape of Fray Luis." Similarly Cape Bonavista was so named by the Corte-Reals, who gave to Trinity Bay the name of " St. Eyria's Bay," after a well-known Portuguese saint.

As it was now the beginning of September and they had already coasted this mainland for over 600 miles without coming to the end of it, Gaspar decided to send home the two caravels containing the Indians while he proceeded farther southwards to discover the connection between this land and the islands found by Columbus near the Equator. Gaspar Corte-Real was never heard of more, but the two caravels reached Lisbon in safety, the first on the 9th and the second on the 11th October, 1501.

The Indians excited the greatest curiosity, and though they were addressed in every known language, their replies could not be understood. As the country was only a month's sail from Lisbon and produced timber, King Manuel was much pleased with this discovery and determined to send back Michael Corte-Real in the following spring. On 15th January, 1502, his half-share of the lands already discovered was ratified, and he himself invested with the captaincy of any fresh lands to be discovered in that year.

Setting sail from Lisbon on 10th May, 1502, with three ships, he appears to have reached Newfoundland towards the end of June. It may have been on this occasion that St. John's received its present name, for it figures on the maps recording the results of the expedition as St. John's River, his festival falling on 24th June. It was decided that each of the three vessels should explore a particular part of the coast and should meet together again at St. John's on 20th August. It was on this occasion, apparently, that names were given both to Cape St. Francis, to the south of Conception Bay, and to Ferryland, which was named *Farelhão*, or the Rocky Promontory. Aquafort harbour was probably named " Fresh-water River " and Fermeuse, *rio Fermoso*, or the Pretty River. Cape Race or Razo was so named either from its barren appearance or from its resemblance to a cape of the same name at the mouth of the Tagus.

On 20th August two of the ships returned to St. John's, but Michael's ship failed to appear. In fact he was never heard of more. King Manuel was much distressed at the loss of these two pioneers, and sent out a fresh expedition in the summer of 1503, but the two ships returned in the autumn without having found any trace either of Gaspar or of Michael.

Meanwhile the merchants of Bristol had again despatched expeditions to those parts, inspired, it seems, by the Portuguese. On 19th March, 1501, Henry VII had granted to Richard Warde, Thomas Ashurst, and John Thomas of Bristol, along with João and Francis Fernandes and João Gonzales of the Azores, permission to undertake explorations in the west with a monopoly of the trade thither for ten years and licence to enter one vessel free of duty at Bristol during four years. In September 1502 they returned with " three men brought out of an Iland forre beyonde Irelond, the which were clothed in beestes' skynnes and ate rawe flesh and were rude in their demeanure as beestes." On the twenty-sixth of the same month Henry VII granted a pension of ten pounds each to Francis Fernandes and John Gonzales " in consideracion of the true service which they have doon unto us to our singler pleasure as Capitaignes into the newe founde lande." On 9th December, 1502, fresh letters patent were issued to Fernandes, Gonzales, Ashurst, and to Hugh Eliot of Bristol for permission to make further explorations in the West with a monopoly of trade to the region explored for forty years, and permission to enter two vessels free of duty at Bristol during five years. Under these and the former letters patent, expeditions were sent out both in 1503, 1504 and 1505, but we do not know which parts they visited.

In 1506 the rights of Gaspar and Michael were transferred to their brother Vasco Annes Corte-Real, and as proof that the Portuguese had now begun to fish on the Banks, a tax was imposed in the following month upon the cod brought to Vianna from that region. About the same time the French seem to have begun to visit the Banks. We first hear of them in 1504, and as the Portuguese frequented the harbours to the north of Cape Race, the French had recourse to those along the south coast of New-foundland to the westward of Cape Race. In 1508 a ship called the *Pensée* of Dieppe showed the fishermen of Normandy the course to the harbours south of Cape Bonavista. In 1509 one of these vessels brought home to Rouen seven Indians and a canoe.

In October 1511 an agreement was concluded in Spain with one Juan de Agramonte for a voyage of discovery to Newfoundland, but there is no record to show that this expedition, which was to be piloted by Bretons, actually took place. English, Portuguese, Breton and French fishermen continued their yearly voyages to the Banks, but it was not till 1520 that a fresh exploration was made by João Alvares Fagundes of Vianna in Portugal. Setting sail with the Portuguese fishermen bound for the Banks, he appears to have explored the coast from Nova Scotia to Placentia Bay. Chedabucto was called the " Bay of Freshwater," as supplies were obtained there. Our Cape North, the extremity of Cape Breton Island, was named the " Big Cape," while Cape Ray received the name of the " Beautiful Cape." To our St. Pierre and Miquelon he appears to have given the name of the " Eleven Thousand Virgins," a festival celebrated on 21st October. On 13th March, 1521, the islands along the coast he had explored were made over to Fagundes, who appears shortly after to have taken out a colony to those parts.

The next explorations along the North American coast were undertaken by the expeditions sent out by Francis I of France under the command of the Florentine, Giovanni da Verrazano, in 1524 and 1526, and the Spanish expedition under Estevan Gomez in 1525, which are considered in another chapter. But it was not until 1534 that the geography of those regions was clearly revealed by the work of one of the most celebrated French explorers.

Jacques Cartier, who was placed in charge of two ships in 1534, had been born in St. Malo in 1491. We know little of his early life except that he appears to have made a voyage to Brazil. He must in any event have been an expert navigator before being placed in command of such an expedition fitted out by the Crown. The course to Newfoundland was well known, so setting sail on 20th April Cartier reached Cape Bonavista early in May. As ice was still about he did not proceed northwards until ten days later, reaching the strait of Belle Isle, then called the Bay of Castles, on 27th May. The western end of this had until then been called the Grand Bay. Cartier anchored first at Blanc Sablon, and then on 10th June at a port called Brest, probably Bonne Esperance harbour on the Labrador coast. Leaving his two vessels here, he proceeded with his longboats for some distance along the coast of Labrador, which he found so inhospitable that he thought it must be the land God gave to Cain. Near Cumberland Harbour he met a large ship from La Rochelle, which shows how well known this fishing-ground had then become.

Setting sail from Brest on Monday, 15th June, Cartier proceeded down the west coast of Newfoundland, which he explored as far as the Bay of St. George, when a storm drove him out into the gulf. This led to his discovery of the Bird rocks, Brion Island and the Magdalens, which latter he took to be mainland. Following this westward, he coasted the southern shores of the Gulf of St. Lawrence round to the Baie de Chaleur, which he was disappointed to find was not a strait leading to the East. At Gaspé he met with a tribe of Indians from the Upper St. Lawrence, and seized two of their number to take with him back to France. A mirage prevented him from proceeding up the St. Lawrence along the Gaspé shore, but instead he rounded Anticosti and headed up the Channel between that island and Labrador. He now realised that he had found the opening of which he was in search, but as the season was late and he did not know his way back to the strait of Belle Isle, he decided to postpone the exploration of it until the following year. Proceeding eastward along the north shore of the gulf, where he heard of more French fishing vessels, he reached Blanc Sablon on 9th August, and arrived safely at St. Malo on 5th September.

In the spring of 1535 a fresh expedition was prepared, and with three ships Cartier made his way to a harbour on the coast of Labrador opposite to Anticosti, which on 10th August he named

143

the Bay of St. Lawrence. Owing to a careless reading of his narrative, this name was afterwards applied to the whole gulf, and finally to the river up which he now made his way as far as the island of Orleans near the present city of Quebec. He took up his quarters for the winter in the river St. Charles, which here enters the St. Lawrence.

On Sunday, 19th September, with his smallest vessel and two longboats, he set off to explore the upper reaches of the river, and on 3rd October reached the Huron-Iroquois village of Hochelaga on the present site of Montreal, where further progress westward was checked by the rapids of Lachine. Cartier had now made his way inland nearly 900 miles from the ocean, and had discovered a magnificent river as well as a vast extent of territory.

His object, however, like that of Cortes and Pizarro, seems to have been to find gold, and he received at Hochelaga the impression that up the river Ottawa there existed a mysterious kingdom of Saguenay rich in jewels and precious stones. He also heard of the River Richelieu leading towards Florida, but spent the winter at Stadacona enquiring about the wealth of Saguenay.

Although Cartier returned safely to France in the summer of 1536, no attempt was made to penetrate to this rich kingdom of Saguenay until the summer of 1541, when Cartier was again sent back to the St. Lawrence, and took up his quarters at Cape Rouge, nine miles above Quebec. He made a fresh exploration of the rapids at Hochelaga, but in the spring of 1542 set out to return home owing to the hostility of the Indians. Roberval, the captain who was to lead the armed forces to the conquest of Saguenay, met Cartier in the harbour of St. John's in Newfoundland, and though he commanded him to return to the St. Lawrence, Cartier, thinking he had already secured some gold and precious stones near Cape Rouge, continued his voyage to St. Malo. Unfortunately the gold and precious stones turned out to be of no value.

Roberval made his way up the St. Lawrence to Cartier's quarters at Cape Rouge, and in the spring of 1543 proceeded in longboats as far as the Lachine rapids. No kingdom of Saguenay could be found, and after losing many of his people, Roberval returned to France a ruined man.

Although the various Western European nations continued to frequent the Banks in increasing numbers during the remainder of the sixteenth century, no further progress was made in the revelation of the North American continent in spite of the voyages of Grenville and others to Virginia, until the coast of New England was explored by Samuel de Champlain from 1604 to 1606. From their permanent quarters on the Bay of Fundy the French sent expeditions southward each summer, and it was due merely to bad luck that they did not reach the Hudson in 1606. Champlain was actually in sight of Martha's Vineyard in that year when head winds drove him back.

Two years later he transferred his activities to the St. Lawrence, discovering Lake Champlain in 1609 and the course of the river Ottawa in 1613. In his map of 1613 he shows all these regions as well as Davis Strait, Hudson's Strait and Hudson's Bay, which latter regions he took from a map made by Henry Hudson which was published at Amsterdam in 1612. In 1615 he explored Lake Huron, and in the autumn of that year crossed Lake Ontario.

In conclusion, perhaps one should say a word to explain the transfer of the name Labrador from Greenland to the mainland of North America.

Greenland is always described as Labrador on the maps of this region previous to the middle of the sixteenth century, but in 1558 there was published at Venice what purported to be a correct map of these regions by the Brothers Zeni on which Greenland was called Engronelant. Subsequent cartographers, therefore, such as Mercator placed this new Greenland to the north of the old Labrador-Greenland. In course of time the water between these two was described as Davis Strait, from which time Labrador has remained as the description of the great peninsula lying between the Gulf of St. Lawrence and Hudson's Strait.

NOTES TO CHAPTER VI

1. *Calendar of State Papers and MSS. relating to English Affairs in the Archives of Venice,* vol. i, pp. lxiv, lxxi, and cxxxv *et seq.,* London, 1864.

2. Wright, T., *Political Poems and Songs,* etc., London, 1861, vol. ii, p. 172.

3. Biggar, H. P., *The Precursors of Jacques Cartier,* pp. 1–4.

4. R. Eden's translation of Varthema in Hakluyt, R., *Principal Navigations,* vol. iv, p. 560, edition of 1812, and Jones and Badger's edition, Hakluyt Society (1863), vol. xxxii, p. 38.

5. The documents relating to Cabot's voyages have been printed in Biggar, *op. cit.,* pp. 6–31.

6. Biggar, *op. cit.,* pp. 99–100.

7. The inscription of the Wolfenbüttel map is reproduced in H. Harrisse, *Jean et Sébastien Cabot,* Paris, 1882, p. 186. See also article by H. P. Biggar in *Revue Hispanique,* vol. x, p. 493.

8. Eden, R., *A Treatyse of the Newe India,* London, 1553, fol. 119.

9. Biggar, *op. cit.,* No. xvi, p. 31.

10. Damian Goes, *Chronica do felicissimo Rei dom Emanuel,* Lisboa, 1566, fol. 65.

CHAPTER VII

THE SEARCH FOR A WESTERN PASSAGE

W I T H I N a very short time after Columbus's first discovery, capable observers, as we have shown, disbelieved his claim to have reached the outermost islands of Asia with only a short further distance to traverse to the rich kingdoms that Polo had described. It soon became clear that a land barrier lay across the route of any who would sail farther west, and in place of the somewhat unsystematic searching for Mangi and Cathay not far from the Antilles, which was Columbus's aim in his third and fourth voyages, the search for a westward-leading strait through the continental land mass of the new world was begun. It is with this striving to discover a western passage, on which so much of the exploring activity of the first quarter of the sixteenth century turns, that we are concerned in this chapter. Before attempts emerge into the clear light of day, there is a period when there is doubt, when thought is confused, a period for which we have few facts and a great deal of speculation. This early period may be said to have closed with the return of Columbus from his fourth and last voyage in 1505, and we have already traced its main outlines. There were, as we have shown, two independent lines of advance having no common inspiration : the first, or as we may call it the Columbian, to the westward of the Antilles and southward, and the other to the north-west, where Cabot and the Corte-Reals showed the way to the fishermen and were followed some thirty years later by Jacques Cartier.

The link between the two is to be found in Sebastian, son of John Cabot, and we begin our story of the search for a westward passage as distinguished from a search for the Indies themselves in the New World at the point where he first appears clearly as one who was a skilled pilot with special knowledge.

How did Sebastian Cabot become a believer in the existence of a passage to Asia by the north-west ? If we accept Dr. Williamson's [1] hypothesis of the date of his birth, it is possible that a few years after being brought to Bristol as an infant, he sailed, a mere boy, with his father in the *Mathew* in 1497. That voyage, of course, did not lead to the discovery of the kingdom of the Grand Khan as John Cabot had hoped. Did Sebastian get his notion from his father's second voyage in 1498 ? We must remember that, as Winship points out [2], there is no certainty that Sebastian went on either voyage. Moreover, it is not certain that any members of the second expedition returned to civilisation, though probably they did, and the La Cosa map of 1500 favours this conclusion. So also does the patent granted to Alonso de Hojeda on 8th June, 1501, with its references to the English and the need to check their activities. If the younger Cabot did not get his ideas of a passage from either of his father's voyages we must ascribe them to the indirect outcome of other later voyages.

When did the younger Cabot sail to seek a north-west passage ? There are two theories at least. Winship argues that the voyage took place in 1508–9, in the last year of the reign of Henry VII. He says also that there is almost sufficient evidence to prove that Sebastian made another voyage, probably before 1512 if not before 1509, but he is alone in thinking this. Dr. Williamson argues that the important voyage took place in 1508–9. The second theory is that Sebastian did not sail to the north-west except in company with his father, who sought a passage to the land of spices in 1498 [3]. There are strong arguments against the latter theory. Can we believe that at that early date it was clearly realised that Asia had not been reached ? It is probable also that Sebastian was a mere boy at the time. Certainly in 1505 Sebastian was granted a pension for service and attendance in and about the port of Bristol, but there is no mention of discovery

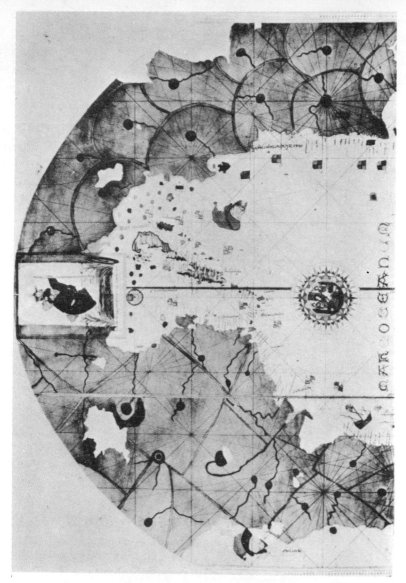

WESTERN PORTION OF THE WORLD-MAP OF
JUAN DE LA COSA, 1500.

(From A. E. Nordenskiöld, *Periplus*. Stockholm, 1897.)

The author sailed with Columbus and Hojeda. The mainland areas depicted are interpreted by Nordenskiöld as representing Eastern Asia, but Harrisse takes them to be a delineation of the new lands, which implies discoveries by unrecorded expeditions.

The position of the picture of St. Christopher may have been chosen only for symmetry or it may conceal doubt of the existence of a strait to the west of the Antilles. The islands are placed to the north of their true position possibly for reasons connected with the policy of the Spanish sovereigns for whom the map was drawn. But against this assumption it may be urged that the map was not intended for publication and was unknown to Spain's foreign rivals.

The presence of an English flag on the northern coast and the nomenclature bear witness to a knowledge of the Cabot discoveries.

(*See p.* 155.)

work.   Moreover, five ships sailed in 1498, and almost certainly only two went with Sebastian.   Where the evidence is largely provided by historians writing after the event, and when their accounts are based on statements coming indirectly from Sebastian himself, care is necessary before conclusions are arrived at, and no conclusions can be regarded as final.

In the interval between 1505 and 1512 we have no certain knowledge of his movements, and all is conjecture, but in the latter year we find him definitely engaged as map-maker with the Anglo-Spanish expedition against Guienne under the Marquess of Dorset.   At that period Ferdinand was contemplating the despatch of an expedition for the exploration of the new-found lands, and Cabot was summoned to Court to state what he knew about those regions.   In October 1512 he was appointed to the Spanish service, and steps were taken to procure Henry VIII's consent to release him from his English obligations.   In March 1514 he was definitely established in Spain, and for the first time we can learn from the words of a contemporary what was the special knowledge that made his employment of value.

Ferdinand and his counsellors and experts were at last entirely convinced that the only way to find compensation for the immense sums expended in exploration and colonisation was to obtain a share in those Asiatic markets where Portugal was winning so much profit.   It must be remembered that in 1514 Cortes' wonderful conquests were as yet undreamed of, and it seemed as though Spain, for all her expenditure of effort and money, had acquired nothing but a few comparatively valueless islands.   There was no longer any doubt that across the westward sea route to Asia there lay the immense continental mass of the New World.   That somewhere there was to be found a passage through that continent they were convinced by what they thought to be scientific reasons.   It is in connection with those arguments that we have our first detailed description of Sebastian Cabot and his information.   In the Third Decade of Peter Martyr written to

Pope Leo X, and published in 1516, there occur certain striking passages which demand quotation at length, as illustrating his methods of thought that were so essentially modern, and the care with which he collected his facts.

" The time has come, Most Holy Father, to philosophise a little, leaving cosmography to seek the causes of Nature's secrets. The ocean currents in those regions [of the Antilles] run towards the west, as torrents rushing down a mountain side.   Upon this point the testimony is unanimous.   Thus I find myself uncertain when asked where these waters go which flow in a circular and continuous movement from east to west, never to return to their starting-place ; and how it happens that the west is not so constantly overwhelmed by these waters nor the east emptied.   If it be true that these waters are drawn towards the centre of the earth, as is the case with all heavy objects, and that this centre as some people affirm is at the equinoctial line, what can be the central reservoir capable of holding such a mass of waters ? And what will be the circumference filled with water which will yet be discovered ?   The explorers of these coasts offer no convincing explanation.   There are other authors who think that a large strait exists at the extremity of the gulf formed by this vast continent, and which, as we have already said, is eight times larger than the ocean.   This strait may lie to the west of Cuba, and would conduct these raging waters to the west, from whence they would again return to our east.   Some learned men think the gulf formed by this vast continent is an enclosed sea whose coasts bend in a northerly direction behind Cuba in such wise that the continent would extend unbrokenly to the northern lands beneath the polar circle bathed by the glacial sea.   The waters, driven back by the extent of land, are drawn into a circle, as may be seen in rivers whose opposite banks promote whirl-pools ; but this theory does not accord with the facts.   The explorers of the northern passages, who always sailed westwards, affirm that the waters are always drawn in that direction, not, however, with violence, but by a long and uninterrupted movement."

So far we have a curious theory of ocean currents and a most interesting reference to a western passage which some do, and others do not, believe in. Peter Martyr goes on to write of Cabot :

" Amongst the explorers of the glacial region a certain Sebastian Cabotto, of Venetian origin, but brought by his parents in his infancy to England, is cited. It commonly happens that Venetians visit every part of the universe, for purposes of commerce. Cabotto equipped two vessels in England at his own cost, and first sailed with three hundred men towards the north, to such a distance that he found numerous masses of floating ice in the middle of the month of July. Daylight lasted nearly twenty-four hours, and as the ice had melted the land was free. According to his story he was obliged to tack and take the direction of west-by-south. The coast bent to about the degree of the strait of Gibraltar. Cabotto did not sail westward till he had arrived abreast of Cuba, which lay on his left. In following this coast-line, which he called Baccalaos, he says that he recognised the same maritime currents flowing to the west that the Castilians noted when they sailed in southern regions belonging to them. It is not merely probable therefore but becomes necessary to conclude that between these two hitherto unknown continents there extend large openings through which the waters flow from east to west. I think these waters flow all round the world in a circle, obediently to the Divine Law, and that they are not spewed forth and afterwards absorbed by some panting Demogorgon."

Here we have expressed a belief in not one, but several straits, between the newly discovered lands. Peter Martyr gives further details of the Cabot voyage. He relates that the term " Baccalaos " is used because the waters swarm with fish like tunnies, which he says, incorrectly, the natives call by this name [4], and he talks of bears. He proceeds :

" Cabotto frequents my house, and I have him sometimes at my table. He was called from England by our Catholic King after the death of Henry, King of that country, and he lives at Court with us. He is waiting from day to day to be furnished with ships with which he will be able to discover this mystery of nature. I think he will leave on this expedition towards the month of March of next year, 1516. . . . But this is enough about the strait and about Cabotto."

At the end of his letter to Leo X, Peter Martyr again returns to the question of the current and the passage. He is still puzzled in 1516 as to the current which drives the waters of the Gulf of Paria towards the west. He says this matter was discussed when Captain Andreas Morales and Gonzales Oviedo came to visit him. They differed on the subject. Morales says the force of the waters is broken by a great body of land believed to be a continent. The waters are drawn in a circle, and passing out through narrow straits spread and lose their force. Oviedo agrees that the continent is closed, but not that the land mass breaks the force of the current. Peter Martyr adds that he once questioned Admiral Diego Columbus, son and heir of the great discoverer, who had crossed the seas four times, and he said : " The continent is open, and there must exist between the two bodies a strait through which these turbulent waters escape to the west. In obedience to a decree of Heaven, they circulate throughout the entire universe." The project of the year 1516 was never carried out. Ferdinand of Aragon died in January 1516, and as his successor Charles V remained for some time in the Low Countries, Cabot's scheme was dropped.

The major part of the above quotation is of interest in relation to the idea of a western passage, but the remarks concerning Cabot's voyage are also of great interest, and they have received various interpretations. Harrisse applies them to the voyages of John Cabot in 1497 and 1498. Dr. Biggar applies them to the 1498 voyage. Out of this in part arises the accusation made against Sebastian that he suppressed his father's achievements. Dr. Williamson classifies all the existing evidence bearing on Cabot's voyage into two periods. The first is between the years 1512 and 1548, when it was not to the interest of Sebastian to disclose to his Spanish masters any knowledge of a western passage in the north. Peter Martyr's accounts come under this heading, and also that of Gomara, these being the most notable. Secondly, there is the period after his return to England in 1548, and testimony based on this or on documents left extant after his death. In this later category come, notably, the accounts of Ramusio, of Sir Humphrey Gilbert, and of Richard Willes. From a consideration of all the evidence, Dr. Williamson concludes that Sebastian Cabot made a later voyage than those of 1497 and 1498 with two ships, passing through Hudson's Strait, and believing Hudson's Bay to be an arm of the Pacific Ocean. His encounter with ice, the rigours of the north, and the unwillingness of his men caused him to return and proceed south down the coast of Labrador to Newfoundland, and thence farther south looking for a western passage which he failed to find. On his return to England Cabot did not find an atmosphere favourable to the propagation of his ideas, but his subsequent activities show an amazingly strong belief in the existence of a western passage.

In 1512, as we have said, he went to Spain as map maker with the army of the Marquess of Dorset, which was to attack France, and obtained permission to transfer his services. He made rapid progress, and, possibly in reward for his work in planning the abortive project of 1516, he was appointed in 1518 Pilot-Major to Spain, an important post previously held by men as noteworthy as Amerigo Vespucci and Juan Dias de Solis, and it was held by Cabot himself for thirty years. He is mentioned by Richard Eden as associated with a projected English transatlantic voyage in 1517, but there is no proof of this.

The subsequent actions of the Pilot-Major were startling in

character. No doubt jealousy played a part. The Portuguese navigator, Magellan, had been sent to find a western passage in 1519 and had succeeded, while Sebastian had been passed over. In the years 1520–21 he was negotiating with Cardinal Wolsey and the English crown with regard to an expedition to Asia by the north-west. Because of international complications, and because Henry VIII was more enthusiastic than the merchants whose help it was proposed to enlist, the scheme fell through. The Drapers' Company of London objected on more grounds than one, and talked slightingly of Sebastian, who "as we here say was never in that land hym self, all if he makes reporte of many thinges as he hath hard his ffather and other men speke in times past " [5]. Later, in the years 1522–3, come what Harrisse calls his " treacherous intrigues with Venice." Against Harrisse's accusation of impostor and traitor, others defend Cabot as no worse than others of his time. Sebastian told the Venetian friar, Sebastian Collona, whom he met in London, according to his account of the affair, that he had means of showing Venice " a passage whereby she would obtain great profit : which is the truth, for I have discovered it " [6]. He tells how he refused the offer of the King of England for the sake of his native Venice. We can well understand him saying, as Gaspar Contarini, Venetian Ambassador in Spain, relates in his letter of 1522 to the Council of Ten : "I most earnestly beseech you to keep the thing secret, as it would cost me my life." The controversy over the Molucca Islands, whether they were in the Portuguese or Spanish spheres, arose a little later, and led to the conference of Badajoz of 1523–4. No doubt Cabot was kept busy in Spain by his official duties, and he discontinued his negotiations with Venice. With his voyage to the Plate estuary, which took place in 1526, we will deal later.

From a consideration of these efforts we turn to Central America and the neighbouring regions. We have already noted that there is good reason to believe that early voyages had been made to the coasts of the continent to the north-west of the

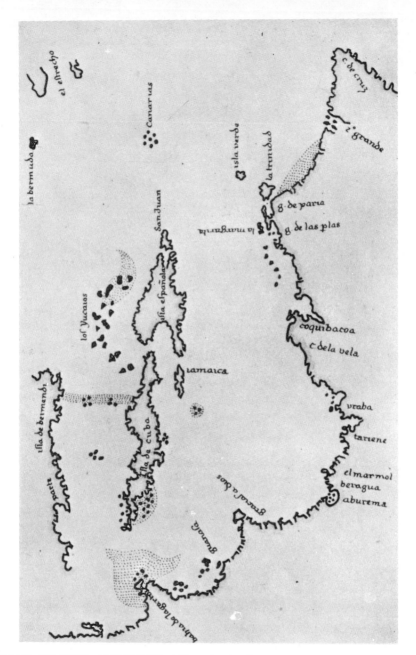

MAP OF THE ANTILLES AND ADJACENT COASTS FROM THE
FIRST EDITION OF PETER MARTYR'S *DE ORBE NOVO*, 1511.

(Reproduced in K. Kretschmer, *Die Entdeckung Amerikas*, Atlas. Berlin, 1892.)

The Seville edition of the Decades in the British Museum contains the map, but
does not show its full extent, details towards the edges being absent. The width of the
Atlantic is greatly minimised. "El estrecho" in the north-east represents the Straits of
Gibraltar. This is the first printed special map of any part of the New World. It is not
referred to in the text of Peter Martyr's work.

(*See* p. 155.)

Antilles. The La Cosa map, and the Cantino and Canerio *mappae mundi* indicate this. The documents begin with the work of Juan Ponce de Leon, but the map, added by Peter Martyr to certain issues of the First Decade, published in Seville in 1511, bears an interesting inscription. On the verso of that map we have : " At the north there have been discovered marvellous countries and lands of which . . . see the engraved representation." The region north of Cuba bears the legend " Isla de beimeni parte " [7]. There is no mention of this in the text. Evidently there had been enterprises, whether to seek the marvellous or to obtain slaves. For a number of years it was thought that islands were situated to the north in the Floridean area. There were, first, the " Isla Bimini " (Bimene or Beniny), probably corresponding to the most southern part of Florida ; secondly, " Boiuca " or " Agnaneo," corresponding to a district on the east coast and already surmised to belong to the continental region ; and thirdly, the " Isla Florida " (" Terra Florida " and " La Florida "), which included the entire apex of the peninsula. These were no doubt regarded as potential sources of slaves. Peter Martyr wrote in the Seventh Decade, in 1525, that the Spaniards had carried off 40,000 slaves from the Lucayan Islands, the modern Bahamas. He mentions also that natives of the large neighbouring islands of Bimini and of the Florida coasts cross the sea to the Lucayos to capture doves. In the Second Decade (1514), he says that among the countries to the north of Veragua is " an island called by us Boiuca and by others Agnaneo : it is celebrated for a spring whose waters restore youth to old men " [8].

In 1512 Juan Ponce de Leon went with two vessels, taking Anton de Alaminos as pilot, in search of the island of Bimini and of the "Fountain of Youth." He landed, says Martyr, in an island, and " he named it Florida because he discovered it on the Feast of the Resurrection which is called Pasqua Florida " [9]. He spent more than six months exploring the region, but was driven out by natives and returned to Porto Rico. He led a second expedition from Porto Rico on 20th February, 1521, with two ships carrying men and horses. His purpose was to plant a colony in Florida, and ascertain whether it was an island or whether it was a continental land connected with the Mexican regions just described by Cortes. The expedition lasted at least five months. A landing was made on the west coast of Florida, but the pioneers suffered from Indian attacks and re-embarked, one ship going to Vera Cruz and one to Cuba with de Leon, who died there of a wound.

We know that in 1516 Diego Murielo went on a trading cruise from Cuba. More significant is the expedition from Cuba of F. H. de Cordova, in 1517, to capture slaves on the Lucayos or Bahama Islands. Storms caused the frustration of this ; the Spaniards were again attacked when on the Florida coasts, and Cordova died of his wounds in Cuba. But the expedition led to two important projects. Diego Velasquez obtained a grant which led to the conquest of Mexico. Secondly, the pilot Alaminos persuaded Francis de Garay, governor of Jamaica, to embark on exploration of the mainland. Permission being obtained, he despatched an expedition under Alonzo Alvarez de Pinedo in 1519, with four caravels, to discover some strait in the mainland. The western passage sought was not found, but the geography of the northern shores of the Gulf was established. Probably Pinedo sailed up the Mississippi, and brought news of lands abounding in gold, in pygmies, and in giants.

In 1520 Lucas Vasquez de Ayllon, an auditor of the island of Santo Domingo, aspired to discover land and found a colony. He despatched Francisco Gordillo to the north, who returned with Indian slaves against orders. De Ayllon went to Spain with one of the Indians, who told of a giant king and many provinces. In June 1523 he was granted a royal cedula to send out vessels in 1524. They were to run 800 leagues along the coast, or till lands already discovered were reached, and if any strait leading to the west was discovered, he was to explore it. On his return to the West Indies his project was delayed. He did not actually sail himself until June 1526, when he left Puerto de la Plata with three vessels, taking colonists possibly to the number of 500 or 600 and 100 horses. Misfortunes came to the settlement he attempted to establish, and the enterprise ended in failure and the death of the leader from fever.

Vasco Nuñez de Balboa does not enter our story as a seeker for a western passage. His discovery of the South Sea, i.e. the Pacific Ocean, gave, however, a very great stimulus to the search. Balboa sailed from Spain with Rodrigo de Bastidas in 1500. A resident in Española, his pecuniary liabilities seem to have embarrassed him, and he resolved to leave the island, of necessity secretly. The opportunity arose. In 1509, Hojeda left San Domingo to found the settlement of San Sebastian on the mainland and arranged for the " bachiller " Enciso to follow later with supplies. Enciso left in 1510, and the story goes that Balboa concealed himself in a cask " of victuals for the voyage," conveyed from his farm to the ship. The historian, Oviedo, however, says that he concealed himself in the folds of a sail. Certainly he later appeared unexpectedly to embarrass Enciso. The vessel went first to Cartagena and later on to San Sebastian in Darien. Here the pioneers endured great suffering, and the stormy character of Balboa found its opportunity. He recollected that when he was with Bastidas, on the west side of the Gulf, they found an Indian town in a fertile area near a great river. He advocated a move to what proved to be Darien, where the Indians did not use poisoned arrows. But troubles had not ended. Some malcontents argued that Enciso had no authority because they were now out of Hojeda's area, and in that which had been allotted to a rival captain Nicuesa. Nicuesa was invited to come from Nombre de Dios, but the welcome turned to anger when he claimed the gold that had been found in his province, and ultimately he was sent to Spain in an unseaworthy brigantine on 1st March, 1511, and never heard of again. Balboa was a participator in these quarrels. He disliked Enciso intensely, and charged him with being a usurper. Later the "bachiller" left for Spain and Balboa's unconventional behaviour was duly reported. Subsequently Balboa occupied himself with the territory surrounding his settlement. We have the usual story of the search for gold and fighting with Indians. Balboa seems to have been something of a diplomatist, playing off native rulers against each other with success.

Forty leagues from Darien was the country ruled by the cacique Comogre, an ally of the Spaniards. We are told that slaves and gold had been presented to the Spaniards. When the fifth part of the latter that was due to the King of Spain was being weighed out before the natives, the son of the cacique was puzzled by the squabbles that arose. Why quarrel over the metal? Towards the sea and southward there was a country rich in gold awaiting conquest, and his people would assist against their enemies. This is the first mention of the South Sea, of the Pacific Ocean, with the possible exception of the stories told to Columbus in Veragua.

Balboa did not act immediately. He and the hardier of his followers, who had escaped violent ends and death from fever, returned to Darien. Provisions were at a low ebb, men were fewer. The district had been stripped of its resources, Balboa relying on terror as the means of keeping his grip. News came. He was appointed Captain-General, and had reason to be glad. But this was more than outweighed by news from Spain that Enciso had been stating a case against the adventurer. A new governor was coming, Pedro Arias de Avila. Balboa resolved to make a great effort to atone for his stormy past, and set out for "the other sea" early in September 1513. His achievement will never cease to arouse admiration, think what we will of the man and his methods. Peter Martyr says the Spaniards "passed through inaccessible defiles inhabited by ferocious beasts, and they climbed steep mountains" [10]. He leaves us to imagine the details of the dangers involved. The tropical climate had already exacted a heavy toll and continued later to thin the ranks of adventurous Spaniards. In addition, we must remember the ever-present danger of attack from Indians. Balboa, leading rather less than 200 men, accompanied by slaves and the dogs which we know the Spaniards used to terrorise natives, seems to have made good use of glass beads, mirrors, copper bells and iron hatchets to secure Indian guides for hidden native trails. On 25th September, 1513, the leader reached the peak from which he viewed the Pacific Ocean. In the words of Peter Martyr [11] :

" A Quarequa guide showed him a peak from the summit of which the southern ocean is visible. Vasco looked longingly at it. He commanded a halt and went alone to scale the peak, being the first to reach its top. Kneeling upon the ground he raised his hands to heaven and saluted the South Sea : according to his account he gave thanks to God and to all the saints for having reserved this glory for him, an ordinary man, devoid alike of experience and authority. Concluding his prayers in military fashion, he waved his hand to some of his companions, and showed them the object of their desires. Kneeling again, he prayed the Heavenly Mediator, and especially the Virgin Mother of God, to favour his expedition, and to allow him to explore the region that stretched below him. All his companions, shouting for joy, did likewise. Prouder than Hannibal showing Italy and the Alps to his soldiers, Vasco Nuñez promised great riches to his men. ' Behold the much-desired ocean ! ' " Clearly the solemnity of the event was fully realised. A notary drew up a list of those present. A heap of stones was erected in altar form as a symbol of possession, and the name of Castile was inscribed here and there on the trunks of trees. Peter Martyr says the Spaniards made the descent from the ridge to the shore in four days. " Great was their joy : and in the presence of the natives they took possession, in the name of the King of Castile, of all that sea and the countries bordering on it " [12]. Later Balboa disregarded the warnings of the Indians against storms, and sailed on the waters of the Gulf of San Miguel. There must be no delay, he argued, " God and all the heavenly host favoured his enterprise, and that he was labouring for God, and to propagate the Christian religion, and to discover treasures to serve as the sinews of war against the enemies of the Faith " [13].

Balboa was told of the Islands of Pearls, but postponed voyaging to them and made his way back to Darien, he and his men suffering terrible hardships from thirst, toiling under a tropical sun. They arrived early in 1514, and Balboa sent letters and presents to King Ferdinand. His achievement could not fail to impress, and he received the title of Adelantado of the South Sea. None the less, the new governor of Darien, Don Pedro Arias de Avila, generally referred to as Pedrarias, left Seville in 1514 to assume his government. Balboa led the residents to welcome him, singing *Te Deum Laudamus*. Events proved that the two men could not endure each other. Balboa interested himself in the South Sea, and had ships constructed for exploration. Pedrarias accused his enemy of conspiring against him, and recalled him. Balboa was arrested, put in irons, and later condemned to death for treason. In 1517, at the age of forty-two, the discoverer of the Pacific Ocean was executed in the public square of Acla.

In the Eighth Decade of the New World, Peter Martyr draws a moral from the factiousness that impeded the work of the explorers :

" But for the jealousy of the Spaniards, who can never agree among themselves in their keen dispute about honours, all these countries would already be conquered. How each is the declared enemy of his companions in this dusty squabble of ambition, which blinds them : how nobody can endure to be commanded by the others, I have already sufficiently explained in my preceding Decades, when I spoke of the quarrels between Diego Velasquez, Viceroy of Fernandina, and Hernando Cortes ; and again between Hernando Cortes and Panfilo Narvaez or

Grijalva, who gave his name to a river in the province of Yucatan :
again of Cristobal Olid's defection from Cortes and the rivalry
between Pedro Arias, governor of the mainland, and Egidius
Gonzales, and finally of that general conflict of contradictory
interests in searching for the strait giving communication between
the south and north oceans " [14].

It is interesting to consider the activities of certain of these
adventurers in so far as they were concerned in the search for a
western passage. Pedro Arias, Peter Martyr tells us elsewhere
in the same Decade, was engaged in the search. But Egidius
Gonzales, Cristobal Olid, Francisco Fernandez (a lieutenant of
Pedrarias), and Francisco de las Casas are described as " four
captains who fairly pant with desire to discover the strait."
At Barcelona in 1519 a royal order directed the governor of
Castilla del Oro (Golden Castile, the mainland) to give to Egidius
or Gil Gonzales the vessels built by Balboa in preparation for
the exploration of the South Sea. Andres Niño, who acted as his
partner and pilot, had served with Balboa, and was inspirer of the
expedition. The ships were not handed over by Pedrarias, but
as the outcome, exploration was later carried out. In the Fifth
Decade Gil Gonzales is said to be captain of a fleet which explored
from Panama on the South Sea [15]. They " sailed so far westwards that they believed themselves to be behind Yucatan. . . .
The ocean on their right hand was so turbulent that they believed
some undiscovered strait must exist between the continent and
Yucatan." But, says Martyr, they would not venture into the
raging waters with their half-rotten ships. In the Sixth Decade
he describes Gonzales as sailing from the Isle of Pearls off the
coast of Panama in January 1523 with four little vessels [16].
The orders of the Emperor and the instructions of the Council of
the Indies were to visit unexplored western coasts, " to discover
whether there exists between the known point of the continent
and the frontiers of Yucatan some strait dividing these immense
regions. I may say at once that the Spaniards did not discover the

strait." Later he describes renewed efforts [17]. "He embarked about the Ides of March of this year 1524, seeking to discover the much-desired mystery of the strait." The outcome of
this was exploration by land in Nicaragua. Gonzales discovered
the lake, but was not sure whether it emptied into the South Sea.
" He thinks, nevertheless, that this body of water connects with
the northern ocean, and that the much-desired strait may be
found there, in which opinion he is sustained by several pilots.
If you wish to know my opinion on this subject, I would say that
Gonzales thus excuses himself for not finding the strait." Then
later he says : " We are ignorant whether or no a strait dividing
these vast countries exists " [18]. In the Seventh Decade there is
further reference to the Lake of Nicaragua and the work of
Gonzales, and we are told that the Council of Española is
anxious to avoid a collision between Gonzales, Pedrarias and
Cristobal de Olid. If they meet there is to be no violence,
by order ! " The explorers are devoured by such a passion to
discover this strait that they risk a thousand dangers ; for it is
certain that he who does discover it—if ever it is discovered—
will obtain the imperial favour, not to mention great authority.
If, indeed, a passage between the South and the North Seas is
discovered, the route to the islands producing spices and precious
stones will be very much shortened, and the dispute begun with
Portugal, which I have mentioned in my first Decades, will be
eliminated " [19].

The collision which the Council of Española was so anxious
to avoid occurred later. Gonzales could find no outlet to the
Lake of Nicaragua, and he encountered Francisco Fernandez,
lieutenant of the governor Pedrarias, and fighting took place,
Egidius being accused of stealing gold. Later we find him in the
area controlled by Cristobal de Olid, and he was taken prisoner
by this rebel from the authority of Cortes.

The conqueror of Mexico, Cortes, played a very considerable
part in the Spanish search for a western passage and shared the

common belief of his contemporaries that a strait did in reality connect the Mar del Norte and the Mar del Sur, the Caribbean Gulf and the Pacific Ocean of our day. Hernan, or Hernando, Cortes, at the age of nineteen, went out to Española as a young adventurer and remained there until 1511, when he accompanied Diego Velasquez on an expedition to the island of Cuba. Later he was entrusted with the conquest of the newly discovered Mexico, on the coast of which he landed in 1519. With the conquest as such we are not concerned, but the last three of his five letters dealing with his conquests and addressed to Charles V provide us with interesting references to a western passage. The third letter was sent on 15th May, 1522, "from the city of Cuyoaccan in this New Spain of the Ocean-sea" [20]. Cortes says, in the course of this epistle, that he had already had " some account of another sea to the south," and goes on to say, " all who possess any knowledge or experience in navigation to the Indies have considered it certain that the discovery of the South Sea in these parts would bring to light many islands rich in gold, pearls, precious stones and spiceries, together with many other unknown and choice productions ; and the same has been affirmed also by persons versed in learning, and skilled in the science of cosmography " [21]. He then relates how he despatched four Spaniards, two by one route and two by another, who took possession of the sea to the south. There is no mention, however, of a strait.

In Cortes' fourth letter, which was written from " Temixtilan of this New Spain," on 15th October, 1524, we have mention of ships building at Zacatula in connection with this exploration of the South Sea, and later in the same letter mention of Cristobal de Olid. He was sent on an expedition, with six ships, and departed from what later came to be called Vera Cruz on 11th January, 1524. His mission was to found a fortified colony, whence in the words of Cortes " the smaller ships and the brigantine with the principal pilot and a cousin of mine named Diego Hurtado, for captain, were to run along the coast of the

Bay of Ascension in quest of the strait that was believed to be there, and to remain until they had explored every part of it : and in case they discovered the strait, they should return to the place where captain Cristobal Olid was," and despatch a ship to Cortes giving him news [22]. He records the fact that he has sent Pedro de Alvarado on an expedition to Utlatlan and Guatemala, and says he will meet Olid " unless the strait divides them." Olid, of course, instead of obeying orders, actually rebelled against Cortes, causing him, Peter Martyr says, to use " unrestrained language."

Later in this letter the writer apologises for further delay with his ships to explore the South Sea, pointing out the difficulties of transporting materials across the isthmus over mountain passes and across large and full rivers, and also that material has been destroyed by fire. Cortes, after explaining that he has always the interests of the Emperor at heart, says, " Nothing seems to remain but to explore the coast lying between the River Panuco and Florida, the latter being the country discovered by the Adelantado Juan Ponce de Leon ; and then the northern coast of Florida as far as the Baccalaos ; because it is considered certain that there is a strait on that coast which leads into the South Sea. If this should be found, it appears to me that it will come out near the archipelago which Magallanes by order of your Highness has discovered, according to a chart I have showing its situation " [23]. He points out that if a strait exists, it will provide Spain with a favourable and shorter route to the east, and, moreover, an all-Spanish route. " I have determined," he says, " to send three caravels and two brigantines to accomplish this object." He will have to borrow, " but if the strait is discovered, it will be of more signal advantage to your Majesty than anything I have yet achieved." But Cortes is not certain. He continues : " and if that discovery is not made, it is possible that others will be, of rich and widely spread lands." It will be useful, he says, to know that such a strait does not exist so that greater attention can be paid to the spice countries. " But may it please our Lord to crown this enterprise with success by the discovery of the strait ! " He goes on to say that he purposes to get ready the ships he has had built on the South Sea, and that they may sail at the end of July 1524, " on a voyage down the coast in quest of the same strait," and if the strait is not to be found, they will reach the land discovered by Magellan [24]. Cortes has laid aside all other schemes, he says, to pursue this object alone, knowing the keen interest of Charles V in the matter.

The fifth letter of Cortes was written on 3rd September, 1526, and is mainly devoted to describing his expedition to the Bay of Honduras, the famous march of 1524–5 [25]. During the course of this he mentions that a ship belonging to Captain Loaysa's expedition to the Molucca Islands arrived on the shore of the South Sea with letters for Charles V giving an account of the voyage, and that he was forwarding these. He has three vessels, he says, at Cacatula, ready to start on an exploring expedition, and proceeds : " I hope to God that, for your Majesty's good fortune and better service, the said voyage shall be made and accomplished ; for even if no strait is found, I feel confident that a way will be discovered in those parts, whereby your Majesty may be yearly informed of what is done at the Especeria." He proceeds to say that if Charles V will grant the mercies he asks for " in certain capitulations respecting that discovery," he will discover and conquer all the Especeria and " so arrange matters that the spices and drugs, instead of being obtained through barter and exchange—as the King of Portugal has them now—may become your Majesty's exclusive property." A little later in the narrative he describes how he despatched a captain to Colima on the South Sea, to follow the coast downwards. The captain was told by natives of a river ten days' march beyond the farthest point he reached, and Cortes thinks that, judging by the volume, breadth and size, this might be a strait. He will send the captain to see.

In May 1528 Cortes landed at Palos in Spain, to lay before the Emperor his case in disputes that had arisen. If he had any remaining faith in a western passage, it must have been quickly dispelled for reasons which will be apparent later.

From affairs in the New World we turn again to the Old. There are three main enterprises to consider, but before we deal with these, with the voyage of Sebastian Cabot to the Plate estuary in 1526, with the attempts of Estevão Gomez to find a passage in the north in 1524–5, and finally with the work of Verrazano, we must mention the expedition of Juan Diaz de Solis. He was commissioned in 1515 to explore the coast south of Brazil. Peter Martyr tells us that he sailed from Spain in September of that year to explore the southern coasts of what, since Vespucci's voyages, was generally supposed to be a continent. The leader met a tragic end in the Plate region, where he landed with some men. We are told that "with fox-like astuteness these Caribs feigned amicable signs, but meanwhile prepared their stomachs for a succulent repast : and from their first glimpse of the strangers their mouths watered like tavern trenchermen" [26]. The men still on board beheld their leader and comrades killed and eaten and, too frightened to land, sailed away northwards, returning to Spain with nothing but a cargo of red wood.

It was as a result of the abortive Badajoz Conference of 1524 that the Spaniards, as we have described, renewed so actively the attempts to discover a route to the east of Asia which would pass only through their dominions. The passage discovered by Magellan was far to the south and was difficult. Gomez was sent to seek a strait to the north in 1524, and in the same year it was decided to entrust Sebastian Cabot with the command of an expedition [27]. Preparations took place in 1525. During the same year, to the sounding of trumpets and the beating of drums, Garcia Loaysa, Knight of St. John, sailed for the Moluccas to follow up the route of Magellan, in spite of Portuguese protests.

Some merchants of Seville, including the English house of the Bristol merchant Robert Thorne, and also the Emperor Charles V, supported the Cabot enterprise. The merchants sought spices, but the Emperor had a wider interest, exploration in South America, and he was personally responsible for the appointment of Sebastian as leader. This divergence of interest led to quarrels. Cabot was not popular with the merchants, and their representatives later caused him embarrassment.

It seems clear that, despite the fact that a number of Spanish navigators had sailed along the coasts of South America, its continental character was not firmly believed in. It was thought that a passage existed to the north of that which Magellan had discovered, and that the Rio de Solis (Plate River) was the key to the mystery. Peter Martyr reports that Magellan had found that " the river is immense " and " its mouth is vast, for many other rivers swell its volume " [28]. Harrisse thinks that the delineation of the great Brazilian rivers in the early maps shows belief in a strait connecting with the Rio de Solis, and leading to the Indian Seas. Can we associate these ideas with the expedition of 1526 ?

Peter Martyr says that Sebastian's squadron will take the same direction as Garcia Loaysa. " He will guide the prows of his ships to the right behind the new continent. . . . He will discover numberless islands scattered through the immensity of the ocean " [29]. Magellan, we are told, had been so intent on reaching the Moluccas that he passed by islands where the sand was mixed with gold and where cinnamon trees grew. Having discovered the islands, says Martyr, Cabot will follow the south coast of the new continent, landing at the colonies of Panama and Nata and sending news. Herrera says that after passing through the Strait of Magellan, one ship was to break away to search the Pacific coast and the rest of the fleet was to proceed to the northwest. Harrisse thinks that Contarini expressed the real truth when he stated to the Senate of Venice, in 1525, that Cabot was to explore the entire coast and thence go to the Indies. This was the Spanish interest, and it was this that aroused the anger of the merchant backers.

Harrisse provides us with a full account of subsequent events, based mainly on the *Islario* of Alonso de Santa Cruz, who sailed on the expedition, on Oviedo's *General History of the Indies*, and on the Ribero map of 1529 [30]. Four ships sailed on 3rd April, 1526, from San Lucar de Barrameda, and according to a cedula of 25th October, 1525, their purpose was to accomplish "the discovery of the islands of Tharsis, Ophir and Eastern Cathay" via the Straits of Magellan. They proceeded via the Canaries and Cape Verde Islands. Then Cabot steered S. by W. and S.S.W. instead of south, either because of incompetence or because of a secret order. Passing slowly through a zone of calms and baffling winds, the vessels reached land in the neighbourhood of Pernambuco. There, at a Portuguese factory and fort, Cabot enquired into the misdeeds of some of his officers and was told of precious metals in the Plate region, and also that some survivors of the de Solis expedition were here and there on the coast. Southerly winds impeded progress, and it is argued that the Pilot-Major of Spain should have chosen a better season. Months passed in sailing south, the flag-ship struck a rock and was lost at Santa Catalina, and it was only in February 1527, about ten months after leaving Spain, that the vessels entered the estuary of the Plate River.

The river was explored, and the courses of the Parana and Paraguay Rivers followed, the gold and silver of which they had heard, doubtless that of Peru, being the lure. Forts were built at San Salvador, and at Sancti Spiritus, farther in the mainland. There was fighting with Indians, disciplinary troubles, and physical hardship. In March or April 1528 Diego Garcia arrived with an expedition from Spain sent by a merchant syndicate to explore the Plate River. He pushed on, and Cabot returned to his base and despatched the *Trinidad*, with Roger Barlow and Hernando Calderon, with news for the merchants of Seville and the Emperor, respectively. Tales of wonderful lands, of gold and silver, and cinnamon and pepper, did not bring the desired reinforcements and supplies. Charles V ordered relief to be sent, but nothing was done. Cabot made renewed efforts early in 1529, but Indian attacks destroyed Sancti Spiritus and made San Salvador dangerous. Famine threatened. In November 1529 the twenty-four survivors out of the original company of 200 sailed for Spain, meeting Garcia on the way, he also having giving up his quest. They reached home in July 1530 with only a number of Indian slaves, picked up on the way back, to show for their labours. There was no word of a western passage and no precious metal.

Very soon after landing information was lodged against the commander at Seville, a judicial enquiry ordered, and Cabot arrested. The promoters had been betrayed. Men had been executed and marooned. The array of charges against Sebastian was imposing, and he was fined and sentenced to banishment for four years at Oran to serve at his own expense against the Moors. Significantly, however, Charles V compensated his Pilot-Major for the fines and cancelled the banishment, Cabot continuing his official duties for many years. Clearly this shows that Sebastian was not responsible for the failure in the eyes of his royal master, and that there was a secret understanding. But Harrisse holds that to Cabot alone was the failure due, he being diverted from his original purpose by tales of gold and silver, related by the Portuguese and the survivors of the de Solis expedition.

In 1538 Cabot attempted to transfer his services to England. Perhaps the failure of his effort to the south-west had once again turned his thoughts to the north-west. He actually came to England in 1548, but neither in the reign of Edward VI nor in that of Mary did he direct any exploration towards the north-west. The English were bent at this time on finding a north-eastern passage. The " worthy old gentleman " died, probably, in 1557.

The last of the Spanish efforts to discover a western passage that need concern us was contemporary with the unfortunate voyage of Sebastian Cabot to the River Plate, and like it was an evidence of the acute interest in the subject in Spain, at the period of her disputes with Portugal that followed on Magellan's success, as we shall see in the next chapter. We turn once again to the Decades of the New World, to quote the following : " It has also been decided that a certain Estevão Gomez, an expert navigator, shall seek for a new route, leading to Cathay, between the Baccalaos and Florida, which belongs to us. He will be given only one caravel and his only instructions will be to search whether amongst the multitude of windings and the vast diversities of our ocean any passage can be found leading to the kingdom of him whom we commonly call the Grand Khan " [31]. Dr. Biggar, in his *Precursors of Jacques Cartier,* prints various relevant documents with translations [32]. In the agreement of 27th March, 1523, between Gomez and Charles V we have the following : " Forasmuch as you, Stephen Gomez . . . offer to go and discover Eastern Cathay, of which you have notice and information, where you hope to discover as far as our Molucca Islands, which all falls and lies within our limits and spheres of influence ; and seeing that along this said route to Eastern Cathay there are many islands and provinces hitherto undiscovered, very rich in gold, silver, spices and drugs, I accepted under the following conditions and terms . . ." [33]. Many details follow, of no present interest to us. These two statements give us a clear idea of the purpose of the venture.

Estevão Gomez was, like Magellan, a Portuguese navigator who transferred his services to Spain. He had visited the East Indies, sailing from Lisbon, and possibly had also come into contact with the Portuguese fishermen who frequented the Newfoundland Banks. He urged the Emperor to send an expedition to seek a strait to the south-west, but received no higher appointment than pilot under Magellan in 1519. He was in the vessel that deserted at the entrance to the strait which Magellan discovered, and returned to Spain. Later, as we have seen, he was entrusted with the seeking of a passage farther north.

There is a lack of agreement on the details of the voyage that he made, his original narrative having been lost. The early historians only make brief allusions to it, e.g. Peter Martyr, Oviedo, Gomara, Alonso de Santa Cruz, etc., and they are not in agreement. Did he sail on 3rd August, 1524, as sometimes stated, or at the close of that year ? Did he commence to search the coast in the north and proceed south, or the converse ? It is really not important for our purpose. Did he find, or think he had found, a western passage ? Alonso de Santa Cruz, who must have known Gomez personally and had access to official documents, says, in the *Islario* : " The pilot Stephen Gomez of whom we have already spoken, in the expedition made by him at the command and by licence of the Emperor, our master, in search of and in order to discover Cathay or the eastern city of India, as well as that so-much-sought-for strait or passage leading to the sea commonly called the South Sea, discovered during the ten months he was absent, a large number of islands along the coast of this continent and especially a very wide deep river which he named Deer River, on account of the number of these which he found there. . . . Gomez sailed for some distance up this river, thinking it was the strait of which he was in search. . . . And although he shared the general opinion about the strait or passage which as we have already stated separates the Cod-fish land continent from the land called the Labrador's Land [probably Greenland], yet he was convinced it was unnecessary to attempt it because of the cold in those parts, which would always be a bar. This opinion and his excuse for not attempting that passage were accepted as so reasonable that no further attempt has ever been made to proceed with this matter, although of great importance to your Majesty's interests and service, since through that channel a claim was laid to the trade and conquest of the Moluccas and to many more islands in those parts belonging of right to your royal crown " [34]. Then Santa Cruz proceeds to argue that even if there should be an open passage there, the cold would not be congenial to Spaniards accustomed to different temperatures, and urges a project which anticipates the Panama Canal, and which we will mention later. We notice that the Deer River disappointed Gomez. Dr. Biggar, from whose translation I have quoted, thinks this was the Bay of Fundy, but Harrisse argues that it was the Penobscot River.

Peter Martyr's remarks on the voyage are terse : " Gomez who returned ten months after his departure found neither the strait nor Cathay, as he had promised to do. I had always thought this good man's ideas were groundless and I openly told him so." He continues : " he nevertheless discovered agreeable and useful countries, corresponding exactly with our latitude and polar degrees " [35]. But of what use is it to find things which we have in Europe ? Fortune must be sought in the south. Everything at the Equator is rich. He proceeds : " Your Holiness will learn a laughable fact and a singular rumour concerning this voyage, which rapidly exploded. Estevão Gomez found nothing he expected to discover but rather than return with empty hands, he violated our instructions which forbade him to use violence against any natives and filled his ship with people of both races all innocent and half naked, who had lived contentedly in huts. Hardly had he reached the port whence he had sailed than an individual, hearing of the ship's arrival with a cargo of slaves, mounted his horse and without waiting for further information galloped to us and quite out of breath exclaimed : ' Estevão Gomez has returned with a ship load of cloves and precious stones.' He hoped to be well rewarded, and without comprehending the stupidity of this man the partisans of Gomez went about the Court with exclamations of joy. They loudly proclaimed that Gomez had brought not slaves (esclavos) but cloves (clavos), cutting off the first half of the word." Peter Martyr describes the ridicule that followed [36].

With the compromise effected with Portugal by the Treaty of Saragossa in 1529, Spanish interest in a western passage in the north waned, and no further effort was made to continue exploration in that region. The quest passed into the hands of the French. From the first years of the sixteenth century onwards French fishermen had visited the fishing-grounds of Newfoundland and Acadia. There is evidence, too, of early voyages to Brazil. De Gonneville's vessel L'*Espoir*, which left Honfleur for the East Indies, lured by reports of valuable cargoes of pepper, cinnamon, etc., in 1503, by accident touched on the coast of Brazil. On the way back an area was reached where for some time men of Dieppe and St. Malo and other Normans and Bretons had traded, bringing back dyewood, cotton, monkeys, parrots, etc. But the early French efforts were also directed to privateering against the Portuguese. The great Jean Ango became the directing force in French maritime affairs, and men inspired by him angered Portugal and Spain by their attacks on shipping.

Francis I had ascended the throne of France in 1515, and in 1519 had been a rival of Charles V in the claim to the title of Emperor. War broke out between the two monarchs in 1521, and their rivalry was reflected in affairs in the New World. Peter Martyr says, in his Sixth Decade, " Numerous French pirates and soldiers of the king of France, with whom we are at war, have blockaded all the ways both by sea and by land. In such difficult times we do live ! " [37]. One episode is especially interesting. The French pirate Jean Fleury, also called variously Juan Florentin, or Juan Florin, who has been confused with the Florentine explorer Verrazano, seized that part of the Aztec wealth which Cortes despatched from Vera Cruz to the Emperor. Peter Martyr notes that the two vessels stopped at the Azores for fear of French pirates, one already having suffered from the breaking loose of caged jaguars. One vessel arrived in Spain later under escort. He says, " The treasure destined for the Emperor is on the other vessel which has not yet arrived : but it is said that it amounts to 32,000 ducats of smelted gold in the form of bars. Were all the rings, jewels, shields, helmets and other ornaments now melted the total would amount to 150,000 ducats. The report has spread I know not how that French pirates are on the watch for these ships. May they come safely in ! " The treasure-laden vessel never arrived. Jean Florin seized the Aztec wealth after a combat a few leagues from Cape St. Vincent. The wonderfully worked objects in silver and gold went to the coffers of Francis I, who is credited with having made the remark that he knew of no provision in Father Adam's will that made his brother of Spain sole heir to all the treasures of the earth [38]. Significantly enough, this was but a short time before the expedition of Verrazano to the New World.

The pirate Florin was one of the most brilliant of the seamen inspired by Jean Ango, who had relieved many a Spanish vessel of its valuable cargo. Ango played a great part in the life of Dieppe and in French maritime affairs. His country house at Varenge-ville was the centre of a Florentine renaissance, one of the havens, along with Rouen and La Rochelle, for exiled artists, merchants and pilots from the Italian city. Among the Florentines at Dieppe were Giovanni and Girolamo Verrazano. The silk merchants of Lyons had always been interested in the East, and a syndicate furnished Giovanni de Verrazano with the means for carrying out a voyage of discovery towards Cathay. The plan originally was to sail by the north-eastern passage, the possibilities of which were no doubt indicated to Verrazano by the Italian Gaspar Centurione ; he had conceived the idea of a spice route from Cathay overland from Central Asia, by way of Moscow to Riga.

The information available relating to the voyage is scanty and raises many difficult problems. On his return Verrazano wrote a letter to Francis I, the original of which has been lost. Two versions of the letter exist, differing considerably. The one was published by Ramusio in his collection of voyages in 1556, and

PORTION OF A MAP OF VESCONTE DE MAGGIOLO, 1527.

(From a facsimile by Prof. E. L. Stevenson in the British Museum.)

The first map of the New World in *portolano* style. The basis was undoubtedly a map incorporating data derived from the Verrazano voyage. A *streito dubitoso* is shown traversing Honduras. To the north only a narrow isthmus separates the Atlantic Ocean from the " Sea of Verrazano." The region visited by the Florentine voyager is indicated by its nomenclature and by the attachment of the royal flag of France.

(*See p.* 177.)

later translated by Hakluyt, to be published in his great work of
1582. The other is the version first printed in 1841, the Carli
letter, being an enclosure in a letter from Fernando Carli at
Lyons to his father in Florence, 4th August, 1524. With the
ingenious deductions made from this single source of information
we are not concerned. I will quote only a passage from Hakluyt's
version [39]. It is headed " The relation of John de Verrazano, a
Florentine, of the land by him discovered in the name of his
Majestie. Written in Dieppe the eight of July 1524." It
commences thus :

" I wrote not to your Majestie, most Christian King, since the
time we suffered the tempest in the North partes, of the successe
of the four Shippes, which your Majestie sent forth to discover
new lands by the ocean, thinking your Majestie had bene already
duely informed thereof. Now by these presents I will give your
Majestie to understand, how by the violence of the windes we
were forced with the two ships, the Norman and the Dolphin (in
such evill case as they were) to land in Britaine. Where after wee
had repayred them in all poynts as was needefull, and armed them
very well, we tooke our course along by the coast of Spaine, which
your Majestie shall understand by the profite which we received
thereby. Afterwards with the Dolphin alone we determined to
make discoverie of new Countries, to prosecute the navigation
we had already begun, which I purpose at this present to recount
unto your Majestie to make manifest the whole proceeding of the
matter.

" The 17 of January the yeere 1524, by the grace of God we
departed from the dishabited rocke by the isle of Madèra,
apperteining to the king of Portugal, with 50 men, with victuals,
weapons and other ship-munition very well provided and furnished
for 8 moneths ; And sayling Westwards with a faire Easterly
winde in 25 dayes we ran 500 leagues and the 20 Febuarie we were
overtaken with as sharpe and terrible a tempest as ever any
saylors suffered : whereof with the divine helpe and mercifull

assistance of Almighty God and the goodnesse of our shippe, accompanied with the good happe of her fortunate name, we were delivered, and with a prosperous winde followed our course West and by North. And in other 25 dayes we made above 400 leagues more, where we discovered a new land never before seene of any man either ancient or moderne and at the first sight it seemed somewhat low, but being within a quarter of a league of it, we perceived by the great fires that we saw by the Sea coast that it was inhabited : and saw that the lande stretched to the Southwards." There is no notice of a western passage here. There are details of natives and their habits, of divers sorts of trees, of vines like those of Lombardy, of a land " very apt for any kind of husbandry of corne, wine and oyle." However, in the cosmographical portion, appended to the Carli letter, we find the following : " My intention was to reach by this navigation to Cathay, in the extreme east of Asia, expecting however to meet with new land such as was found as an obstacle, but I had reason to suppose that it was not hopeless to penetrate to the eastern ocean. This opinion was held by all the ancients and it was positively believed as certain that our ocean was one and the same as the eastern one of India, without any interposition of land. Aristotle affirms this . . ." [40]. Verrazano, although he ranged the Atlantic coast of North America from the Spanish sphere in the south to the area explored by the Portuguese in the north, failed, of course, to find a strait. Hakluyt asserts that Verrazano went thrice to the east coast of North America to find a route through to the Pacific. There are good grounds for believing from cartographical evidence that he made a second voyage at least. Cartographical evidence, too, proves conclusively that he made the first.

The map made by his brother Girolamo in 1529 indicates " Gallia Nova," and states that it was discovered five years before by Verrazano. The nomenclature shows the influence of France and of Florence. Interesting for our present purpose is the western sea indicated, separated from the Atlantic Ocean by a narrow isthmus. This influenced certain later work and is to be seen in the map of 1529, in the Maggiolo map of 1527, and notably in the globe of Ulpius of 1542 and in Michael Lok's map of 1582.

The Maggiolo map of 1527 is of particular interest. Not only does it show the " Sea of Verrazano," separated from the Atlantic Ocean by an isthmus a few miles wide, but a " streito dubitoso " is marked, a doubtful strait across Honduras. The relationship to ideas of a western passage in the central region, ideas which we have already described, is clear but difficult to trace definitely. The strait thus localised is to be found in the treatise of a Belgian monk, Franciscus Monachus, in 1526. Finally we note that the Münster map of 1540, of schematic academic type and which had a wide circulation, shows clearly the influence of the " Sea of Verrazano," which is merged with a northern passage. We have the inscription, " Through this strait lies the way to the Moluccas."

The search for the Western Passage did not, of course, end with the voyage of Verrazano, renewed efforts being made towards the north-west. But we have witnessed the gradual and far from uniform dispelling of the belief that a passage existed between the Straits of Magellan in the south and the colder latitudes of North America. The narrow isthmus that separated the Caribbean Sea from the Pacific Ocean, i.e. the North Sea from the South Sea, served as a land bridge in default of a sea passage. While Pedrarias was governor he organised the construction of a road from Panama on the South Sea to Nombre de Dios on the north. Richard Eden printed, along with the first three Decades of Peter Martyr's *New World*, a translation of *The Natural History of the West Indies*, by G. F. de Oviedo y Valdés, first printed in 1526 in Toledo. In it this passage occurs : " It hath byn an opinion among the Cosmographers and Pylottes of late tyme, and other which have had practise in thynges touchynge the sea, that there shulde bee a strayght of water passynge from the North Sea of the firme, into the South Sea of Sur, which nevertheless hath not byn seene nore founde to this daye. And suerlye yf there be any suche strayght we that inhabite these partes do thynke the same shulde bee rather of lande then of water " [41]. He then discusses the route from Nombre de Dios to Panama. Thick woods, mountains, rivers, valleys, make the twenty leagues difficult, but it can be done. But better, he says, to enlist the aid of the Chagre River to shorten the route. Certainly, he argues, the isthmus route brings Spain 7,000 leagues nearer the spices of the South Sea. Later, of course, the land route became a focus for traffic between the two seas and a magnet for raids on the wealth of New Spain.

The project of making a western passage where nature had failed to provide it soon entered the minds of men. Alonso de Santa Cruz, in the *Islario General* of 1560, from which we have already quoted, says :

" Should the great cares that burden your Majesty allow your magnanimous heart to conceive of a matter so useful and necessary as the junction of the South Sea with the Western ocean across that isthmus from Panama to Nombre de Dios, which the lie of the land favours so much that out of a total of 17 leagues 12 are traversed by a river so even and easy that brigantines and barks are able to sail up it . . . only 5 leagues would require to be excavated." He then points out that this is a far smaller project than linking the River Nile to the Red Sea ! [42]. This is not the earliest mention we have of such a scheme. The Spanish government opposed it, however. Not till the rise to power of the United States of America, and the demand for a canal through the isthmus to link the east and west coasts strategically and commercially, was the project of an artificial western passage energetically advanced. The 1876 report urged that the Nicaragua route was best, using the lake which had raised the hopes of Egidius Gonzales, but the later decision favoured a Panama canal. When it opened for traffic in 1915,

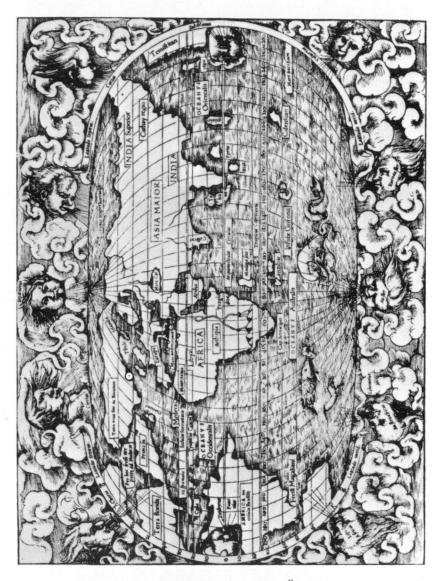

WORLD-MAP OF SEBASTIAN MÜNSTER, 1540.

(From A. E. Nordenskiöld, *Facsimile Atlas*. Stockholm, 1889.)

Editions of Ptolemy revised by Münster were published at Basle in 1540, 1541 and 1542, and had a wide circulation. The 1540 map shows the "Sea of Verrazano" merged with a northern passage. An inscription is attached stating that "Through this strait lies the way to the Moluccas."

(*See p.* 177.)

engineers had created at last what the Spaniards sought for in vain, a short route through from the waters of the Atlantic to those of the Pacific.

NOTES ON CHAPTER VII

1. Williamson, J. A., *The Voyages of the Cabots*.

2. Winship, G. P., *Cabot Bibliography*, 1900.

3. See Henry Harrisse, *John Cabot the Discoverer of North America and Sebastian his Son*, London, 1896; and H. P. Biggar, " Voyages of the Cabots and Corte-Reals," *Extrait de la Revue Hispanique*, 1903.

4. Actually the term " Baccalaos " is thought to be Basque in origin, and a designa- tion for codfish. A word akin to it is used also in Portuguese and Spanish.

5. Quoted from Williamson, J. A., *The Voyages of the Cabots*, p. 99.

6. Quoted from *ibid.*, p. 95.

7. See Harrisse, H., *Discovery of North America*, p. 134.

8. *De Orbe Novo*, vol. i, p. 274.

9. *Ibid.*, vol. ii, p. 24.

10. *Ibid.*, vol. i, p. 283.

11. *Ibid.*, vol. i, p. 286.

12. *Ibid.*, vol. i, p. 288.

13. *Ibid.*, vol. i, p. 289.

14. *Ibid.*, vol. ii, p. 340.

15. *Ibid.*, vol. ii, p. 183.

16. *Ibid.*, vol. ii, p. 214.

17. *Ibid.*, vol. ii, p. 226.

18. *Ibid.*, vol. ii, p. 235.

19. *Ibid.*, vol. ii, p. 283.

20. See Folsom, G., *The Despatches of Hernando Cortes*, London, 1843.

21. *Ibid.*, p. 337.

22. *Ibid.*, p. 401.

23. *Ibid.*, p. 417.

24. *Ibid.*, pp. 418–19.

25. See de Gayangos, D. P., *The Fifth Letter of Hernan Cortes to Charles V*, Hakluyt Soc., 1868, pp. 148-9. The five letters of Cortes are available also in a translation by MacNutt, F. A., *Letters of Cortes*, 1908.

26. *De Orbe Novo*, vol. i, p. 401.

27. The best account of Sebastian Cabot's expedition to the Plate estuary is to be found in Harrisse, H., *John and Sebastian Cabot*, 1896.

28. *De Orbe Novo*, vol. ii, p. 153.

29. *Ibid.*, vol. ii, p. 289.

30. An inscription on the Ribero map of 1529, referring to the La Plata area, runs as follows: "This country was discovered by Juan de Solis in 1515 or 1516. There Sebastian Gabotto now is in a fort which he has constructed. It is very well appropriated for yielding breadstuff and wine in great abundance. The river is extremely large and abounding with fish. The belief is that there is gold and silver in the interior."

31. *De Orbe Novo*, vol. ii, p. 241.

32. Biggar, H. P., *The Precursors of Jacques Cartier, 1497–1534*, Ottawa, 1911.

33. *Ibid.*, p. 147.

34. *Ibid.*, p. 193.

35. *De Orbe Novo*, vol. ii, p. 416.

36. In one of the interesting inscriptions made on the Diego Ribero map of 1529, reference is made to Gomez as follows: " Tierra de Estevan Gomez—Country of Estevan Gomez which he discovered by order of his Majesty. It contains numerous trees and fruits like those of Spain, much rodovallo [a kind of fish], salmon and soles. No gold has been found." Elsewhere on the map he points out that gold is not found because the area is " too much out of the way of the tropic."

37. *De Orbe Novo*, vol. ii, p. 240.

38. See de la Roncière, C., *Histoire de la Marine Française,* Paris, 1906, vol. iii, for interesting references to the voyage of Verrazano and its background.

39. Hakluyt, R., *Principal Navigations* (Maclehose edition), vol. viii, p. 423.

40. Brevoort, J. C., *Verrazano the Navigator,* New York, 1874, p. 114.

41. Eden, Richard, *The First Three English Books on America,* edited E. Arber, 1885, p. 234.

42. Biggar, H. P., *Precursors of Jacques Cartier,* p. 194.

CHAPTER VIII

THE FIRST CIRCUMNAVIGATION

T H E First Circumnavigation is a title which describes one of the results of the expedition despatched under the command of Ferdinand Magellan in 1519. But the circumnavigation of the globe was only an incidental outcome of that adventure. It was not part of the plan, which was based on a motive very different from that of simply accomplishing a feat of navigation. A consideration of the plan is necessary to an understanding of the voyage ; and it will introduce us to some interesting problems of geographical science, and of the strategy of empire as practised in the days when Portugal and Spain led the movement of European expansion.

The desire to open a direct sea-borne trade with Eastern Asia was, as we have shown, the inspiration both of Spain under the leadership of Columbus and of Portugal under that of Bartolomeu Dias and Vasco da Gama. The manifestations of that desire were controlled by the geographical conceptions of the period. The globe of Martin Behaim, which embodies the accepted doctrine of the late fifteenth century, depicts the tripartite world, the world of the three continents of Europe, Africa and Asia, with Asia stretching so far round the globe as to lie within a practicable distance of Western Europe. Omitting a possible arctic passage by the north-east, there were thus two obvious seaways to Asia : by the west, and by the south-east round the Cape of Good Hope.

Columbus made the western voyage, and on his return in 1493 it was believed that Spain had the archipelago of Eastern Asia at her command. At that date the Portuguese had discovered the Cape of Good Hope and the entrance to the Indian Ocean, but they had not yet completed the passage across it to the Indies. Portugal, however, had staked a claim, and was in possession of papal bulls authorising the conquest of heathen lands *usque ad Indos*. Spain lost no time in seeking similar recognition from the spiritual authority of Christendom, and in 1493 Pope Alexander VI issued bulls which accorded to Spain the right to make discoveries and conquests in a region inaccurately described as west and south of a meridian passing through the Atlantic Ocean. The bulls were important as establishing a principle. The detail was decided by the two Powers concerned, who negotiated the Treaty of Tordesillas in 1494, and agreed upon the meridian passing 370 leagues west of the Azores and Cape Verde Islands as the dividing line between their respective discoveries.[1] Thus the meridian of Tordesillas passed from pole to pole through the Atlantic. Nothing was said about a corresponding meridian in the opposite part of the world to complete the division of the globe into two hemispheres. That remained a latent question until the progress of exploration should render it active. But when that stage was reached in the second decade of the sixteenth century, it was common ground to Spaniards and Portuguese that the principle of 1493–4 governed the matter, and that the complementary meridian should be 180 degrees east and west of the primary one.

Until his death in 1506, Columbus clung to the view that the continent forming the western border of the Caribbean Sea was Asia, and that South America or the *Mundus Novus* was a peninsula projecting from Asia. There has been a tendency to regard his contention as representing the thought of his contemporaries. In reality opinion was divided on the matter, and from 1500 an increasing number of geographers held that the Americas must be a fourth and hitherto unknown continent distinct from Asia.[2] This concept involved a modification of the project for a westward

[1] See Chapter III, p. 54.
[2] See Chapter V.

route to Asia. If the Americas were distinct, there must needs be another ocean beyond them, an ocean which must be entered and crossed before the shores of Cathay and Cipangu could be reached. Three possibilities of entry suggested themselves : a north-west passage through or round North America, a tropical channel penetrating Central America, and a south-west passage through or round South America. But before any west-bound ship actually passed the American obstacle, the progress of general discovery gave firmer definition to the elements of the problem.

In the East the Portuguese made rapid strides. Vasco da Gama reached India from the Cape of Good Hope in 1498. Lopes de Sequeira reached the Straits of Malacca in 1509. Two years later Albuquerque captured the city of Malacca, and by so doing opened the gate to the eastern shores of Asia and to the vast archipelago which Columbus had vainly imagined he had found. In 1512 Antonio d'Abreu passed through the gate and attained the Moluccas, the Spice Islands already described by Ludovico di Varthema, an Italian wanderer who had visited them in Asiatic shipping at the close of the fifteenth century.

In the West the American coasts became better known, and the three possibilities above mentioned were investigated. In the north-west continuous failure never extinguished the optimism of successive believers, although it is to be noted that an influential school of cartographers joined North America to Asia (as in fact they are almost joined), and so ruled out the possibility of the North-West Passage. But in spite of theoretical and practical discouragement, the north-western faith remained vigorous though barren. The central channel, west of the Caribbean, was perhaps less ardently believed in, and hopes were virtually at an end after the coasting voyages of 1517–18. The South American coast was found to stretch far beyond the tropics into the South Atlantic. Vespucci revealed this in his voyage under the Portuguese flag in 1501–2. Frenchmen were on the coast of Brazil certainly from 1504 ; but they were primarily traders, and are not known to have discovered anything new. A voyage from Lisbon in 1513–14, described in a rare German pamphlet, *Newen Zeitung aus Presil Land,* is thought to have reached a point beyond the River Plate. Juan de Solis entered that estuary in 1515–16, and was killed there by the Indians. The reports of his comrades, whilst not conclusive, suggested that the Plate was not the opening of a through channel to the west. The South-West Passage was not yet found. Nevertheless, it appeared by 1518 to offer the most promising line of investigation, simply because its possibilities had not been fully examined. The captains who were coasting South America had met with no ice barrier. They had not completed their task. Hundreds of miles of feasible navigation were as yet unattempted, and at any point therein the corner leading westwards might be turned. The enterprise of the South-West Passage awaited its man.

Ferdinand Magellan[1] was born in Portugal about the year 1480. His family was noble, but not wealthy, and he was twenty-five before he had any chance of winning distinction. At that age he sailed for India, in the fleet which accompanied Francisco d'Almeida in 1505 ; and he served under Almeida until 1509. He was an officer in the first expedition to Malacca, commanded by Lopes de Sequeira. After reaching Malacca in September 1509, the squadron met with disaster, losing sixty men by treachery at the hands of the inhabitants. This caused Sequeira to return to India. Magellan is said to have saved the life of a comrade, Francisco Serrão, during the fighting, and the result was a friendship between them which had historical consequences. Magellan continued his career under the next viceroy, Affonso de Albuquerque, and was present at the second taking of Goa in 1510. In the following year, Albuquerque captured Malacca, and

---

[1] More correctly, Fernão de Magalhães. But the present writer must confess his preference for established and familiar forms. The irritation and confusion arising from the substitution of the unfamiliar outweigh the advantage of the accuracy so attained. Such accuracy may justly be described as pedantic, since it yields no advance in historical knowledge.

THE GLOBE OF JOHANNES SCHÖNER, 1520.

(Re‑drawn for K. Kretschmer, *Die Entdeckung Amerikas*, Atlas. Berlin, 1892.)

A portion of the most complete of the extant globes constructed by the Nuremberg mathematician. It is of the academic type, and the delineation of the coast of eastern Asia corresponds with that of Behaim. Not only are northern and southern passages shown, but there is also a strait through the central isthmus leading to a not‑far‑distant Cipangu. There, as an inscription tells us, there is gold in great quantities.

both Magellan and Serrão were members of his force.   Varthema, the Italian traveller, had given information of the Moluccas, or Spice Islands, many years previously.   The Straits of Malacca were the gate which led to them, and no time was lost in pushing through.   Early in 1512 Antonio d'Abreu reached the Moluccas and opened the direct spice trade.   It is unlikely that Magellan went with him, but certain that Serrão did.   There was as yet no attempt to conquer the native princes of the Moluccas, but some Portuguese factors, including Serrão, remained in residence there to collect cargoes.   Serrão corresponded with his friend Magellan, and assured him that the longitude of the Moluccas must be such as to place them within the Spanish hemisphere of exploitation, if the meridian of demarcation should be drawn in the eastern seas.   Serrão was not alone in holding this opinion.   The majority of the Portuguese navigators seem to have believed in it, although actually it is untrue.

Later in 1512 Magellan returned to Portugal after an absence of seven years.   He served in Morocco, and was accused of financial irregularities which lost him the favour of King Manuel. There were two other men similarly unfortunate, Ruy Faleiro, the astronomer, and Christopher de Haro, the Lisbon head of a great international trading firm.   Faleiro had a somewhat unbalanced mind, but considerable scientific attainments, wherewith he lent support to Magellan's belief on the longitude of the Moluccas. De Haro had already been taking part in the Indian trade.   Some of his ships had been destroyed on the Guinea coast, and he could obtain no redress.   He passed over to Spain in the hope of securing a more lucrative share in the spice trade by the westward passage, which it was in the power of the Spanish Government to promote.   Magellan was contemplating a like transfer of allegiance.   He computed that the Moluccas were just within the Spanish hemisphere, and he had heard of lands lying farther to the east—Borneo, the Philippines, Formosa, China and some fabulous countries reported by the Asiatics at Malacca.   It seemed to him that there existed a vast and legitimate field for Spanish enterprise. Its exploitation was sooner or later inevitable, and he determined to be the exploiter. In 1517 he and Faleiro entered Spain, where Christopher de Haro had prepared the ground. The King of Spain, known to history as the Emperor Charles V, sanctioned the enterprise on 22nd March, 1518.

Magellan undoubtedly betrayed his natural allegiance. It was a common offence in his age, and particularly among the Portuguese, who threw off a multitude of renegades in the sixteenth century, to sell commercial and colonial secrets to the English and French. Some of them were persecuted Jews, to whom the term traitor cannot fairly be applied. Magellan had not that excuse, but his temptation was great. He saw a chance of founding a new colonial empire by making a great discovery, but he could hope to be employed only by his country's rivals. The world, in hailing him as one of its great men, has tacitly agreed that honour was well lost.

The preparations were considerably delayed. The Portuguese Government protested against the voyage, and its agents intrigued secretly to stir up trouble for Magellan. His Spanish officers were insubordinate and jealous of the authority of a foreigner. He insisted on employing a nucleus of Portuguese colleagues whom he could trust, but this naturally prejudiced his relations with the Spaniards. The crews were of divers nationalities. The majority of the men were Spaniards, but there were also Portuguese, Italians, Frenchmen, Greeks, and one Englishman, " Master Andrew of Bristol," who was not destined to survive the voyage. A notable individual was Antonio Pigafetta, an Italian soldier of fortune and a knight of Rhodes, for he wrote the fullest account of the expedition which has been preserved. At length all obstacles were overcome, and in September 1519 Magellan sailed from San Lucar with five ships. His intention was to reach the Moluccas by searching for the South-West Passage even into the Antarctic circle. In default of finding the passage, he was to go by the Cape ; but, at all costs, he was to reach the Moluccas and plant the Spanish flag in them.

Six days' sailing brought Magellan to Teneriffe. Here a caravel overtook him with warning from his friends in Spain that some of the officers intended mutiny. It was probably no news to him, but he was not in a position to anticipate the blow, for the revolt itself would constitute the only evidence of the intention that would secure credence from the Spanish authorities. He passed on southwards to the latitude of Cape Verde, where he reprimanded Juan de Cartagena, captain of the *San Antonio,* for his insolent behaviour. In the doldrums of the equatorial belt there were sixty days of slow progress, during which Cartagena again offended and was deprived of his command. The baffling winds edged the fleet westwards until the coast of Brazil was sighted in the neighbourhood of Pernambuco. Magellan coasted south, and reached Rio de Janeiro on 13th December, 1519. He remained for two weeks, and then sailed on to the River Plate. Here, in January 1520, he made an exploration of the estuary in case it should lead to the desired channel ; but the investigation proved what was already suspected, and the explorers passed on. At the end of February they entered the Gulf of San Mathias, which may have been reached by the 1513–14 expedition reported in the *Newen Zeitung.* It was a possible opening of the passage, and had to be examined as such. The fruitless search occupied the greater part of a month, after which the goal was acknow- ledged to lie yet to the southward. The next halt was on 31st March at Port St. Julian. The southern winter was about to set in, and further progress was for the time impossible. Magellan determined to wait at Port St. Julian for the spring. He reduced the rations, and the men grumbled. Some of the officers gave vent to their fears or their ill-will, and urged a return to the northward. It was a situation which every sixteenth-century commander had to face as the rigours of the south drew near. Richard Hawkins tells us that there was always a demand to put back, in order to winter in the tropics, and adds that he had never known of its being acceded to without the abandonment of the voyage as the consequence. Magellan, without precedent to guide him, was quite firm. He would die, he said, before he would turn back, and he would continue the voyage as far as might be necessary to find the strait.

The answer was a sudden mutiny. Three ships revolted by night, the *Concepcion*, the *San Antonio* and the *Victoria*, and Magellan found himself obeyed only by his own *Trinidad* and by the *Santiago*, a small vessel which remained loyal. There could be no question of allowing the malcontents to go home. The object of the voyage was to establish an empire besides making a discovery, and every man and ship was indispensable. Magellan struck cunningly and hard. He believed that he had many friends on board the *Victoria*, and he sent a boat's crew of trusty men to parley with those who commanded her. His emissaries gained access to her deck, and provoked a scuffle, in which they killed the rebel captain, whereupon the rest returned to their duty. The balance of force was now with Magellan. With his three ships he blocked the mouth of the anchorage, and prevented the exit of the two others. The *San Antonio* tried to force her way out, but was taken after a half-hearted fight. The *Concepcion* then surrendered, and the mutiny was over. Retribution was stern but limited. Magellan executed one ringleader, Gaspar Quesada, who had himself murdered a loyal officer. Juan de Cartagena had been the chief author of the whole conspiracy, but he held the King's commission. It was probably for this reason that Magellan refrained from his formal execution, but in Spain there were well-known methods of taking life without the shedding of blood. Cartagena was marooned on a desolate coast, together with a priest who had stirred up disaffection. That was all : several others were sentenced to death, but pardoned ; and the whole proceeding constituted a nice balance between the vindication of authority and the preservation of the man-power so essential to success. It is difficult to concur with those who have described Magellan's conduct as brutal and heartless. To do so is to urge that perversion of ethics which condones the crime and reproves its suppression.

Magellan had some months to wait at Port St. Julian before the winter should be past. He suffered a further disaster in the loss of the *Santiago*, which was wrecked whilst examining the coast to the southward. Her crew escaped to the shore, and reached Port St. Julian after a perilous march. It was at first supposed that the country was uninhabited, but one morning a native appeared. Whether he was an exceptional person, or whether the explorers were growing fanciful, is not clear, but to them he seemed to be a member of a race of giants. " So tall was this man," says Pigafetta, " that we came up to the level of his waistbelt. He was well enough made, and had a broad face, painted red. . . . His hair was short and coloured white, and he was dressed in skins." Others followed, of like appearance, and so arose the legend of the gigantic Patagonians, alternately confirmed and denied by subsequent expeditions to this coast. The truth seems to be that the Patagonians are tall men, but not the monsters that heated imaginations have made them. The frequent corroboration of the tale is interesting to the student of historical evidence.

On 24th August, 1520, the fleet, reduced to four sail, left Port St. Julian. It halted for two more months in the mouth of the Santa Cruz River in 50° S. At length, in the latter half of October, the spring was setting in. Four days' sailing revealed a cape, beyond which " we saw an opening like unto a bay." It was, although none yet knew it, the entry of the Straits of Magellan.

It may be well to anticipate by giving a brief description of the straits. The entrance from the Atlantic, marked on the north side by Cape Virgins, is in approximately $52\frac{1}{2}°$ S. Thence, the channel runs westwards to the First Narrows, well under a mile in width, and south-westwards to the Second Narrows, some seventy miles from the entrance. After the Second Narrows the strait turns in a southerly direction, and widens out in Broad Reach, about fifteen miles wide. At Cape Froward is the southernmost point of the mainland of America, almost on the 54th parallel ; and this also marks the half-way limit of the passage. From Cape Froward the strait runs north-west by west to its Pacific exit at Cape Pillar, formerly called Cape Deseado.

Navigators entering from the Atlantic generally found the first half of the strait, to Cape Froward, comparatively easy sailing. The shores were not mountainous, and Broad Reach afforded reasonable space for the manœuvres of a sailing-ship. Yet, even here the tides were strong, and the bottom foul with jagged rocks. These were a serious cause of anxiety, for it was often necessary to anchor, and the hempen cables were quickly chafed through. It was impracticable to carry more than four or five anchors, and once they were lost the ship was helpless. After Cape Froward had been turned the conditions changed rapidly for the worse. The passage was narrower, the currents swifter, projecting reefs more numerous, and the shores were a tangle of cliffs and mountains which split up the wind into furious squalls from unexpected directions. The main force of the wind was generally from the west, and therefore contrary, and the available refuges were so few that it was often necessary to run back a long distance in the wrong direction before it was safe to bring up. It was here that sails and anchors were lost, hulls strained, and men's hearts broken by unremitting toil, on a diet at best of seal-flesh and penguins, at worst of mussels and limpets. Even with the best of commanders the passage was largely a matter of luck. Drake made it in sixteen days, the quickest time recorded in his century. Richard Hawkins took forty-six days, and Thomas Cavendish fifty-one.

Magellan knew nothing of what lay before him. On rounding Cape Virgins he suspected that the strait was found, but could not

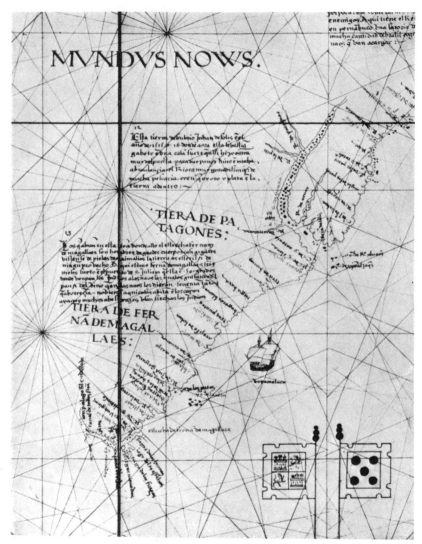

THE STRAITS OF MAGELLAN, FROM THE MAP OF DIEGO RIBERO,
1529.

The general direction of the channel discovered by Magellan is well delineated,
although the details are necessarily imperfect. The map is also interesting for its record
of the discoveries in the River Plate, made by the expedition of Sebastian Cabot, commenced in 1526. The flags represent the Spanish and Portuguese standards, placed on
either side of the meridian of demarcation.

(*See p.* 197.)

be sure. He sent two ships ahead to reconnoitre, for fear of desertion precluded him from doing that work himself. They passed rapidly through both the Narrows into Broad Reach, and returned in a few days with flags flying and guns firing to announce success. They had not been right through the strait, but the strength of the tides left no room for doubt of its nature. Magellan accordingly entered. The narratives give no account of the difficulties ; but we know from later stories what they were, and that Magellan must have encountered them in full force, for his passage was a tedious business. After passing Cape Froward, as the map shows, there were alternative channels to be explored, and none knew which was the right one. Magellan had therefore to disperse his ships on different quests, and the *San Antonio* took the opportunity to desert. Her commander was indeed loyal, but the pilot Estevão Gomez incited the crew to mutiny and sailed for Spain. They took with them their unlucky captain, wounded and in irons, and they told such a plausible story against him that he was thrown into prison on arrival. He was not released until the remainder of the expedition came home, two years later, and the truth was revealed. This record was paralleled fifty years afterwards when the *Elizabeth* deserted Drake in like manner, contrary to the will of her captain, John Winter. But Winter has been branded as a traitor for more than three centuries, and has been exonerated only by documents quite recently discovered.

On 28th November, 1520, Magellan, with his three remaining ships, passed out of the strait into the South Sea. His passage had occupied thirty-eight days, and nothing but his personal ascendancy had won success. For it is evident that if he had shown the slightest weakness, there would have been a general demand to turn back.

The greatest hardships were still to come, for the extent of the unknown ocean proved a terrible surprise. The general mis-calculation of longitudes, which pushed the bounds of Asia

much farther eastward than they actually lie, had led to the
erroneous notion that the Moluccas must lie within the Spanish
hemisphere. It had also the effect of reducing the estimated
width of the Pacific, and no one was prepared for the length of
the passage which lay between Magellan and his goal. He had
already declared, whilst asserting his will, that he would go on
until all were reduced to eating the leather bindings of the
yardarms. This proved a true prophecy, for they did chew
leather before they came to the islands of Asia. The shipping of
the sixteenth century had barely reached the stage of development when, with infinite suffering and heroism, the Pacific could
just be crossed. That in itself was a great advance on the state
of affairs that had prevailed when Magellan himself was born.
But it was not until the days of Captain Cook that the ship was
fit to master the ocean, and to explore it at will in comfort and
security. The hardihood displayed by the pioneers of the early
period has never been surpassed, but they paid dearly for
immortality.

After leaving the straits the expedition turned northward to
avoid the belt of the strong westerly winds which blow in that
latitude. The voyagers passed parallel to the Chilean coast, but
not in sight of it, until they were north of the island of Juan
Fernandez. Then, on 16th December, they turned in a direction
west-north-west, diagonally across the tropics and the Equator.
It was two months before they saw any land, and then only a
deserted island with no anchorage. Eleven days later they sighted
another island, which yielded neither food nor water. It was
now a question whether endurance or hardship would be
victorious. " We ate biscuit," records Pigafetta, " but in truth
it was biscuit no longer, but a powder full of worms. . . . We
were forced to eat the hides with which the mainyard was
covered to prevent chafing against the rigging. . . . We had
also to use sawdust for food, and for rats we paid half a ducat
apiece." Some died of hunger, and some of scurvy, and almost

all were extremely weak. A storm would have destroyed them, but the weather was uniformly kind. It was for this reason that Magellan named his ocean the Pacific, and also, no doubt, in order to impress those at home with the attractions of his new route to the Indies.

Insoluble as was the problem of longitude, the latitude of the Moluccas was approximately known to Magellan. In spite of this he crossed the Equator and pressed on to the northward of the required parallel. It seems probable that he was seeking the rumoured lands lying to the north-east of the Moluccas—the mainland of China, or the islands thought to lie off it. He might reach them sooner than the Moluccas themselves, and might there refit before appearing in the spice region, where he knew he would have to dispute the supremacy with the Portuguese.

At length, on 6th March, 1521, after ninety-eight days of hope deferred, he sighted a group of islands. Their inhabitants were unpleasant people, who stole everything they could lay hands on ; but at least they provided fruit and vegetables, and the plague of scurvy was stayed. Magellan named them the Islands of the Ladrones, or robbers, and passed on. A few days later (16th March) he came to an island which formed part of a larger group, now known as the Philippines. He called them the Archipelago of St. Lazarus, and realised that he had made an important discovery. He found a settled population under regular government. Intercourse was facilitated by the fact that he had with him a Malay slave, acquired during his former service in the East, and that this man's language was understood by the new people.

Here was an opportunity to establish a base of Spanish power in the East Indies. Magellan preached Christianity and talked politics to the island chiefs. He concluded a treaty with the King of Sebu, whereby the Spaniards were to have the exclusive privilege of trade ; and the trade might be valuable, for already they had seen gold in the possession of their new friends. A brother of the King of Sebu lay sick and at the point of death. A

O

Spanish priest baptised him, and in five days he rose from his bed, and led his people to destroy the temples and the idols they contained. The voyage had succeeded in demonstrating the westward passage to Asia, and Spanish prestige seemed established among Asiatics as yet undiscovered by the Portuguese.

The King of Sebu had a rebellious vassal in the neighbouring island of Mactan. Magellan determined to give an illustration of Spanish power by subduing the rebel chief. There were some who urged caution, in view of the weakness and scanty numbers of the white men. But their leader was in winning vein, and set upon the conquest of the whole archipelago—the true *conquistador* counted odds only to discount them. On 27th April, 1521, he landed with sixty Spaniards on the beach of Mactan, telling his native friends to look on and see how Christians could fight. It is easy for us, who know the outcome, to denounce his rashness, but it was by just such rashness that Cortes was at that moment winning an empire for Spain on the other side of the vast Pacific. Fortune favoured Cortes, but not Magellan. She had given him the hard choice of achieving fame by bartering his allegiance, and now, perhaps, she exacted retribution for the acceptance of her terms. As his handful gained the shore they were surrounded by hundreds, some say thousands, of enemies. The Spaniards fought well, but were beaten down under showers of spears, arrows and stones. The whole affair lasted, or seemed to last, an hour, until Magellan, many times wounded, was killed whilst trying to retreat in good order. Pigafetta stayed by him to the end, and then with the survivors took to the boats and returned to Sebu.

Not only was Magellan dead, but the entire prospect of the expedition was clouded. Prestige was everything, and it was as easily lost as gained. The King of Sebu had indeed seen white men fight worthily, but he had seen them beaten, and their spell was broken. On 1st May he invited the Spanish officers to a ceremonial, and there murdered them in cold blood. Of twenty-seven who landed only two escaped. Pigafetta would have gone, but was disabled by a wound received at Mactan. The three ships weighed anchor and departed from Sebu under the shadow of a double disaster.

There were now 115 men remaining, and as the *Concepcion* was unseaworthy, it was decided to burn her and continue the voyage with the *Trinidad* and the *Victoria*. The task before the survivors was to complete the exploration of the eastern archipelago, to investigate the Moluccas, and to return by the most promising route to Spain. They sailed westward to the coast of Borneo, where they visited the great city of Brunei. The name " Borneo," now applied to the whole island, represents the Spaniards' corruption of " Brunei." Here, and in the adjacent waters, they lingered for several months ; and it was not until 8th November, 1521, that they sighted the Moluccas and anchored off Tidore. There and at Ternate the people received them well, and in course of trade the Spaniards obtained cargoes of spices. They found that the Portuguese were developing the trade of the Moluccas, although as yet without establishing sovereignty or planting permanent garrisons there. They heard also of the death of Francisco Serrão, Magellan's old comrade, who had borne a part in inspiring the expedition. He had lived at Ternate since 1511, playing for his own hand, and mistrusted by the Portuguese authorities at Malacca. Early in 1521 he was poisoned, although whether by native enemies or at the instigation of his own country-men is not clear. By December the Spaniards had completed their cargoes and had concluded treaties of friendship and Spanish protection with the island chiefs. This was the work of Sebastian del Cano, who was now in command. Whether Magellan would have done more we cannot tell. He had the spirit of a *con-quistador*, but resources had grown small. His successors accom-plished as much as was to be reasonably expected.

The time for departure drew near, and it was at this point that the project of circumnavigation was definitely adopted, for one only of the two remaining ships.   The *Victoria* was to pass through the Indian Ocean and round the Cape of Good Hope.   The *Trinidad* was to re-cross the tropical Pacific in the hope of reaching Panama.   It was recognised that there was no chance of returning by the Straits of Magellan, since the prevailing winds already experienced would be contrary ; but north of the line it was hoped that they would prove more favourable.

We may follow the fortunes of the *Trinidad* first.   She was found to be leaky and in need of heavy repairs, and it was not until April 1522 that she sailed from Tidore with fifty-four men. They struggled against continuous head winds in the North Pacific, until hunger and disease forced them to turn back.   They regained the Moluccas, only to find that a strong Portuguese squadron had arrived from Malacca, and to these Portuguese the few survivors surrendered.   Two-thirds of them had perished in the attempt to make the eastward passage of the Pacific, a feat which no Spanish vessel was destined to accomplish for more than forty years to come.   Not until 1565 did Andres de Urdaneta discover the correct course and season for sailing, and by so doing establish the Spanish trade-route from Asia by way of Central America to Europe.   Prior to that date a number of Spanish captains crossed the Pacific to the Asiatic islands, but not one of them retraced his course.   Of the luckless crew of the *Trinidad*, only four survived Portuguese captivity, to return, years later, to their native land.

Meanwhile, the *Victoria*, with forty-seven Europeans and a few Asiatics on board, had quitted the archipelago in the opposite direction.   Her commander, Sebastian del Cano, who had been one of the mutineers at Port St. Julian, had now a chance to retrieve his reputation.   The road home was known, but it was a question whether ship and crew would be strong enough to follow it—half round the world with enfeebled men, scanty victuals, worm-eaten timbers, and rotten gear.   Some were for shirking it and giving themselves up to the Portuguese.   " But the greater number," says Pigafetta, " valued honour more than

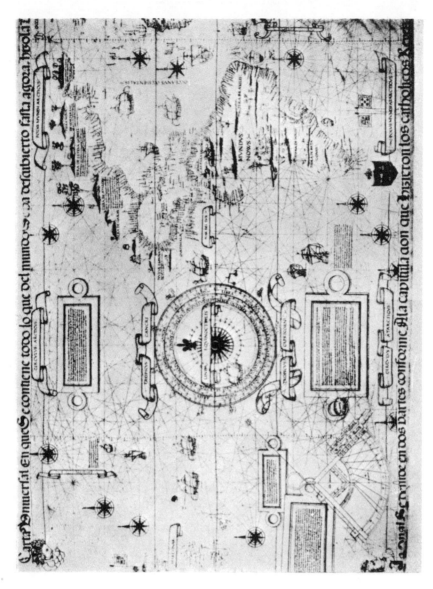

THE PACIFIC OCEAN, FROM THE MAP OF DIEGO RIBERO,
1529.

Three copies of this map exist, preserved respectively in the Ducal Library of Weimar, in the Propaganda Fidei at Rome, and in the Library of the Duke of Brunswick at Wolfenbüttel. The present illustration is from a printed reproduction of the Rome copy in the British Museum. On the extreme left is seen the Spanish flag upon the newly discovered Archipelago of St. Lazarus or Philippine Islands.   The western coasts of the Americas, except in the neighbourhood of Panama, are shown to be unexplored. The general outline of South America is remarkably well proportioned.

(See p. 197.)

life, and resolved at all hazards to attempt the return like Spaniards." When they rounded the Cape there were about thirty of them left. More died as they struggled north through the Atlantic. They were obliged to seek food at the Cape Verde Islands, where the Portuguese made prisoners of a boat's crew. It was with eighteen white men and four Asiatics that the *Victoria* accomplished her last stage to Seville. She arrived on 8th September, 1522, three years after setting out.

The results of this great voyage may be stated as follows : First, it revealed the Pacific Ocean in its true magnitude, as may be seen from the official Spanish map drawn by Diego de Ribero in 1529, and embodying mainly the knowledge gained by Magellan. It should be noted, however, that Magellan had crossed the ocean on a single narrow track, its width of accurate information limited by the range of visibility from the tops of his ships. On either side of that track all was still unknown, and it was by no means certain that there existed nothing but the empty sea, which was all that Ribero felt justified in depicting. Magellan began the revelation of the Pacific, but that was all. For a variety of reasons geographers argued that great lands would be found to the north and to the south of the belt he had traversed. Two and a half centuries were to elapse before these beliefs should be fully tested by Cook and their substantial unsoundness demonstrated.

Secondly, the voyage gave to Spain a footing in the Far East. It is true that by the Treaty of Saragossa, 1529, Charles V sold to Portugal his claim to the Moluccas. But the sale did not include the Philippines. They remained potentially Spanish, and were effectively occupied in 1564. The possession endured for more than three centuries. By means of it the Spaniards exploited a share in the trade of Asia, operated a regular trade route across the Pacific, and played a worthy part in the earlier stages of the exploration of that ocean.

Finally, Magellan's achievement was a notable contribution to the establishment of European supremacy over Asia, one of the dominant factors in that period of world-development which is now drawing to its close. Magellan was a great European in an age when great Europeans were turning the tide of history. Behind them lay the centuries in which Asia had sent forth its Huns, its Mongols and its Turks to lay waste the lands of Western civilisation. Before them stretched the centuries in which Western civilisation was to overawe the East—and they were the leaders of the resurgence. It was accomplished, not by marching masses such as followed Attila or Genghiz Khan, but by daring individuals and little ships' companies, taught by Magellan and his like that the white man's initiative was a lever to overturn the static edifices of Asiatic power. We of this generation can appreciate their greatness, our admiration sharpened by the pang of regret. For once again the tide is turning. The grasp of Europe is relaxing, and Asia bestirs herself after centuries of quiescence. To what end we cannot tell, but it can hardly be a good end for Europe. We who read history know at least that. It tells us that the expectation of some self-denying ordinance, whereby the strong shall not exploit their strength, is nothing but a dream. And we look in vain for men like Magellan and those crews of Renaissance humanity whom he fashioned into heroes.

AUTHORITIES FOR CHAPTER VIII

The standard English work on the subject is F. H. H. Guillemard's *Life of Magellan*, London, 1890. It is full, accurate and based on a wide survey of the evidence. Some of its interpretations are questioned in J. Denucé's monograph *La question des Moluques et la première circumnavigation du globe,* Brussels, 1911, which submits doubtful points to minute examination, and is especially valuable for the antecedent circumstances of the voyage. E. F. Benson's *Ferdinand Magellan*, London, 1929, is a vigorously written biography intended for the general reader.

CHAPTER IX

THE NORTHERN PASSAGES

THE long familiarity of Englishmen with northern waters, which tradition carries back to the days of King Arthur, marked them out in many men's minds as predestined among Europeans to search out the northern passages. As early as 1496 John Cabot, speaking we must believe as the mouthpiece of the merchants of Bristol, demanded a patent of discovery for " all parts, regions, and coasts of the eastern, western, and *northern* seas," while the Adventurers of 1501, men of the same city and of the Azores, made use of the even more specific phrase, " all parts, regions and territories of the eastern, western, southern, *arctic* and northern seas." Nevertheless, it was not for the sake of northern territories or northern waters in themselves that men turned their ships' prows polewards ; the northern lands were to be stepping-stones, the northern seas were to be passages, to the sun-enriched south. For it was an accepted principle of natural law that as the strength of the equinoctial sun drew from the earth rich spices, both sweet and pungent, and luxuriant exotic fruits, so too his rays engendered precious metals and precious stones within the earth.

The view of a thoughtful man was well expressed in an Address to King Henry VIII, delivered by an Englishman in 1541, and long since formulated by him when as a young merchant in Seville he had bent his mind to the problem of securing for his own country a share in the rich spoils pouring in from the newly revealed " under-side of the globe." His words were these :

" Now . . . we shall speak of the part of the land that is . . . toward septentrion, which is called the New Found Land, which was first discovered by merchants of Bristol. . . . What commodity is within this land is not known, for it hath not been laboured, but it is to be presupposed that there is no riches of gold, spices, nor precious stones, for it standeth far aparted from the equinoctial, whereas the influence of the sun doth nourish and bring forth gold, spices, stones, and pearls. But whereas our merchants of Bristol did enterprise to discover, and discovered that part of the land, if at that season they had followed toward the equinoctial, no doubt but they should have found great riches of gold and pearls as other nations hath since that time. Now by this your Grace may well apperceive what part of the Universal is discovered and what there resteth to discover. It is clearly seen by the Cosmographia that of four parts of the world, the three parts be discovered : for out of Spain they sail all the Indies and Seas Occidentals, and from Portugal they sail all the Indies and Seas Orientals, so that between the way of the orient and the way of the occident they have compassed all the world . . . and also by the way of the meridian there is a great part discovered by the Spaniards. So there resteth this way of the north only for to discover, which resteth unto your Grace's charge, for that the situation of this Realm is more apt for it than any other, and also for that your Grace hath taken far enterprise to discover this part of the world already, and such an enterprise ought not to be left off " [1].

It is easy, in the light of modern knowledge, to dismiss schemes such as this for discovery by way of the Arctic as the idle and foolish dreams of ignorant and irresponsible minds. But a proposal to cross the Pole by sailing ship in the sixteenth century presented itself to contemporary thinkers in much the light that a proposal to cross it by submarine or airship presented itself in the twentieth century : there were likely to be great hazards, success was doubtful, but it was a matter demanding careful consideration, and not to be rejected out of hand. It is not therefore proposed in this essay to deal with the actual Polar voyage which were undertaken later than our period, but rather to examine the Cosmographical Ideas that governed their inception, influenced their acceptance or rejection, and ruled their promoters' minds.

These ideas were drawn from two main sources, the authority of the past, as gathered by careful comparative study from the works of ancient writers of repute, and the experiences of the present, with the inferences, often contradictory and debatable, that could be drawn from them. Every educated man of the Renaissance gave at least lip-service to the principle that "experience is the mother of wisdom," but the formal education of the day, both at the school and at the university, was, in England at least, divorced from current progress, and consequently the written word, alike of classical and medieval scholars, and of their contemporary scholiasts, often carried disproportionate weight.

For English views on the Polar Regions it is natural to turn first to the geographical section of the *Opus Majus* of Roger Bacon as the work of the first modern writer on the subject, but Bacon deals with the matter only in identally, and by theoretical reasoning arrives at the conclusion that there must be two large ocean basins, one round either Pole, united by a meridional belt of water. The *Opus Majus*, moreover, remained practically unknown, save through the copious borrowings of Pierre d'Ailly; the latter's interest in high latitudes, like Bacon's, was but slight, and hence we must look elsewhere for information. We find it in a treatise written a century after Bacon, for presentation to King Edward III, which was devoted entirely to the subject in question. This was the book called *Inventio Fortunatae*, " *qui liber incipit a gradu 54, perveniens usque ad Polum* " : it dealt, that is to say, exclusively with the realms lying beyond the Seven Climates of Hipparchus and Ptolemy, realms which were deemed by these ancient writers to be uninhabitable.

Richard Hakluyt knew of this book through handling the manuscripts of John Dee, and through enquiries made concerning it from Mercator ; he assigned its authorship, for reasons that will presently appear, to Nicholas of Lynn, prefixing this scholar's name to the relevant extracts from Dee and Mercator, which he printed in the *Principal Voyages*. Nevertheless, there is no direct evidence on the point, for the *Inventio Fortunatae*, though known, for example, to Las Casas when he wrote about 1570, was anonymous, and has now disappeared.

Such fragments of its contents as can be pieced together have reached us in an extraordinarily circuitous fashion. A certain Fleming, Jacobus Cnoyen van Tsertoghenbosch, at some unknown date, " travelled the world," says Mercator, " like Mandeville, but noted with better judgment what he saw. He wrote in the Flemish tongue all that had been discovered before his day about the Northern Regions," and one of the sources upon which he drew was the lost work under discussion. His manuscript came into the possession of Abraham Ortelius, the great Flemish cartographer, who lent it to his friend Mercator at Duisburg, the latter basing upon it the delineation of the Polar Regions in his famous world-map of 1569, and since the " Mercator" projection, then first employed, made it impossible to show the Pole on the general map, a special inset upon a Polar projection was added. This inset was accompanied by a long note upon the source employed, part of which Hakluyt quotes, while adding his own comments.

Now Mercator as a young man had formed an intimacy with John Dee, when that clever young Welshman, fresh from his Cambridge honours, had recommenced his studies at the University of Louvain. It was natural therefore that when Dee, who from 1550 onwards had placed his great learning at the disposal of the venturers for Cathay, wished for more detailed information upon the Far North, he should write to his friend Mercator. This, however, was not until 1577, by which date Mercator had returned the Cnoyen manuscript to Ortelius, who had lent it once more and lost sight of it. All that Mercator could

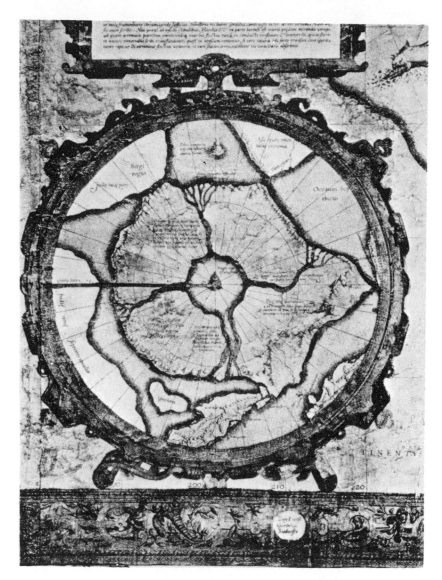

THE POLAR REGIONS AS DEPICTED BY GERARDUS MERCATOR, 1569.

(Inset from *Nova et aucta orbis terrae descriptio*, 1569.   Original in the Stadtsbibliothek, Breslau.)

The four Polar lands separated by in-drawing-channels are girt about by mountains and enclose a Polar Sea in which stands the Black Rock.   The Magnetic Pole, placed according to Mercator's own calculations, is in the sea between the extremities of Asia and America.   The boundary of the map is latitude 70° and the Polar passages are indicated as extremely difficult.

(See p. 202.)

do was to transcribe his old notes, made eight or nine years earlier, and send them to Mortlake. Dee, in his turn, retranscribed them at the close of his *Volume of Great and Rich Discoveries,* written for the furtherance of the search for the North-East Passage and Strait of Anian, and it is from this manuscript [2], mutilated by fire, and in places almost illegible, that they must be deciphered to-day. The story that Jacobus Cnoyen has to tell is that in 1364 there came to the Court of the King of Norway eight persons, including two priests, who related to their lord strange particulars of their home in North or Dusky Norway, said to be far away to the north-west, where in winter the sun was hidden for three months. One of the priests was descended from a man of Brussels, the other from the first colonists of that distant settlement, who had been placed there by King Arthur of Britain. Details of this part of the story are drawn by Cnoyen from a version of the *Gestae Arthuri,* which was familiar also to Mercator, who therefore cuts his notes short with the comment : " Here is much more *De Situ Septentrionis,* found at the beginning of the *Gestae Arthuri.* "[1] It appears, however, from the fragmentary remainder, that according to its authority, Arthur, after wintering in the north of Scotland, at a time when part of his army was already in Iceland, sailed away to the north in May, but was warned by natives to come no farther on account of dangerous indrawing seas; he therefore turned aside and left colonists in the islands between Scotland and Iceland, and also in a region called "Grocland." " It appears, therefore," comments Mercator, " that the indrawing sea only begins beyond Grocland." The following year a second fleet of twelve ships sailed for the north on 5th May, carrying colonists to the number of 1,800 men and about 400 women : five of the ships were lost in a storm, but the rest arrived at their destination on 18th June. Writing elsewhere, John Dee ascribes these events to about the year A.D. 530, but from the mutilated Cnoyen manuscript the date is missing. The story now returns

---

[1] This version of the Arthurian legends has not been traced.

to the priests at the Norwegian Court, of whom one is said to have had an astrolabe, a strange and rare possession at that time and place, and it is he who takes up the tale. It seems that four years earlier, that is to say in 1360, there had come to the Northern Islands an English Minorite, a good astronomer (" etc.," says Mercator's note tantalisingly), who, leaving his companions, had travelled alone, for the purpose of describing the Isles and the Indrawing Seas in his book, which he subsequently delivered to the King of England. He it was who gave his astrolabe to the priest in exchange for a Testament, and his description of what he had seen was apparently in the same terms as that of the *Gestae Arthuri* with some added details. Within the Arctic Circle was a circle of lands pierced by nineteen channels, or indrawing seas, the narrowest only three-quarters of a mile broad, so that within it the current rushed too strongly for a ship to pass through in safety. These lands terminated in latitude 78° in a girdle of high mountains, beyond which the nineteen indrawing channels gathered into four indrawing seas, separating four level lands, two inhabited and two uninhabited. Finally, these four seas gathered into a single whirlpool, where the water was sucked down as into a funnel, extending for 4° around the pole, and having in its centre a shining bare black rock, thirty-two miles in circumference and all of magnetic stone. So far the account seems to be a schematisation of the most striking features of far northern lands in general—the intricate channels, the dreaded races and whirlpools, the lofty, forbidding, bare cliffs, and the magnetic pole. The schematisation was in harmony with early Cosmological notions which placed the seat of the winds and tides at the Pole. " The Philosophers," says Hakluyt, " describe four indraughts of this Ocean Sea, in the four opposite quarters of the world, from whence many do conjecture that as well the flowing of the sea, as the blasts of the wind, have their first original " [3].

The Minorite narrator went farther, however, and spoke of a land where the sea froze each winter to the west, but lay open to the east, a contrast not uncommon ; of an inhabited region, too, where the people were but four feet high, surely the Eskimo ; and of more than one spot where, from the remains of wooden ships, and of great house timbers that lay about, he was aware that there had been people dwelling in former times who had gone away. There is mention, too, in sentences rendered fragmentary by mutilation, of wooded lands, and even of forests of brasil, the valuable wood that gave a red dye.

Now at this period the wooded shores of America discovered by Leif Ericsson were not forgotten, and there are records as late as 1347 of ships coming from Greenland " that had been to Markland." Moreover, it was at about this time that some of the Western settlements in Greenland had been abandoned in the face of Eskimo (or Skraeling) aggression. It is not impossible therefore that a learned English friar visited Arctic lands, that he met men returning to Norway from some remote colony, and recorded his impressions in a book in which he also gave due weight to cosmological theory. English merchants had permission to resort freely to the dominions of the King of Norway as early as the reign of Henry III, and Hakluyt refers to a privilege granted by Edward III to the men of Blakeney in Norfolk in respect of their trade to Iceland. He records, too, how a Commission appointed under King Henry IV to examine the grievances suffered by Englishmen at the hands of the Hansa merchants, had before them merchants of Lynn, " pitifully complaining " that in the year 1394 the men of Wiemar and Rostock had assaulted Norbern in Norway, held the merchants of Lynn there residing to ransom, and burnt their houses and mansions in the same place to the number of twenty-one. When it is added that there was an important Franciscan house at Lynn, that the Friars of this Order were among the world's greatest travellers, and that according to Bale [4], Nicholas of Lynn wrote a treatise De usu astrolabii about 1370, it will be agreed that Hakluyt had some grounds for naming this Nicholas as the " Minnebroder " of Cnoyen's compilation, although from a footnote to Dee's manuscript, which is possibly Hakluyt's, he or another reader thought also of one Hugo de Hibernia as the author ; this was yet another Minorite, who, flourishing in 1360, wrote a work *Itinerarium quoddam* (otherwise unknown), as Bale once more records [5].

It is perhaps more pertinent to note that restrictions on the movements of English merchants " to Iceland, Helgoland and Finmark " appear only to have been enforced in the fifteenth century, which becomes therefore a period of fading English knowledge of the North.   Nor is it to be forgotten that restrictions upon fishermen, as opposed to merchants, are almost impossible to carry into effect, and the whale fisheries of Greenland, described in Ivar Bardsen's fourteenth-century narrative [6], may have attracted Englishmen thither.   Such unlettered men leave no trace upon the written record, as is seen in the parallel case of the fishermen on the Newfoundland Banks, which were frequented for well nigh fifty years before Sir Humphrey Gilbert arrived in 1583 as to an unknown shore.   A scrap of documentary evidence, too, has survived, which points indirectly to a wider English knowledge of the North in the fourteenth century than prevailed at a later date.   This is a little rhyming cosmography, written about 1385, which in cataloguing the countries of the world in turn, comes at last to those of the north-west quadrant :

> " On the North Sea on, on
> Stand Flanders and Brabant,
> Hainault, Sagony, Lorraine, and Swedia,
> Alemain, Denmark, Norway, and —— [illegible]
> Veneland, Gotland, Iceland, Greenland,
> Maydenland, Hakesland, Friseland. . . ."

Not one of the last four names appears in the text of the stereotyped Latin Cosmographia of which the verses purport to be a vernacular epitome.   " Maydenland " and " Friseland " are reminiscent of the names of the so-called " imaginary islands " of the fourteenth-century seaman's charts, as is the " Brasil " mentioned in the friar's description ; and these charts were not works of imagination, each feature that they showed derived eventually from some report of actuality, however distorted in transmission.

"Friseland," whatever may have been its origin, became associated in the mid-sixteenth century with an island figuring in an elaborate story of adventure, dated by a curious coincidence not ten years earlier than that of the Oxford friar. Two Italians, the brothers Zeni, were said to have travelled from land to land in the North, and three hundred years later, their narrative and accompanying chart showing Friseland, Drogio and Estotiland, found, it was claimed, among family papers, was edited and published by a descendant. It obtained wide acceptance as an authentic documentary record, and was republished almost immediately by Ramusio in his *Viaggi* [7], nor need it be denied a substratum of truth, although the greater part is now seen to be an obvious fabrication. There is nothing inherently impossible in an Italian vessel reaching Iceland or the Faroes in the mid-fourteenth century, and in the travellers hearing of Christian people still farther west. Ramusio has a well-authenticated and perfectly credible narrative of a voyage made by some Italian merchants in 1432, with a cargo from Crete which they hoped to sell " in the West." Caught in a south-westerly gale somewhere off Ireland, the little vessel ran before the wind for weeks, and was at last shipwrecked on Rusten Island in the Lofotens within the Arctic Circle. Norwegian fishermen succoured the crew, and they were taken safely to Bergen.

John Dee believed that the Zeni's " Friseland," with " Estotiland " to the west of it, were among the countries colonised by King Arthur, and hence rightful appanages of the English Crown. Consequently, the features of the Zeni chart, side by side with those derived from the *Inventio Fortunatae*, are to be found on the map which he drew in 1580 for Queen Elizabeth to accompany his summary of the claim he put forward on her behalf for the British Empire of the North [8]. In the map which he prepared in 1583 for Sir Humphrey Gilbert's venture, he used the same sources, although he differed from other authorities in indicating a clear passage-way alike to the north-east and to the north-west running south of the girdle of Polar lands. The map of Johann Ruysch, published in the Rome edition of Ptolemy of 1508, which follows most faithfully the details of the *Inventio Fortunatae*, and must have been derived from that work in the original Latin, shows these passages blocked in either direction by the linking of certain of the Polar lands with the north coasts of Europe and Asia.

Such links were the cartographical expression of an inference drawn by orthodox thinkers from the fact of the existence of the Eskimo or Skraelings, for since the whole population of the earth was descended from the three sons of Noah, it followed that all inhabited lands must be linked together. A similar chain of reasoning led to the conclusion that the new continent of America must be joined with North-east Asia, so that the so-called Strait of Anian could not really exist, and the Arctic Ocean was merely a great gulf, the shore of which swung round from Labrador by Tartaria to Norway.

If this were true, then there was no Northern Passage to Cathay, the South Sea, or the Moluccas, and the English adventures were foredoomed to failure. That they must fail on this account was the opinion of the eminent scholar, Julius Caesar Scaliger, who described this Arctic Gulf in a widely esteemed work [9], published in 1557, the year following Stephen Burrough's discovery of Vaigatz Strait. Not only was there no through passage, he maintained, but the shore of the Gulf could not be sailed to Scythia or Tartaria, since the winds were continually from the north, and westerly or south-westerly winds were practically unknown. In the sunless winter, too, which lasted ten months, the sea was transformed into a solid pavement of ice, while in the gloomy summer, the dangers were even greater, since the ice broke up into huge floating blocks like moving islands, crowding one against the other. These, he said, were

THE POLAR REGIONS FROM THE GLOBE OF MARTIN BEHAIM,
1492.

The area shown is that beyond the Arctic Circle. The land " where the polar bear was hunted " is shown beyond Iceland. A ring of Arctic lands encloses the Polar Sea. The Frozen Sea beyond Scythia is land-locked, and this part of the map was copied by Gemma Frisius.

(See p. 216.)

the real Symplegades, or Jostling Rocks, not those of the lying Greeks.

John Dee challenged this view, and contested it point by point, citing his conversations with his friend Richard Chancellor during his lifetime, and the yearly experience of the Muscovy fleet, which passed to and fro without let or hindrance to St. Nicholas, rounding North Cape in 71°. Here was direct evidence of the ready navigability of Arctic waters, and of the existence of favourable winds. In this case the argument by experience was indeed a dangerous one, for the perpetually open waters between North Cape and Bear Island are an anomaly, due to the slow increep of the warm Gulf Stream Drift and to the south-west winds, the high temperature of which this Drift maintains : the average position of the edge of the ice-encumbered seas elsewhere is some 10° farther south. William Bourne [10], however, was not far from the truth when he said that the absence of icebergs there pointed to an absence of land to the north of Norway, while the icebergs off Newfoundland and Labrador took their origin in extensive lands in higher latitudes and floated out from their sounds and rivers. "The great salt sea," he wrote, "never freezeth." Consequently the open water met with for 100 leagues from North Cape northwards might extend right across the Pole, and afford a route to Cathay, although "before that it hath been put to proof," he adds cautiously, "it cannot be known."

William Bourne was an authority upon "sea-causes," and from his home at Greenwich had seen many an expedition set out for the north. John Dee himself had discussed with him the problem of Cathay, and shown him the book of Ser Marco Polo, had shown him perhaps also his own copy of an old manuscript that was then being passed from hand to hand, and that boldly suggested the trans-polar route to the South Sea. This manuscript was from the pen of Robert Thorne, and was the first original of that Address to King Henry VIII which has been already quoted.

Thorne and his friend Roger Barlow were two men whose cosmo-graphical education had been of a practical rather than of an academic type.   They knew nothing of ancient cosmologies, but much of modern sea-charts, maps and globes, with the elements, too, of mathematical geography, the geography of the earth as a sphere.   As English merchants in Seville, they had interests in many lands, north, south, east and west, but their Spanish and Portuguese business associates, as they well knew, drew profits from yet farther afield, from the Spiceries then in dispute between the crowns of Portugal and Spain.   The Portuguese had approached the Spice Islands from the east, the Spaniards from the south, and then from the west : why should not the English approach them from the north ?   The idea probably originated with Thorne, for he says : " God knoweth though by it I should have had interest, I have had, and yet have, no little mind to this business : so that if I had faculty to my will it should be the first thing I would undertake, even to attempt if our seas be navigable to the Pole or no.   For I reason that as some sicknesses are heirs, and come from father to son, so this inclination or desire of this discovery I inherited of my father : which with another merchant of Bristol named Hugh Eliot, were the discoverers of the New Found Lands, of the which there is no doubt if the mariners had been ruled and followed their Pilot's mind, the lands of the Indians, whence all the gold cometh, had been ours " [11].   The elder Thorne had not lived to hear of the conquest of Mexico, but there must have been many like his son to lament that the English expeditions under the Cabots had never pushed their advantage, as the Spaniards themselves at one time feared they would do.

To anyone habitually using a globe, as Thorne and Barlow did, in common with many of their contemporaries, the circuitous character of the routes to the Spice Islands by the Cape or by Magellan's Straits was very strikingly apparent, as too was the fact that a much shorter route lay from England directly across the

Pole. The official seaman's charts of Spain, besides, charted only such coasts as were actually explored, and hence on these the Polar regions appeared as vistas of open sea. It was tempting to argue, too, that the increasing length of summer daylight, explained in every elementary treatise on the sphere, would prevent any undue excess of cold, and would keep the seas open. Nor could it be denied that the absence of the perils of darkness for many months together must be of enormous advantage when penetrating into the unknown.

That there was open water to Iceland, and to the extremity of Norway was well known, and the cosmographers placed both of these lands in 71 or 72°, leaving but 18° or 300 leagues [1] (reckoning 16⅔ leagues to a degree) of uncertain waters before the Pole was reached, and as much again on the far side. True, the older maps had marked these regions as " uninhabitable on account of the cold," but so, too, they had marked the equinoctial zone as " uninhabitable on account of the heat," whereas it had now been abundantly proved to be habitable. Such were the lines of argument adduced by Thorne and Barlow, nor could they be hastily brushed aside. One difficulty remained : while many maps and globes showed the New World as an island or a group of islands, there was yet the possibility that the South Sea was a great gulf, enclosed by land to the north, which would preclude any approach to it from that direction.

It was to ascertain the truth in this matter, as well as to procure native charts of the seas about the Spice Islands, and other local information, that Roger Barlow, with financial assistance from Thorne, embarked with a Spanish expedition, whose destination was the South Seas, in April 1526. This expedition, led by Sebastian Cabot, got no farther than the River Plate, from which Barlow returned in 1529.[2] Undeterred by this disappoint-

---

[1] The " 3 or 4 leagues " of Thorne's Address as printed by Hakluyt is due to an error of transcription.

[2] See pp. 167–9.

ment, however, the two friends did not cease to discuss their plans, and in 1531, a ship of unusual tonnage being for sale in Andalusia, Thorne bought it to use on the proposed voyage by the north. The two men then returned to Bristol to await a suitable opportunity of approaching Henry VIII, but before that opportunity came Robert Thorne was dead, and the ship *Saviour* passed into the possession of his brother Nicholas. Roger Barlow spent the next eight or nine years in building up his private fortune in Pembrokeshire, and only in 1541 did he lay an Address before the King setting out the advantages of the Polar route. There was some rumour at the time that Jacques Cartier was about to set out for the Spice Islands by a short route through the Glacial Sea, and the Privy Council were inclined to look favourably on Barlow's plan, but nothing was done. Nearly ten years later, when Sebastian Cabot was back in England, and there was a general eagerness for an English venture of discovery, the plan was examined yet again, but without result. It could only, indeed, have led to disappointment or disaster, such as actually occurred when John Davis detached from his fleet the *Sunshine*, of 50 tons, and a small pinnace, to seek this northern passage between Iceland and Greenland in 1586. After little more than a fortnight's sailing from north-west Iceland, the *Sunshine* found herself " between two firm lands of ice," and turned back again towards Greenland, which " looked very blew " and was beset with ice. The pinnace was lost in a storm, and although John Davis wrote an optimistic letter to his patron, William Sanderson, a passage was as far from discovery as in the 'fifties.

It was in 1549 that the Earl of Warwick, becoming after an interval once more Lord Admiral, found time and opportunity to set men to work on plans for encroachment on the Spanish and Portuguese monopolies, an idea for which he had already shown enthusiasm as Lord Lisle, patron of foreign pilots and cosmographers. It must remain a puzzle why Sebastian Cabot did not on this occasion press, or seemingly even suggest, the following up of his penetration of a strait to the north-west in 1508–9, a voyage which must be looked on as the first English effort to pass round the Americas to the South Sea. True that the new English edition of his World Map, printed from blocks " cut by Clement Adams," indicated nothing of such discoveries, but there appear to have been manuscript maps of his in certain chosen hands, including the particular specimen which later hung in the Earl of Bedford's library at Chenies, which recorded the voyage in question.

While in the absence of any documentary evidence the considerations which decided the noblemen and merchants of London to attempt the North-east rather than the North or North-west Passage must be a matter of conjecture, it is worth pointing out that there were certain obvious advantages in the route they chose. The Old World was, up to a point, the known world, where " civill people " might be expected en route, and Robert Thorne had long since pointed out the cold lands of Scythia and Tartary, which were considered to occupy the north-east of Asia, as possible markets for woollen cloth. The seas as far as Wardhouse (Vaardhuis or Vardö) were well frequented and known : known, moreover, to be free from the menace of those great floating mountains of ice, which were to be dreaded as far south as 50° in the north-west. Then, too, the scholars and students of cosmography who were called into counsel, such men as Recorde, Eden and Dee, could furnish literary evidence of the existence of a sea way, at least as far east as the great River of Ob, and that from modern writers and modern experience. Such evidence might be valueless to seamen, lacking even the poorest chart or ruttier to guide them, but it carried weight with educated people.

Beyond the Ob, however, lay a coast for the contour of which it was necessary to seek information from antiquity. Here, according to Ptolemy, was Cape Tabin, projecting within the Arctic Circle to 80°, a very formidable obstacle, unless it could be circumvented by some river leading inland to Cathay. And here it may be remarked that the supposition of a river entering two oceans, and so offering a complete trans-continental water-way, presented no difficulty to the sixteenth-century mind, as contemporary maps reveal. This possibility of pursuing the journey by river explains the frequent choice of vessels unsuitably small for long voyages of exploration. Beyond Cape Tabin no further obstacle presented itself, always supposing Asia were not continent with America, and directly southward of Tartaria lay the country of the Grand Khan, to whom the explorers hoped to present that letter of Edward VI, written in Latin, Greek, " and divers other languages," commending them to the humanity of all kings and rulers whom they might encounter with the simple and touching admonition : " Consider you that they also are men."

Two letters [12] written by the Spanish Ambassador, Jehan Scheyfve, who was jealously watching the English preparations for the Willoughby-Chancellor venture, throw light on the dis-cussions and hopes which it was exciting in London. The first, dated 10th April, 1553, is addressed to the Bishop of Arras : " The three vessels which are to set out for the discovery of new lands will be ready in the course of this month. Since I last wrote I have been able to ascertain that they will follow a northerly course, and navigate by the Frozen Sea (*Mare Congelatum*) towards the country of the great Cham China, or the neighbour-ing countries. The English opine that the ancients passed by that sea and joined the Ocean, as Pliny and others wrote : and they believe the route to be a short one, and very convenient for the kingdom of England for the distributing of kerseys in those far countries, bringing back spices and other rich merchandise in exchange. . . . Cabot came to see me recently, and I spoke to him on the subject. . . . I asked him if the said voyage was as certain as it seemed. He replied, Yes, it was. . . ." Scheyfve then went on to suggest that Cham China was part of the Emperor's conquest, to which Cabot retorted that people other than the Emperor and the King of Portugal would consider that it belonged to the first to occupy it ! A reply reminiscent of that given by the King of France [13] to the Spanish Ambassador in 1540, when the Canadian settlement scheme was afoot : " The Popes hold spiritual jurisdiction, but it does not lie with them to distribute lands among kings, and the kings of France and other Christians were not summoned when the partition took place."

Scheyfve's second letter was written to the Emperor himself, and is dated a month later, 11th May, when the expedition was in the Thames, nearly ready to start. The writer was reporting his conversation with certain Portuguese merchants, who had asked him to assist in the repatriation of the Portuguese pilot Pinteado, already engaged to conduct the first English expedition to the Guinea coast. " I did not mention Cabot," writes the Ambassador. " I said it was rumoured that they [the ships lying ready] would follow a north-easterly route, or possibly a north-westerly one. Some said they would steer to the north-east and pass the Frozen Sea, and others that their plan was to follow a westerly course and enter the Strait of the Three Brethren, or pass Cape de las Parras and proceed thence to the Great Cham's country or the neighbouring places. Cosmographers and mathematicians doubt if this passage be practicable, and cannot agree whether it can or cannot be accomplished. Gemma Frisius, in his last chart, published in '49, discourses on that point . . ." [14].

A further echo of this debate as to the most likely route is to be found in Richard Eden's Preface to his translation of the New India from Sebastian Münster, made for the occasion of the same voyage in 1553. After relating the evidence drawn from Pliny and the ancient writers as to a passage actually accomplished by Northern Asia, which is briefly referred to by Scheyfve in his first letter, he continues : " Wherefore, to conclude, if no good can be done this way, it were worthy the adventure to attempt if the voyage may be brought to pass another way, as by the strait called *Fretum trium fratrum*, westward and by north from England, which voyage is sufficiently known to such as have any skill in geography " [15].

The " Strait of the Three Brethren," affording a clear passage by the north-west to the South Sea, appears to have originated as a cartographical feature in the school of Gemma Frisius, the great mathematician and cosmographer of Louvain, who enjoyed the patronage of the Emperor Charles V.   Apart from a little text-book illustration of small interest, all Gemma's world maps have disappeared, including the one which Scheyfve refers to as published in 1549, and containing a discussion of the vexed question of the Strait.   One of his globes, however, survives in a single example, now at the Zerbst Museum, and indicates plainly the author's concept of the Arctic Regions and the Northern Passages.   A land bridge united North-eastern Asia and North-western Europe by way of Greenland, and enclosed a Glacial Sea to the north of Asia, the whole being reminiscent of the delineation in Behaim's famous globe of 1492, and showing no trace of the influence of the *Inventio Fortunatae*.   America thus appeared as an island, no doubt conceived of as the lost Atlantis of Plato's story, a view very widely held, and it was separated from the Polar land bridge by the *Fretum Arcticum, sive trium fratrum*, which was so frequently cited by contemporary writers. The Strait lay in about 64°– 66° N., and its length was not great, owing to the rapid bending away southwards of the American or southern shore.   The northern shore was joined to North-east Asia, and it is here that the puzzling inscription occurs : " Quii people, whom John Scolvus the Dane reached in 1476."   All later references to Scolvus, although some describe him as a Danish pilot, appear to derive from this source, and nothing more is known of his voyage.   It is probably most correctly to be interpreted as a voyage to Greenland, but the " Quii people " are Asiatics, the " Le Quii " (Lequios) of other contemporary maps, and originally the Lu-Chu islanders.

THE GLOBE OF GEMMA FRISIUS, 1537.

(From a photograph supplied by the Director of the Museum, Zerbst.)

The short " Strait of the Three Brethren " in 66° is seen to the right, giving easy access to the Pacific. Asia is continuous with the Polar lands, and there is no access to the Pacific from the Scythian Sea (on the left in 70°).

(See p. 216.)

The position and shape of the Arctic Strait on the globe strongly recall that said to be delineated on Sebastian Cabot's map at Chenies, but Gemma himself mentions the voyages of the Corte-Reals as one of his sources, and it is possible that the name of the Strait commemorates the three Portuguese, or rather Azorean, brothers of that name, of whom two were lost, and the third had a licence to seek them. Gemma's interpretation of their story and of the charts based upon it was certainly that Gaspar Corte-Real had reached Asia, for he places a *Promontorium Corterealis* by the Polisacus River in Cathay. Moreover, an anonymous writer [16], evidently brought up on Gemma's maps and globes " made 70 years since," who is reviving all the old arguments for a north-west passage venture somewhere about 1590, writes as follows : " The Portingale named Cortes Realis came from the South Sea into this our North Sea by that passage at 66 degrees. And at his coming into Portugal he was committed to prison all his life-time for making that passage known," adding in the margin : " The said Cortes Realis made three crosses in the globe, for a sign of his passage, and [it] was named the passage of the three Brethren." Thus the writer has got hold of an apocryphal story, which was, however, very persistent, that these straits had been passed and knowledge of them suppressed, and the whole appears definitely traceable to Gemma's globes and maps. Mercator was at Louvain as one of Gemma's students when the particular globe was in preparation, and undertook with Gasper â Mirica the work of engraving it, which was completed in 1537. In 1538 he himself published a world map on a heart-shaped projection, on which he copied the delineation of the Polar Regions found in his master's work, while in 1540 the same Arctic Strait was shown in somewhat exaggerated form on a world map drawn for Sebastian Münster's edition of Ptolemy, with the legend against it : " Through this strait there is a way to the Moluccas."

The influence of Gemma's views is well illustrated by a

report [17] made in 1541 to the Spanish Ambassador in France at a time when every effort was being used by the Emperor's servants to ascertain the true objectives of the Cartier-Roberval expedition to Canada : "Most honoured Lord, in accordance with your letters I have made enquiries about the New Lands, and have not found any special map of them. Yesterday, after the lecture on the Sphere, delivered by a very distinguished Spanish mathematician, named Jo. Martin Poblatius, whom you may know, physician to the Queen, I had a long talk with the lecturer while accompanying him to the Sorbonne where he was supping ; and as in his lecture he had mentioned the *Zona Torrida,* I took the opportunity of bringing up our matter by remarking that it seemed that the ancients were in error in deeming it uninhabitable. . . . Upon this I asked him if he knew whether this Strait by which Roberval intended to go was open and navigable, and afforded a passage to the Moluccas or to Peru . . . and he said that a pupil of his had been near it, but they saw great mountains of ice in the sea, and therefore dared go no further. Whence, it may be conjectured that the said sea is frozen in winter, and in the warm weather the ice breaks up. . . .

"To-day I have seen my lord Orontius [Finaeus] at his house, and asked him to find out if it would be possible to obtain maps of these New Lands. . . . And as for this Strait, he told me that it was not navigable at all, and that they would have to go by land [Orontius believed that N. America was linked in the north with Asia]. . . .

"As for the situation of the said Strait, its mouth according to the descriptions of Gemma Frisius on the world-map lately made at Louvain [dated 1540 and dedicated to Charles V] lies approximately in longitude 328° and in latitude 66° N. . . ."

That the Strait was much as Gemma Frisius depicted it, with its south-western entry in comparatively low latitudes, was the strong belief of a man whose views on the South Sea commanded respect, namely that Friar Andreas Urdaneta who, at the instance

of Philip of Spain, worked out the return route from the Philippines. It was some years before this event, that is to say, in May
1560, that he wrote to the King begging to be excused from further
work of discovery, on account of his age and his religious habit,
but meanwhile urging the examination of the Strait between
Baccalaos (Newfoundland) and the *Mar del Sur* with a view to
securing it against foreign intrusion, since it offered such an easy
route to China, Peru, and New Spain.

It appears that when he was raising this point, Urdaneta displayed a chart of the Strait to some gentlemen of position in New
Spain, for one of these gentlemen, a certain Salvaterra, subsequently
declared that not only had he seen this chart in 1560, but that
Urdaneta himself had then told him that he (the Friar) had
actually passed through it to Germany [18]. This statement,
obviously an exaggeration, was made to Sir Henry Sidney in
Ireland in 1568, when Sir Humphrey Gilbert was standing by, and
the latter added Salvaterra's testimony to his own arguments for
the feasibility of the North-west Passage, which he had begun to
put down in writing in 1566.

Sir Humphrey Gilbert's *Discourse* [19], which was not actually
published until 1576, a few weeks before Frobisher sailed, was
written down in the first instance as an amplification of material
which he had collected for a debate held before the Queen and
the Privy Council in 1564–5, when Anthony Jenkinson spoke as
the protagonist of the North-east Passage. The two men had
been actively working together to secure the renewal of the search
for Cathay, which the Muscovy Company, busy with new trades,
had left entirely in abeyance, and Sir Humphrey's strong faith in
the north-west, while founded very largely on a study of Gemma
Frisius, had been re-enforced by the striking evidence afforded by
a new and immediately popular world map, that published by
Abraham Ortelius of Antwerp in 1564. So highly did Gilbert
think of this map, that he prepared directly from it the sketch
map with which he illustrated his pamphlet.

Ortelius had not as yet read the *Inventio Fortunatae* (which he used in his world map of 1570), and the Arctic Regions are shown as open ocean, save for the huge island of Greenland, and a promontory of Asia (corresponding with Ptolemy's Tabin), stretching northward to latitude 83°. Labrador is shown as an island, its north coast in 62°, separated by a wide strait from Greenland, and bounded to the south by a strait corresponding to the Gulf and Estuary of the St. Lawrence. The north coast of America he placed between 50 and 58°, i.e. nowhere in latitudes likely to be encumbered by ice, and its western coast, between latitudes 40 and 50° N., was shown as hardly 100 leagues from Cathay. A study of this map lends significance to Gilbert's suggestion that a trading station should be inhabited in the neighbourhood of the Sierra Nevada, for such a station would lie exactly opposite the great city of Quinsay, and within easy reach of Japan and the Moluccas, while in reaching it, and sailing beyond it, there would be no encroachment upon the established prerogatives of Spain and Portugal. Francis Drake set sail about eighteen months after Gilbert's pamphlet was published, and in 1579 took possession of the very area indicated, under the name of "New Albion."

The basis of Ortelius's delineation of the north is not clear, although it certainly includes an attempt to interpret the French data concerning Canada. John Dee, who was in close touch with Gilbert, wrote to Ortelius, who was well known to him, to enquire his authority for features that are peculiar to this map, but unfortunately the famous cartographer's reply has not been preserved.

Sir Humphrey Gilbert's *Discourse*, and the Argument written by Richard Willes for his *History of Travayle* [20] published in the following year, well illustrate the laborious dialectic of the period, the conflicting nature of the evidence, and the absence of any sound canons of criticism of historical documents. Gilbert, in his list of "all the best modern Geographers," ranging from

WORLD-MAP OF ABRAHAM ORTELIUS, 1564.

(From the original in the British Museum.)

Once Labrador is passed, the way is seen to lie freely open to the strait of about 10° width that separates Sierra Nevada from Cathay. Cipangu lies just to the south of the strait and the Moluccas are on the extreme margin of the map. A vast *Terra Australis* stretching to the Moluccas is freely accessible from the Straits of Magellan.

(*See* p. 220.)

Gemma Frisius to Peter Martyr, does not distinguish between cosmographers and historians of standing, such as the two named, and mere compilers of textbooks like Honterus, or map engravers like Tramezine, and he admits that " What moved these learned men to affirm [America to be an island] I know not, . . . but I conjecture that they would never have so constantly affirmed or notified their opinions therein to the world if they had not had good cause."

The appeal to authority is followed by an appeal to reason, that is to say, an argument from general principles, and much of this is very sound, especially the inference of the absence of a land bridge between Asia and America from the dissimilarity of the peoples and animals in the two continents, although the likeness of the Greenland Eskimo to the Hyperboreans of Eurasia led in their case to faulty conclusions in the opposite sense. The argument of the western movement of the waters, so plainly discerned in low latitudes, had of course no real validity, although it had been often used before Gilbert wrote to prove that straits to the South Sea must exist. In seeking to explain the apparent absence of this current in the north-west, he incidentally makes us aware of the method used by pilots of his day to discern the direction and strength alike of currents and undercurrents by means of a weighted sail. Such knowledge was, of course, of the highest importance when there was no means other than dead reckoning of fixing a ship's position.

After the appeal to reason comes the appeal to experience, the cases of voyages through a part of the passage being first alleged, and then the cases of those which were actually continued from sea to sea. Among the latter, the foremost place is given to the two stories, one dating from 57 B.C., the other from A.D. 1160, of " Indians " cast up on the coast of Germany. Three chapters are devoted to examining these stories from every angle, and there is no doubt from the constant references to them in the writings of the Renaissance Period that they exercised a powerful influence on men's minds and imaginations. Actually, if the tales have any foundation in fact, which is not impossible, the castaways must have come from America itself, and have been carried across the Atlantic on the Gulf Stream Drift; but this possibility Gilbert dismisses in a few words, being unaware of the Drift, and satisfied that the natives of America were without sailing vessels. They could have come, he concluded, only by the north-west.

A brief chapter suffices for the dismissal also, to Gilbert's own satisfaction, of the arguments alleged on the contrary part by Jenkinson ten years since at the public debate, that is to say, the argument drawn from the words of a Tartarian fisherman, that from the finding of the rhinoceros's (or unicorn's) horn on Vaigatz Island, and that from the existence of an east-to-west current along the northern coast of Russia: the ignorant fisherman might err, the horn be that of a certain fish, the currents be the overflow of the rivers Dwina and Ob. Thus the North-west Passage is triumphantly proved to be the more certain of the two, and to possess the additional advantages that it involved doubling no cape, and so could be carried out with easterly and westerly winds only, while its use involved no political complications, such as might arise if the Moscovy Emperor perceived a lucrative trade to be passing his shores.

Richard Willes, to whom Gilbert's arguments were familiar, goes over the same ground in somewhat different fashion, following what was then a favourite device of conceding to the opponent each argument and then wresting it back again. The last reason alleged against the feasibility of the passage was the possibility that it would be out of the question to return through it from east to west, and it is a point to be borne in mind in respect of all the voyages to Cathay that the possible necessity of pursuing them, if not round the world, at least right round Asia, seems to have been very generally envisaged. As Willes pointed out, the Strait of Anian between Western America and Eastern Asia, was shown in " Zalterius' table of New France and in Don Diego Hermano de Toledo his Card for Navigation of that region " as no greater in breadth than the Strait of Magellan. It followed that the west-moving current would rush so furiously through it that, as in the case of its southern counterpart, to navigate it in the contrary direction would be well nigh impossible : hence, the English travellers must return by the north of Asia or risk intrusion upon the route of the Portuguese.

This argument he then proceeded to demolish from a two-fold standpoint. In the first instance, was it so certain that this western-flowing current was forced by the *Primum Mobile* to continue round the world ? It was a point on which the learned were not agreed. Or, granting this current, was it true that the Strait of Anian was as narrow as it was delineated on the maps which he had named ? " But in that place there is more sea-room by many degrees, if the Cards of Cabota and Gemma Frisius and that which Tramezine imprinted be true. And reason see I none at all but that I may as well give credit to their doings as to any of the rest. It must be *Peregrinationis historia*, that is, true reports of skilful travellers, as Ptolemy writeth, that in such controversies of geography must put us out of doubt." And on that note of unanswerable wisdom Richard Willes brings his discourse to a close.

Arguments on either side, equally weak or equally unanswerable, according to the point of view of the parties concerned, continued to be brought forward, and John Dee found a sentence " worthy to be written in letters of gold," in the *Geography* of Abulfeda as transcribed by Ramusio : it was to the effect that from Cathay the coast of Asia trended north-westward, and hence it appeared legitimate to conclude that from Muscovy the coast trended south-eastwards, when the bugbear of Cape Tabin vanished. On such slender threads were arguments hung, and on such slenderly based arguments were men found willing to hazard their lives ! Yet, as Gilbert declared, " If you will indifferently compare the hope that remaineth to animate me to this enterprise, with those likelihoods which Columbus alleged before Ferdinand the King of Castile . . . you will think this North-west Passage most worthy [of] travail therein." An idea had led to the discovery of the New World, might not ideas lead equally to the conquest of the northern passages ?

NOTES ON CHAPTER IX

1. Barlow, Roger, *A Brief Somme of Geographie,* Hakluyt Soc., 1932.
2. Brit. Mus., Cotton MSS., Vitellius C., vii., fol. 265 *et seq.*
3. Hakluyt, Richard, *Principal Navigations,* vol. i, edition of 1599.
4. Bale, *Scriptorum illustrium . . . Catalogus,* 1558.
5. *Ibid.*
6. Major, R. H., *Voyages of the Brothers Zeni,* Hakluyt Soc., 1873.
7. Ramusio, *Viaggi,* vol. ii, 1559.
8. Cotton MSS., Aug. I, i (1).
9. Scaliger, J. C., *De subtilitate ad H. Cardanum,* 1557.
10. Bourne, William, *A Hydrographicall Discourse of Five Ways to Cathay,* 1580.
11. Hakluyt, Richard, *Divers Voyages to America,* 1582.
12. *Calendar of State Papers, Spanish,* under date named.
13. Biggar, H. P., *A Collection of Documents relating to Jacques Cartier,* p. 170.
14. *Calendar of State Papers, Spanish,* under date named.
15. Eden, Richard, *A Treatyse of the Newe India,* 1553.
16. Harleian MSS., No. 167.
17. Biggar, H. P., *Documents relating to Jacques Cartier,* No. ccxciii. Here translated from the original French.
18. Gilbert, Sir Humfrey, *A Discourse for a Discovery for a New Passage to Cataia,* 1576.
19. *Ibid.*
20. Willes, R., *The History of Travayle in the West and East Indies,* 1577.

INDEX

Abreu, Antonio de, and Moluccas, 68, 183, 185
Aden, 52, 68, 130
Adventurers, of Bristol, 141, 199
Africa, Portuguese exploration, 45–62 ; Columbus and, 80, 81 ; and Barros, 84 ; 139
Alaminos, Anton de, pilot, 155, 156
Albuquerque, Affonso de, in India and Malacca, 67–69, 183, 184
Alcalá, University, 25 ; 108
Almeida, D. Francisco de, and Antilles, 53 ; and East Africa, 67 ; 68, 184
Americas, municipal government in, 37 ; hispanisation, 38 ; and Castile, 39, 40, 41 ; Spanish legislation in, 42 ; naming of, 126, 127
Andalusia, Muhammadans of, 17 ; and art, 26 ; political power, 30 ; silk, 39 ; and Columbus, 86
Andrade, Fernão Peres de, 69, 70
Ango, Jean, influence of, 173, 174
Antilha (Antilia), search for, 83 ; and Columbus, 94 ; Antilia, 9, and Pinzon, 41 ; 89 ; Antilles, 39 ; and Almeida, 53 ; and Indies, 97 ; 104 ; and new world, 110, 147 ; currents, 150
Aragon, and printing, 24 ; in Mediterranean, 30 ; union with Castile, 31 ; 35, 36, 37, 38, 39 ; Columbus and, 94 ; 96
Arce, Don Martin V. de, tomb, 13
Arco, F. D. de, explorer, 83
Aristotle, 25, 102, 176
Arthurian legend, 203, 207
Aveiro, J. A. de, explorer, 51, 90
Avila, Pedro Arias de, and Balboa, 158, 160 ; 161, 162, 177
Avila, Teresa of, 15
Ayala, Don Pedro L. de, historian, 18, 19

Ayllon, Lucas V. de, 156
Azambuja, Diogo de, 50, 80
Azores, and Portuguese, 45 ; and papal bull, 53 ; 83 ; Columbus and, 93 ; 123, 173, 182

Baccalaos, 151, 164, 170
Bacon, Roger, 201
Badajoz, Conference, 154, 166
Bahamas, 92, 155, 156
Balboa, Vasco N. de, and discovery of Pacific Ocean, 157–160, 161
Barlow, Roger, 168, quoted, 199–200 ; and northern passage, 210–212
Barros, João de, historian, 52, 64, 65, 69, 78, 84, 85
Bastidas, Rodrigo de, 157
Bayuera, Constantio, 116
Behaim, Martin, 83, 90, 91, 181
Bengal, 69, 131
Berardi, Juanoto, 120
Bernaldez, Andrés, quoted, 86
Bimini, 155
Bisagudo, Pero Vaz, 65
Bojador, Cape, 45, 46
Borneo, 129, 185, 195
Borromeo, John, 99, 106
Bourne, William, 209
Brasyl, island of, 132
Brazil, 54, Cabral and, 63–65 ; 121, 122, Vespucci and, 123–124 ; 138, 142, 166, 173, 183, 187
Bristol, 78, 132, 133, 134, 135, 141, 148, 167, 186
Brocar, Arnao G. de, 25

Cabot, John, 5, and spice trade, 129 ; 130, 131, 132, 1st voyage, 133 ; 2nd voyage, 134–136 ; 137, 138, 147, 148, 152, 199

Q